Flow charts for the

Supply Contract

This contract should be used for local and international procurement of high-value goods and related services including design

An NEC document

April 2013

NEC is a division of Thomas Telford Ltd, which is a wholly owned subsidiary of the Institution of Civil Engineers (ICE), the owner and developer of the NEC.

The NEC is a family of standard contracts, each of which has these characteristics:

- Its use stimulates good management of the relationship between the two parties to the contract and, hence, of the work included in the contract.
- It can be used in a wide variety of commercial situations, for a wide variety of types of work and in any location.
- It is a clear and simple document – using language and a structure which are straightforward and easily understood.

NEC3 Supply Contract is one of the NEC family and is consistent with all other NEC3 documents. Also available are the Supply Contract Guidance Notes, Flow Charts.

ISBN (complete box set) 978 0 7277 5867 5
ISBN (this document) 978 0 7277 5933 7
ISBN (Supply Contract) 978 0 7277 5895 8
ISBN (Supply Contract Guidance Notes) 978 0 7277 5931 3

First edition 2009
Reprinted 2010
Reprinted with amendments 2013

British Library Cataloguing in Publication Data for this publication is available from the British Library.

Typeset by Academic + Technical, Bristol

Printed and bound in Great Britain by Bell & Bain Limited, Glasgow, UK

CONTENTS

The number of each flow chart is the same as the number of the clause in the NEC Supply Contract to which it primarily relates.

FOREWORD

I was delighted to be asked to write the Foreword for the NEC3 Contracts.

I have followed the outstanding rise and success of NEC contracts for a number of years now, in particular during my tenure as the 146th President of the Institution of Civil Engineers, 2010/11.

In my position as UK Government's Chief Construction Adviser, I am working with Government and industry to ensure Britain's construction sector is equipped with the knowledge, skills and best practice it needs in its transition to a low carbon economy. I am promoting innovation in the sector, including in particular the use of Building Information Modelling (BIM) in public sector construction procurement; and the synergy and fit with the collaborative nature of NEC contracts is obvious. The Government's construction strategy is a very significant investment and NEC contracts will play an important role in setting high standards of contract preparation, management and the desirable behaviour of our industry.

In the UK, we are faced with having to deliver a 15–20 per cent reduction in the cost to the public sector of construction during the lifetime of this Parliament. Shifting mind-set, attitude and behaviour into best practice NEC processes will go a considerable way to achieving this.

Of course, NEC contracts are used successfully around the world in both public and private sector projects; this trend seems set to continue at an increasing pace. NEC contracts are, according to my good friend and NEC's creator Dr Martin Barnes CBE, about better management of projects. This is quite achievable and I encourage you to understand NEC contracts to the best you can and exploit the potential this offers us all.

Peter Hansford

UK Government's Chief Construction Adviser
Cabinet Office

PREFACE

The NEC contracts are the only suite of standard contracts designed to facilitate and encourage good management of the projects on which they are used. The experience of using NEC contracts around the world is that they really make a difference. Previously, standard contracts were written mainly as legal documents best left in the desk drawer until costly and delaying problems had occurred and there were lengthy arguments about who was to blame.

The language of NEC contracts is clear and simple, and the procedures set out are all designed to stimulate good management. Foresighted collaboration between all the contributors to the project is the aim. The contracts set out how the interfaces between all the organisations involved will be managed – from the client through the designers and main contractors to all the many subcontractors and suppliers.

Versions of the NEC contract are specific to the work of professional service providers such as project managers and designers, to main contractors, to subcontractors and to suppliers. The wide range of situations covered by the contracts means that they do not need to be altered to suit any particular situation.

The NEC contracts are the first to deal specifically and effectively with management of the inevitable risks and uncertainties which are encountered to some extent on all projects. Management of the expected is easy, effective management of the unexpected draws fully on the collaborative approach inherent in the NEC contracts.

Most people working on projects using the NEC contracts for the first time are hugely impressed by the difference between the confrontational characteristics of traditional contracts and the teamwork engendered by the NEC. The NEC does not include specific provisions for dispute avoidance. They are not necessary. Collaborative management itself is designed to avoid disputes and it really works.

It is common for the final account for the work on a project to be settled at the time when the work is finished. The traditional long period of expensive professional work after completion to settle final payments just is not needed.

The NEC contracts are truly a massive change for the better for the industries in which they are used.

Dr Martin Barnes CBE

Originator of the NEC contracts

ACKNOWLEDGEMENTS

The first edition of the Supply Contract was produced by the Institution of Civil Engineers through its NEC Panel. It was mainly drafted by P. A. Baird and J. J. Lofty with the assistance of P. H ggins, N. C. Shaw and J. M. Hawkins.

The NEC3 Supply Contract Flow Charts were produced by Ross Hayes.

The original NEC was designed and drafted by Dr Martin Barnes then of Coopers and Lybrand with the assistance of Professor J. G. Perry then of the University of Birmingham, T. W. Weddell then of Travers Morgan Management, T. H. Nicholson, Consultant to the Institution of Civil Engineers, A. Norman then of the University of Manchester Institute of Science and Technology and P. A. Baird, then Corporate Contracts Consultant, Eskom, South Africa.

The members of the NEC Panel are:

N. C. Shaw, FCIPS, CEng, MIMechE (Chairman)
F. Alderson, BA (Melb), Solicitor
P. A. Baird, BSc, CEng, FICE, M(SA)ICE, MAPM
M. Codling, BSc, ICIOB, MAPM
L. T. Eames, BSc, FRICS, FCIOB
M. Garratt, BSc(Hons), MRICS, FCIArb
J. J. Lofty, MRICS

NEC Consultant:

R. A. Gerrard, BSc(Hons), FRICS, FCIArb, FCInstCES

Secretariat:

J. M. Hawkins, BA(Hons), MSc
S. Hernandez, BSc, MSc

AMENDMENTS

Full details of all amendments are available on www.neccontract.com.

Legend

CHART START

HEADINGS

    Headings in caps
    provide guidance

STATEMENTS

    If a clause is
    referenced, text
    is from the NEC

LOGIC LINKS

    Links go to right
    and/or downward
    unless shown

QUESTION

    Answer question
    to determine the
    route to follow

SUBROUTINE

    Include another
    flow chart here

CONTINUATION

    Link to matching
    point(s) on other
    chart sheets

CHART TITLE

    Chart number,
    title and sheet

Start

HELPFUL HEADING

Statement explaining next step

51.1
Statement using part or all of the NEC text in clause 51.1

Does Option X14 apply?

YES

NO

FC X14
Advanced payment to the *Supplier*

A
sheet
2

B
sheet
2

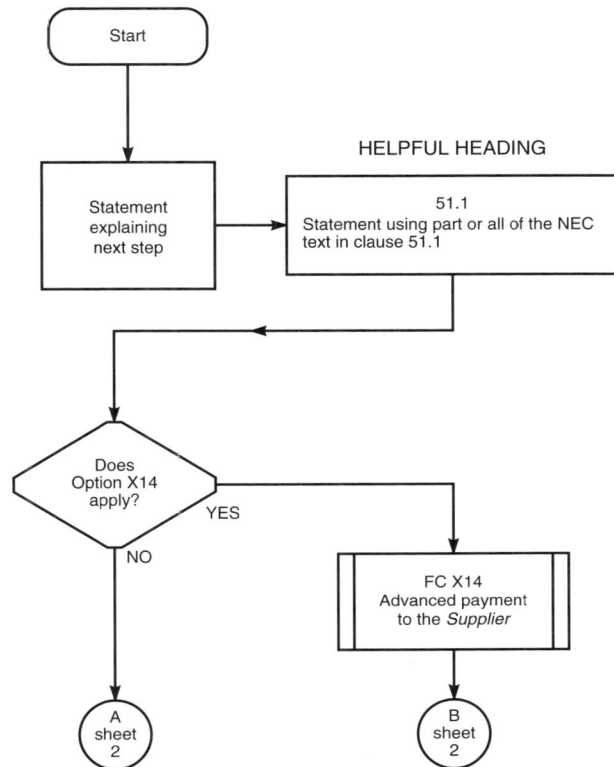

**Flow chart 51 Sheet 1 of 2
Payment**

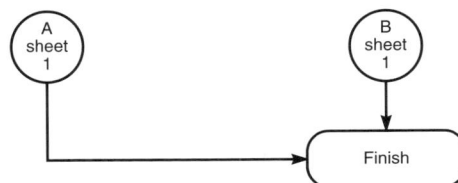

CONTINUATION

A
sheet
1

B
sheet
1

CHART FINISH

Finish

CHART TITLE

**Flow chart 51 Sheet 2 of 2
Payment**

ABBREVIATIONS USED IN THE FLOW CHART BOXES

FC 61	Flow chart for clause 61
FC X7	Flow chart for secondary Option X7
P	*Purchaser*
S	*Supplier*
SM	*Supply Manager*
SC	Subcontractor
CD	Contract Data
CE	Compensation event
DCP	*defect correction period*
GI	Goods Information
PI	Partnering Information
P&M	plant and materials
PAF	Price Adjustment Factor
SR	Supply Requirements

Start

A communication is to be made

FORM OF COMMUNICATIONS

COMMUNICATIONS REQUIRED BY THIS CONTRACT

THE LANGUAGE OF THIS CONTRACT

13.1
This contract requires instructions, certificates, submissions, proposals, records, acceptances, notifications, replies and other communications.

13.1
A communication is in a form which can be read, copied and recorded.

13.1
Writing is in the *language of this contract*.

13.1
The *language of this contract* is stated in the CD.

RECEIPT OF COMMUNICATIONS

13.2
A communication has effect when it is received at the last address notified by the recipient for receiving communications or, if none is notified, at the address of the recipient stated in the CD

CERTIFICATES

13.6
Is this communication a certificate?

YES →
13.6
The *SM* issues his certificates to the *S* and the *P*.

NO

NOTIFICATIONS

13.7
Is this communication a notification?

YES →
13.7
A notification which this contract requires is communicated separately from other communications.

NO

A
sheet
2

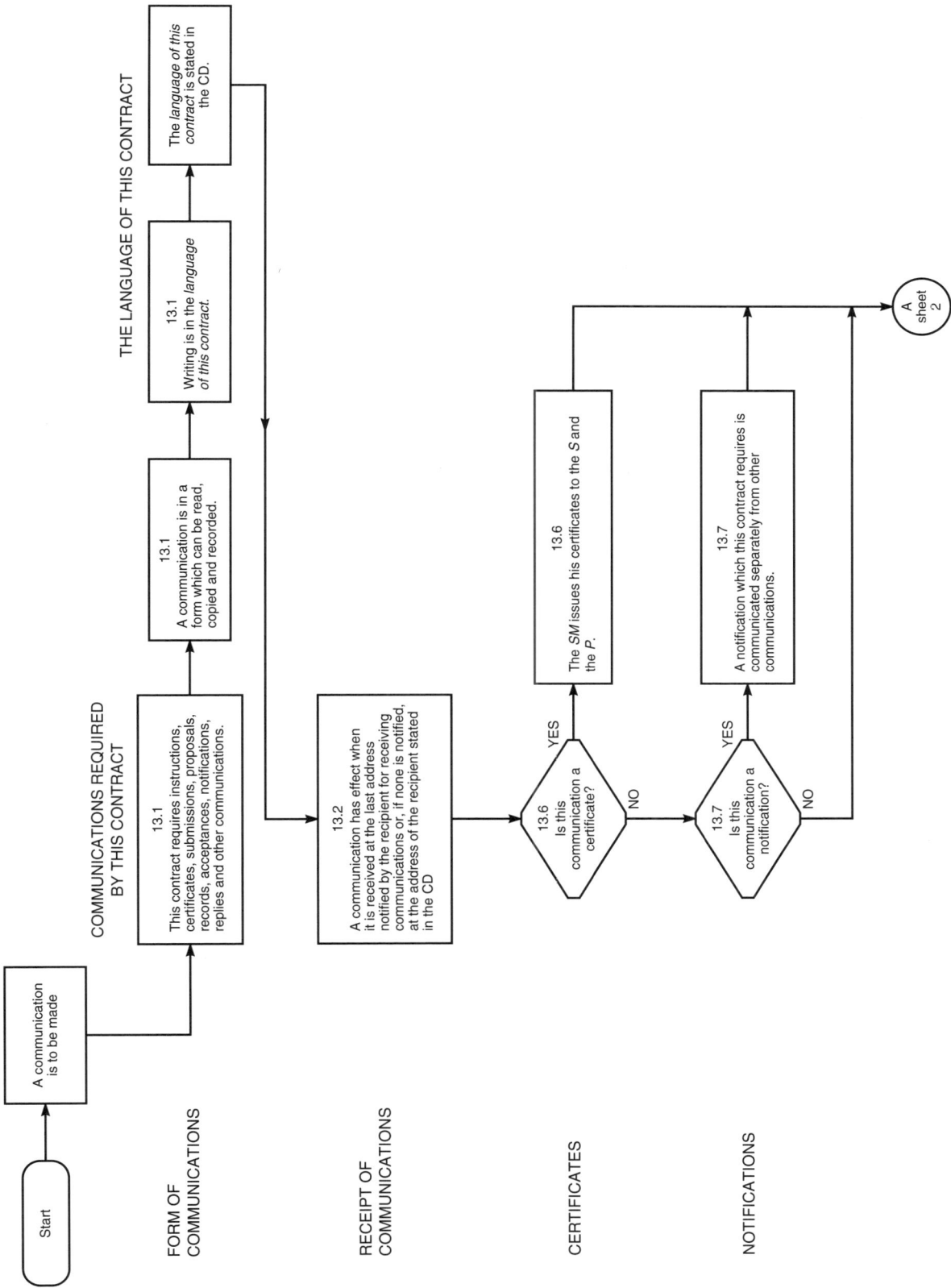

Flow chart 13   Sheet 1 of 3
Communications

REPLY TO A
COMMUNICATION
REQUIRED BY
THIS CONTRACT?

A
sheet
1

13.3
Does this
contract require the
SM or *S* to
reply?

NO

YES

C
sheet
3

RESUBMISSION

REPLY WITHIN PERIOD

13.3
Unless otherwise stated in this
contract, the *SM* or *S* replies
within the *period for reply*.

PERIOD FOR REPLY

The *period for reply*
is stated in the CD.

EXTENSION
TO PERIOD
FOR REPLY

13.5
The *SM* may extend the *period
for reply* to the communication
if the *SM* and the *S* agree to the
extension before the reply is due.

AGREED?

13.5
Do the *SM* and *S*
agree to extend
the period?

YES

NO

EXTENSION NOTIFIED

13.5
The *SM* notifies the *S* of the
extension which has been
agreed.

NOTIFY

FC 13
Notification

TIMELY
REPLY?

Does the *SM*
reply within the period
required?

NO

YES

COMPENSATION EVENT

FC 61
Notify CE 60.1(6)

13.4
Is this
communication
a submission or
resubmission for
acceptance?

NO

YES

SUBMISSION OR
RESUBMISSION
FOR ACCEPTANCE?

B
sheet
3

Finish

THE COMMUNICATION
IS A SUBMISSION OR
RESUBMISSION FOR
ACCEPTANCE

(B sheet 2)

ACCEPTANCE WITHHELD

13.8
The *SM* may withhold acceptance
of a submission by the *S*.

REASON GIVEN

13.4
A reason for withholding acceptance
is that more information is needed in
order to assess the *S's* submission
fully.

NOT COMPENSATION EVENT

13.8
Withholding acceptance for a reason
stated in this contract is not a CE.

SUBMISSION
ACCEPTED?

13.4
Does the *SM*
accept the *S's*
submission?

YES → RESPONSIBILITIES UNCHANGED

FC 14
The *SM*.

NO

INVALID REASON
FOR WITHHOLDING
ACCEPTANCE?

Does
the *S* believe
that the *SM* has
withheld acceptance
for an invalid
reason?

YES → SUPPLIER NOTIFIES

FC 61
The *S* notifies acceptance
withheld as a CE 60.1(8)

NO

RESUBMISSION
REQUIRED

13.4
The *S* resubmits the communication
within the *period for reply* taking
account of the *SM's* reasons.

(C sheet 2)

Finish

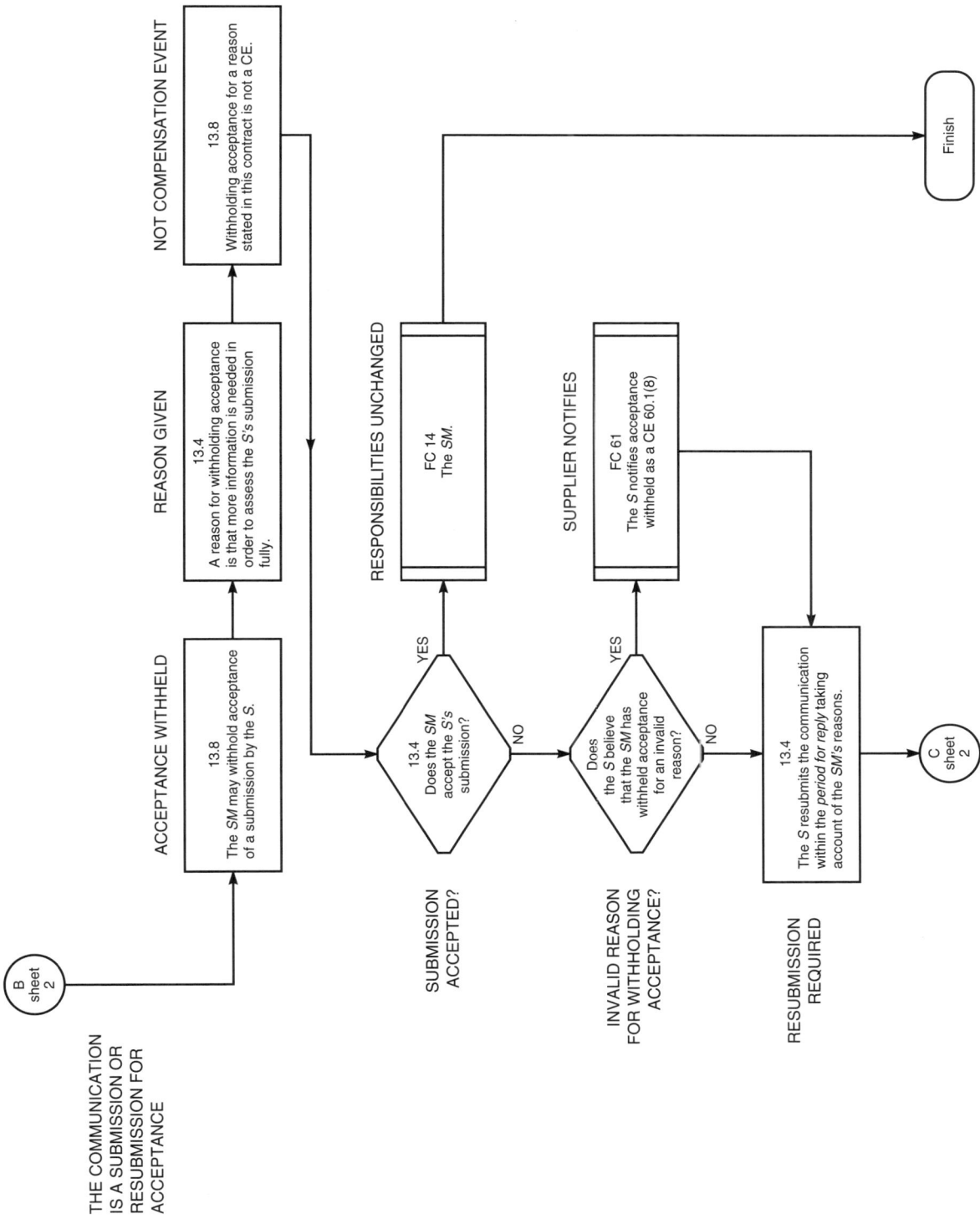

Flow chart 13   Sheet 3 of 3
Communications

Start

What is the issue involving the *SM*?

ACCEPTANCE OF A COMMUNICATION OR SUPPLIER'S WORK

Acceptance?

SUPPLIER RESPONSIBILITIES NOT CHANGED BY ACCEPTANCE

14.1
The *SM's* acceptance of a communication from the *S* or of his work does not change the *S's* responsibility to Provide the Goods and Services or his liability for his design.

SUPPLIER PROVIDES THE GOODS AND SERVICES, AND DESIGNS THOSE PARTS OF THE GOODS AND SERVICES AS STATED IN THE GI

FC 20
Providing the Goods and Services

FC 21
Supplier's design

DELEGATION BY THE SUPPLY MANAGER

Delegation?

DELEGATION OF ACTIONS

14.2
The *SM*, after notifying the *S*, may delegate any of his actions and may cancel any delegation.

NOTIFY SUPPLIER

FC 13
Notification

REFERENCES IN CONTRACT INCLUDES HIS DELEGATE

14.2
A reference to an action of the *SM* in this contract includes an action by his delegate.

INSTRUCTION CHANGING GOODS INFORMATION

Instruction?

GOODS INFORMATION CHANGES

14.3
The *SM* may give an instruction to the *S* which changes the GI.

An instruction to change the GI may change the SR.

SUPPLY REQUIREMENTS

INSTRUCT SUPPLIER

FC 13
Instruction

CHANGE?

Does the *SM* change the GI?

NO

YES

COMPENSATION EVENT

FC 61
Notify CE 60.1(1)

REPLACEMENT OF THE SUPPLY MANAGER

Replacement?

PURCHASER REPLACES

14.4
The *P* may replace the *SM* after he has notified the *S* of the name of the replacement.

NOTIFY SUPPLIER

FC 13
Notification

Finish

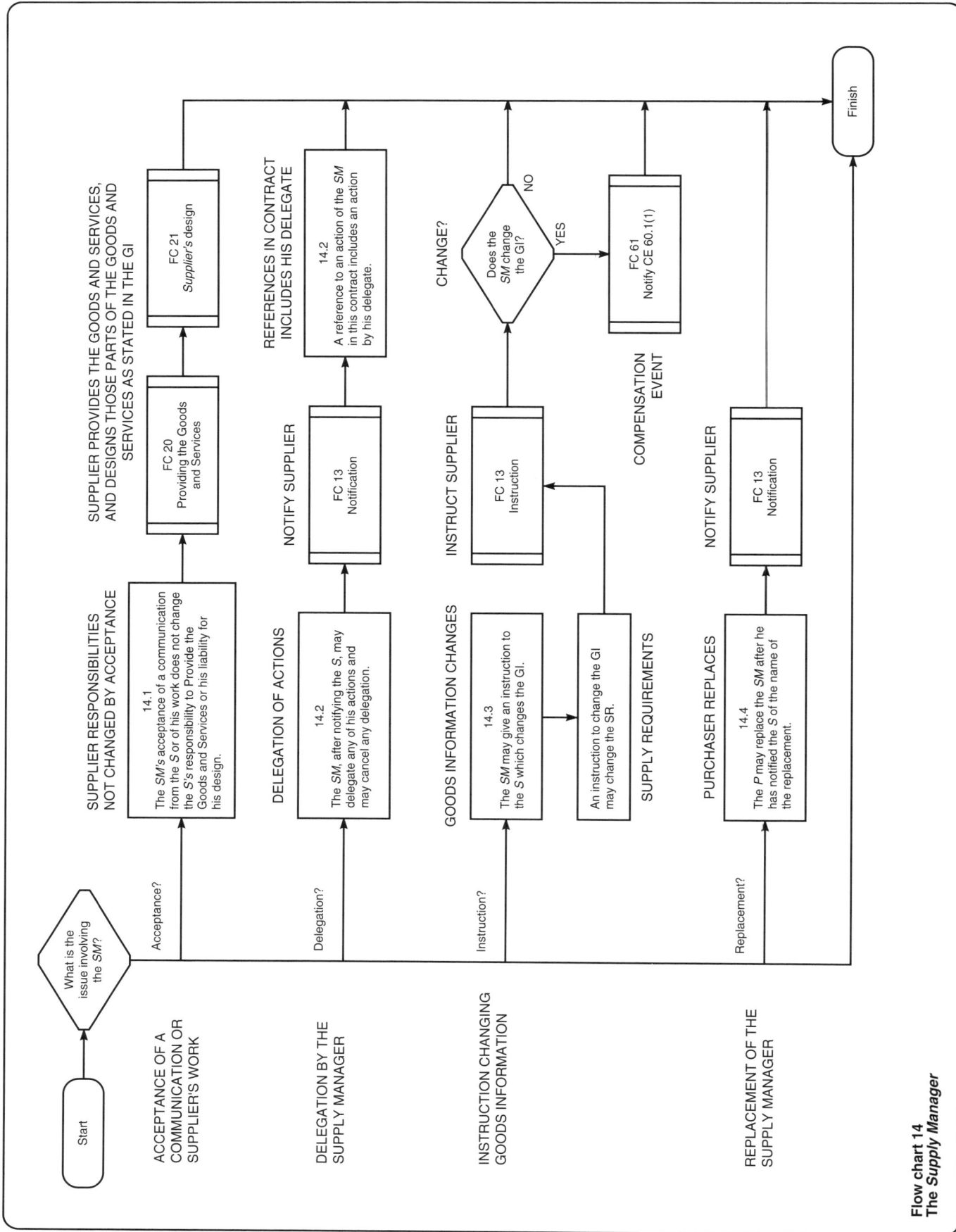

Flow chart 14
The *Supply Manager*

Start

16.1
The *S* and the *SM* give an early warning by notifying the other as soon as either becomes aware of any matter which could
- increase the total of the Prices,
- delay Delivery,
- impair the performance of the *goods* in use or
- impair the usefulness of the *services* to the *P*

16.1
The *S* may give an early warning by notifying the *SM* of any other matter which could increase his total cost

16.1
Does such a notifiable matter occur?

YES → **16.1** Has a CE already been notified?

NO →

YES → **16.1** Early warning of a matter for which a CE has previously been notified is not required

NO →

COMPENSATION EVENT NOTIFIED

FC 13 Notification

16.1 The *SM* enters early warning matters in the Risk Register

11.2(14)
The Risk Register is a register of the risks which are listed in the CD and the risks which the *SM* or *S* has notified as an early warning matter. It includes a description of the risk and a description of the actions to be taken to avoid or reduce the risk

16.2 Is a risk reduction meeting instructed?

NO / YES

INSTRUCTED?

16.2 Either the *SM* or the *S* may instruct the other to attend a risk reduction meeting

RISK REDUCTION MEETING

OTHERS MAY BE INSTRUCTED TO ATTEND

25.3 The *S* obeys an instruction which is in accordance with this contract and is given to him by the *SM*

16.2 Does the *SM* wish to instruct other people to attend?

YES → **16.2** Does the *S* agree to those other people attending?
YES → **16.2** The *SM* may instruct those other people to attend

NO →

16.2 Does the *S* wish to instruct other people to attend?

YES → **16.2** Does the *SM* agree to those other people attending?
YES → **16.2** The *S* may instruct those other people to attend

NO →

16.2 A risk reduction meeting is held

THE PARTIES CO-OPERATE TO RESOLVE THE MATTER

16.3
At a risk reduction meeting those who attend co-operate in
- making and considering proposals for how the effect of the registered risks can be avoided or reduced,
- seeking solutions that will bring advantage to all those who will be affected,
- deciding on the actions which will be taken and who, in accordance with this contract, will take them and
- deciding which risks have now been avoided or have passed and can be removed from the Risk Register

PROPOSALS AND DECISIONS

16.4
The *SM* revises the Risk Register to record the decisions made at each risk reduction meeting and issues the revised Risk Register to the *S*

16.4
If a decision needs a change to the GI, the *SM* instructs the change at the same time as he issues the revised Risk Register

Does the decision need a change to the GI?

YES → **SM's INSTRUCTION** **FC 13** *SM's* Instruction

NO → **Finish**

Flow chart 16 Early warning

Start

NOTIFICATION OF AMBIGUITY OR INCONSISTENCY

17.1
The *SM* or the *S* notifies the other as soon as either becomes aware of an ambiguity or inconsistency in or between the documents which are part of this contract.

Does the *SM* or *S* become aware of such a state? — **NO** / **YES**

NOTIFY OTHER PARTY

FC 13
Notification

INSTRUCTION RESOLVING AMBIGUITY OR INCONSISTENCY

17.1
The *SM* gives an instruction resolving the ambiguity or inconsistency.

FC 13
SM's instruction

SUPPLIER OBEYS AN INSTRUCTION

25.3
The *S* obeys an instruction which is in accordance with this contract and is given to him by the *SM*.

CHANGE TO THE GOODS INFORMATION?
Is the instruction a change to the GI? — **NO** / **YES**

COMPENSATION EVENT

FC 61
Notify CE 60.1(1)

Finish

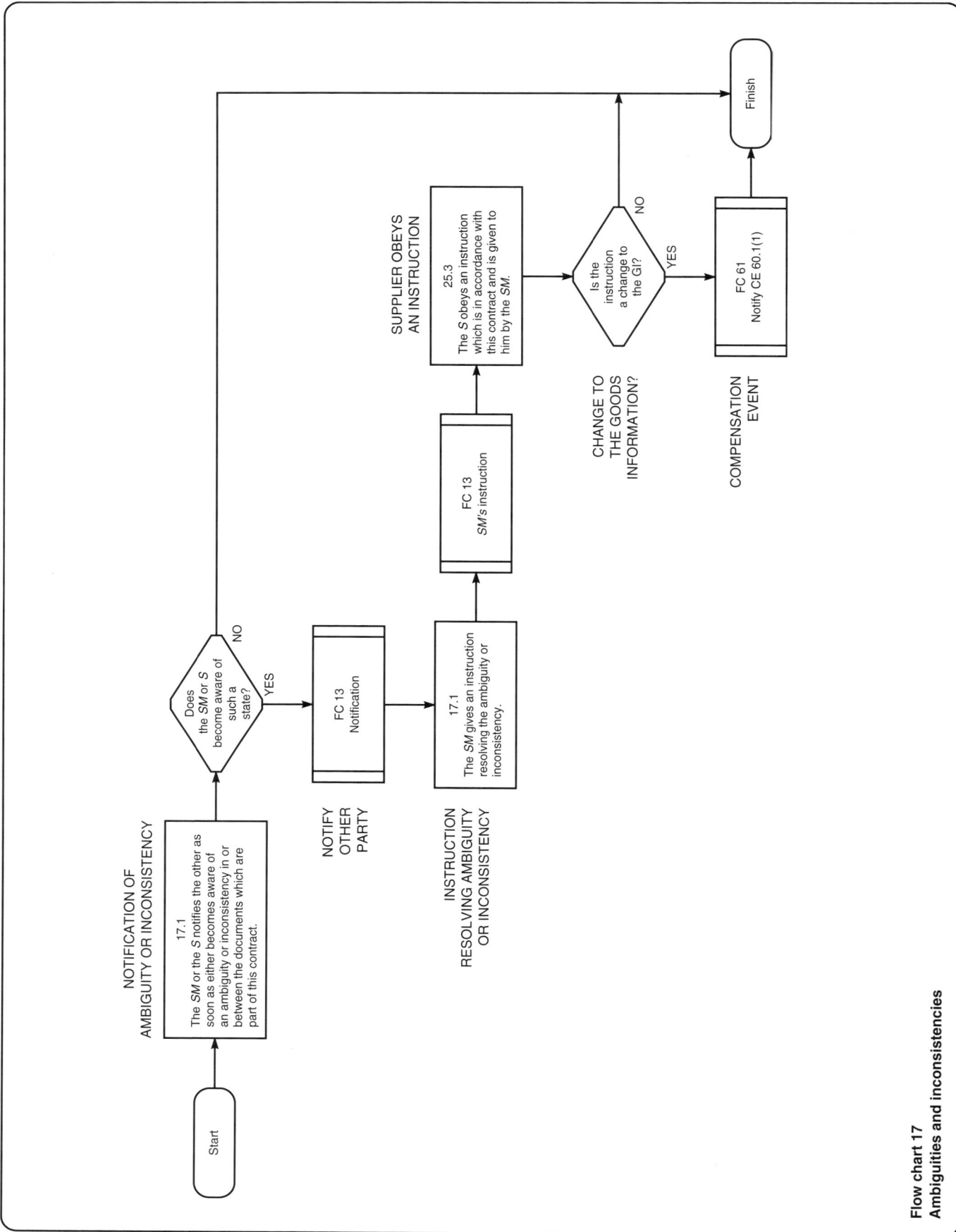

Flow chart 17
Ambiguities and inconsistencies

Flow chart 18

Start → **NOTIFICATION OF ILLEGAL OR IMPOSSIBLE REQUIREMENT**

18.1 The *S* notifies the *SM* as soon as he considers that the GI requires him to do anything which is illegal or impossible.

Does the *S* consider such a state has occurred?
- NO → Finish
- YES → **FC 13** *S*'s notification

DOES SUPPLY MANAGER AGREE?

FC 13 *SM*'s reply

18.1 Does the *SM* agree?
- NO → Finish
- YES →

INSTRUCTION TO CHANGE GOODS INFORMATION

18.1 The *SM* gives an instruction to change the GI appropriately.

An instruction to change the GI may change the SR.

SUPPLIER OBEYS THE INSTRUCTION

25.3 The *S* obeys an instruction which is in accordance with this contract and is given to him by the *SM*.

COMPENSATION EVENT

FC 61 Notify CE 60.1(1) → **Finish**

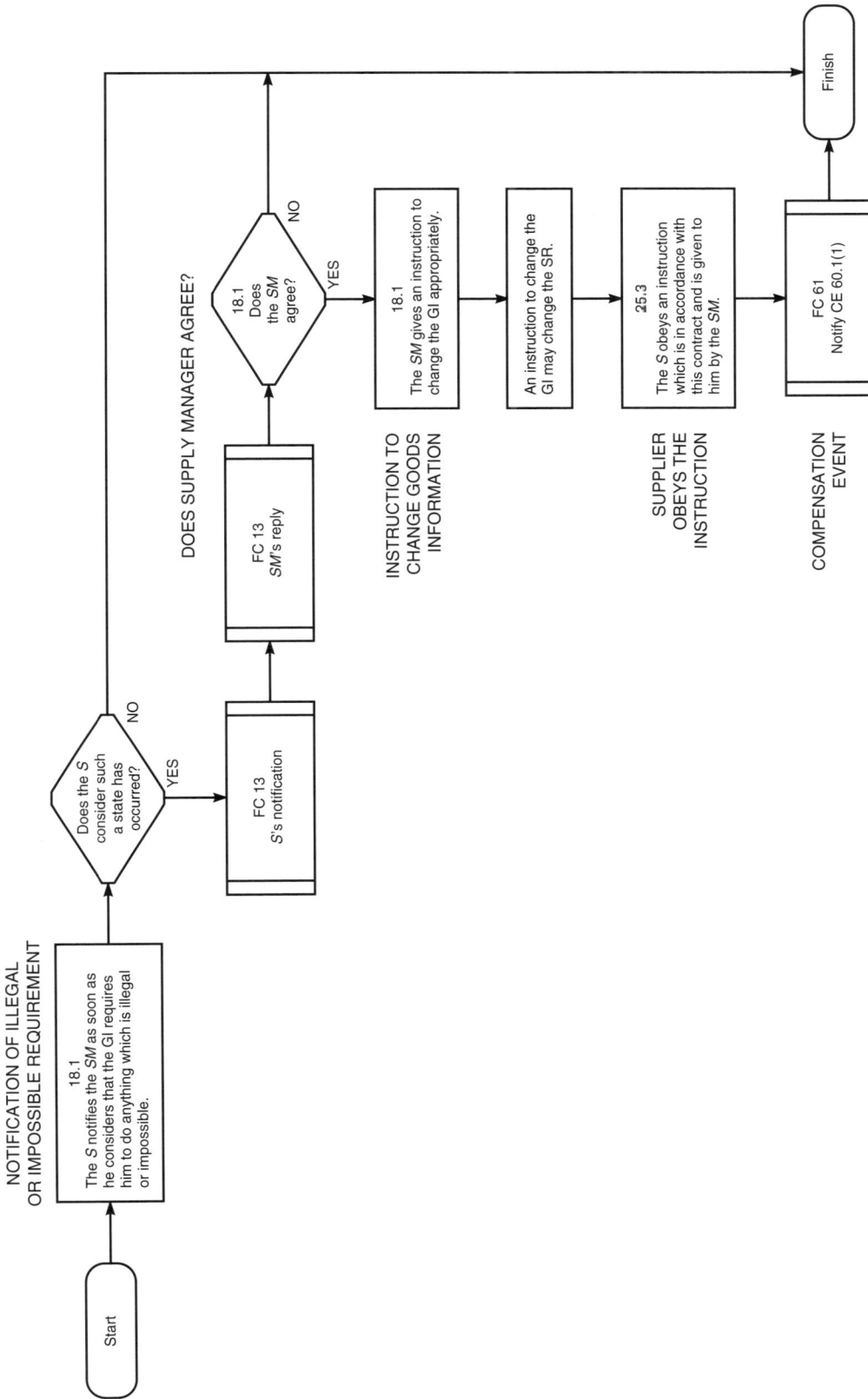

Flow chart 18
Illegal and impossible requirements

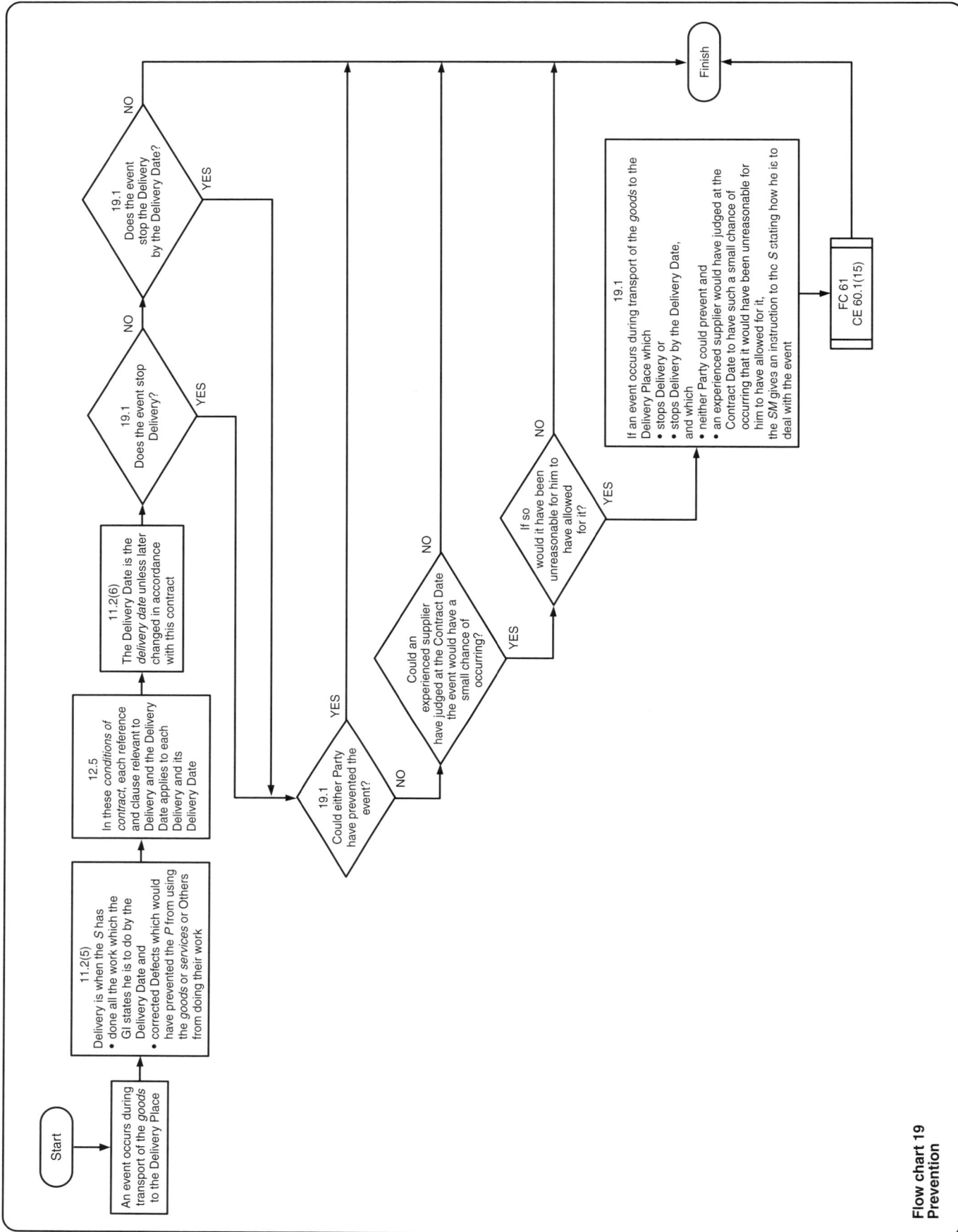

Start

An event occurs during transport of the *goods* to the Delivery Place

11.2(5)
Delivery is when the *S* has
• done all the work which the GI states he is to do by the Delivery Date and
• corrected Defects which would have prevented the *P* from using the *goods* or *services* or Others from doing their work

12.5
In these *conditions of contract*, each reference and clause relevant to Delivery and the Delivery Date applies to each Delivery and its Delivery Date

11.2(6)
The Delivery Date is the *delivery date* unless later changed in accordance with this contract

19.1
Does the event stop Delivery? — NO / YES

19.1
Does the event stop the Delivery by the Delivery Date? — NO / YES

19.1
Could either Party have prevented the event? — YES / NO

Could an experienced supplier have judged at the Contract Date the event would have a small chance of occurring? — NO / YES

19.1
If so would it have been unreasonable for him to have allowed for it? — NO / YES

19.1
If an event occurs during transport of the *goods* to the Delivery Place which
• stops Delivery or
• stops Delivery by the Delivery Date,
and which
• neither Party could prevent and
• an experienced supplier would have judged at the Contract Date to have such a small chance of occurring that it would have been unreasonable for him to have allowed for it,
the *SM* gives an instruction to the *S* stating how he is to deal with the event

FC 61
CE 60.1(15)

Finish

GOODS INFORMATION

11.2(8)

Goods Information is information which either
- specifies and describes the *goods* and *services* and
- states any constraints on how the S Provides the Goods and Services

and is in
- the documents which the CD states it is in,
- the SR or
- an instruction given in accordance with this contract.

SUPPLY REQUIREMENTS

11.2(16)

SR is information which
- describes the *P*'s requirements in connection with the supply of the *goods*,
- states the delivery place,
- describes the requirements for transport of the *goods* and
- describes other information to be provided by the S in connection with the supply of the *goods*.

THE SUPPLIER PROVIDES THE GOODS AND SERVICES

20.1

The S Provides the Goods and Services in accordance with the GI.

THE GOODS AND SERVICES

The *goods* and *services* are stated in the CD.

SUPPLIER RESPONSIBILITIES NOT CHANGED BY ACCEPTANCE

14.1

The *SM*'s acceptance of a communication from the S or of his work does not change the *S*'s responsibility to Provide the Goods and Services or his liability for his design.

TO PROVIDE THE GOODS AND SERVICES

11.2(13)

To Provide the Goods and Services means to do the work necessary to supply the *goods* and *services* in accordance with this contract and all incidental work, services and actions which this contract requires.

Start

Finish

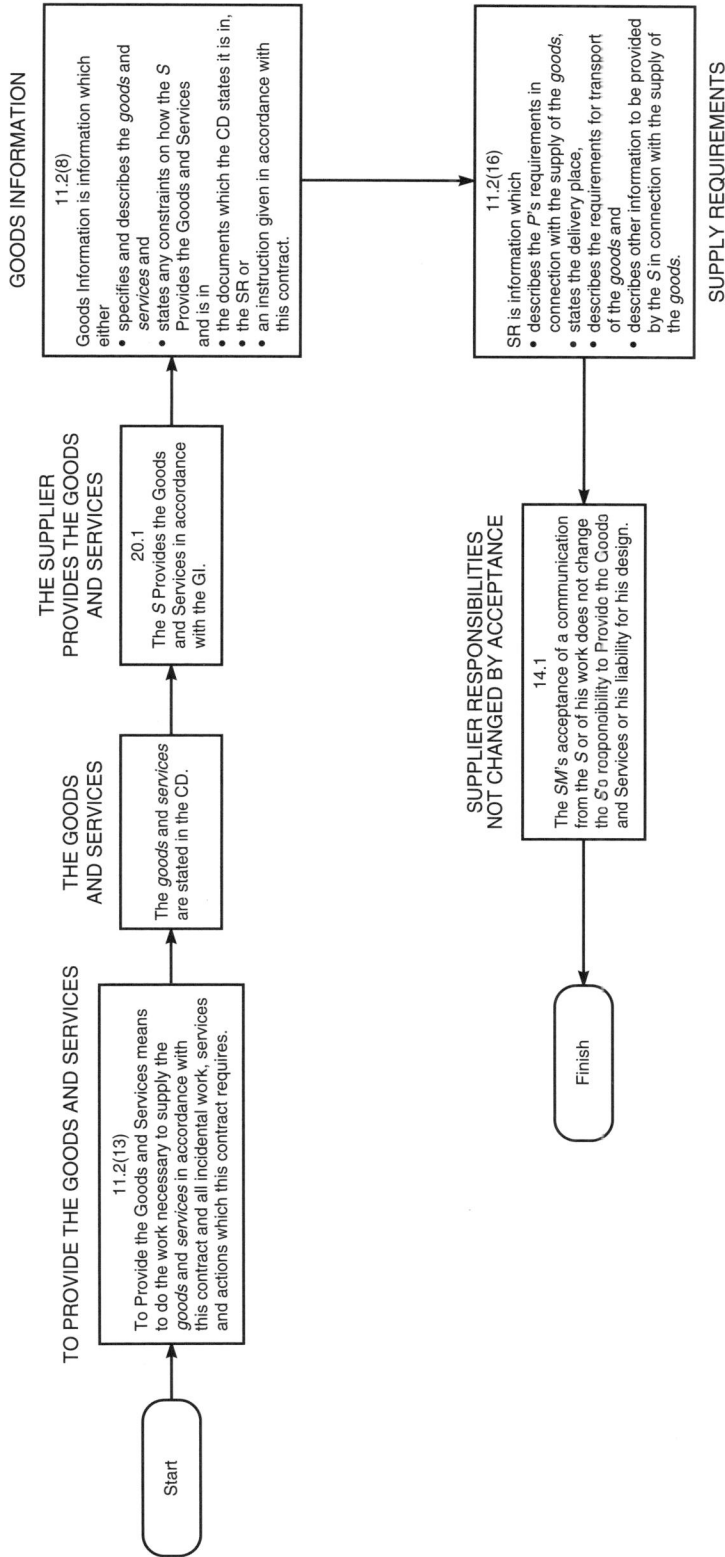

Flow chart 20
Providing the Goods and Services

SUPPLIER DESIGNS

Start

21.1
The *S* designs the *goods* and *services* except for those parts which the GI states the *P* designs.

DESIGN ACCEPTANCE

21.2
The *S* submits the particulars of his design which the GI requires to the *SM* for acceptance.

SUBMIT DESIGN

FC 13
Submission for acceptance

DESIGN TO BE SUBMITTED?

21.2
Does the GI require the *S* to submit his design?

YES —

SUBMISSION IN PARTS

21.3
The *S* may submit particulars of his design for acceptance in parts if each part can be assessed fully.

REASON FOR NOT ACCEPTING

21.2
A reason for not accepting the *S*'s particulars is that they do not comply with either the GI or the applicable law.

SUBMIT DESIGN

FC 13
Submission for acceptance

REVISE DESIGN

The *S* revises the particulars of his design.

AWAIT ACCEPTANCE

21.2
The *S* does not proceed with the relevant work until the *SM* has accepted the particulars of his design.

DESIGN ACCEPTED?

Does the *SM* accept the *S*'s submission?

NO

YES

NO (from DESIGN TO BE SUBMITTED?)

SUPPLIER PROVIDES THE GOODS AND SERVICES

FC 20
Providing the Goods and Services

LIABILITY FOR DEFECTS

FC 88
Limitation of *S*'s liability for Defects due to his design.

Finish

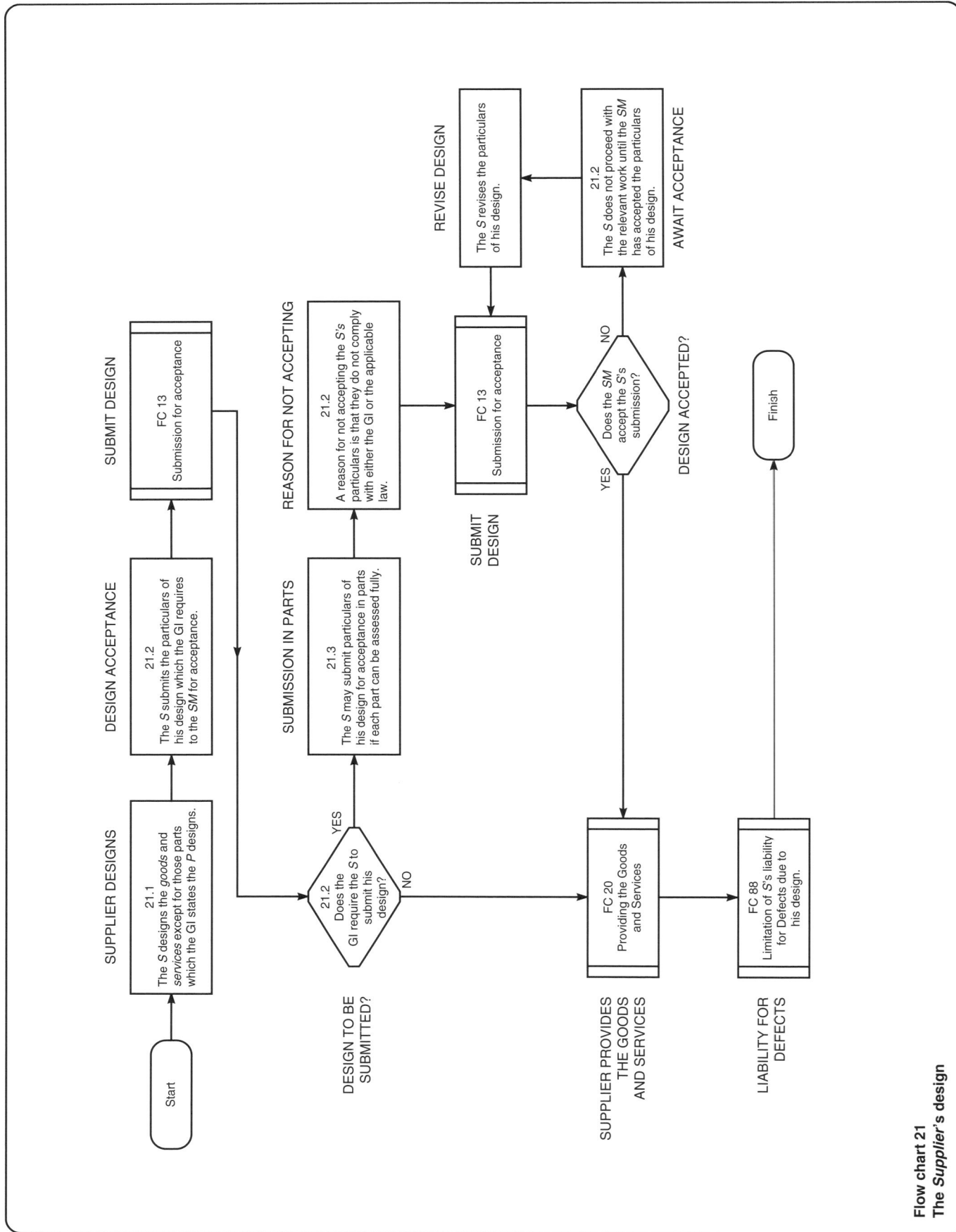

Flow chart 21
The *Supplier's* design

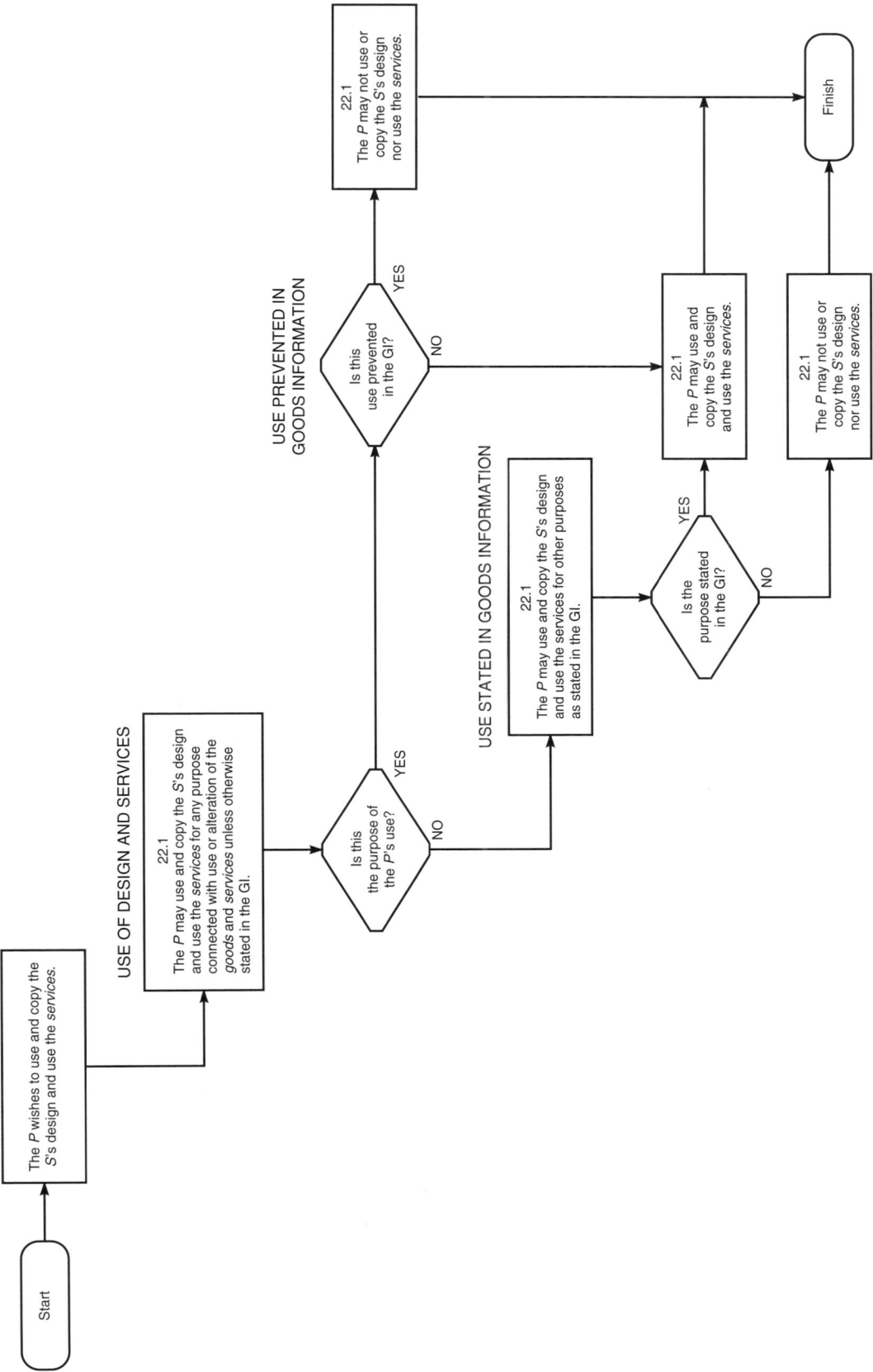

PURCHASER WISHES TO USE SUPPLIER'S DESIGN AND SERVICES

Start

The *P* wishes to use and copy the *S*'s design and use the *services*.

USE OF DESIGN AND SERVICES

22.1
The *P* may use and copy the *S*'s design and use the *services* for any purpose connected with use or alteration of the *goods* and *services* unless otherwise stated in the GI.

Is this the purpose of the *P*'s use?

YES / NO

USE PREVENTED IN GOODS INFORMATION

Is this use prevented in the GI?

YES / NO

22.1
The *P* may not use or copy the *S*'s design nor use the *services*.

USE STATED IN GOODS INFORMATION

22.1
The *P* may use and copy the *S*'s design and use the services for other purposes as stated in the GI.

Is the purpose stated in the GI?

YES / NO

22.1
The *P* may use and copy the *S*'s design and use the *services*.

22.1
The *P* may not use or copy the *S*'s design nor use the *services*.

Finish

Flow chart 22
Using the *Supplier*'s design and *services*

CO-OPERATION WITH OTHERS

SUPPLIER CO-OPERATES WITH OTHERS

Start

11.2(9)

Others are people or organisations who are not the *P*, the *SM*, the *Adjudicator*, the *S*, or any employee, Subcontractor or supplier of the *S*.

WHAT IS NEEDED?

23.1

Do Others need information about the *goods and services*?

YES →

NO →

PROVISION OF INFORMATION

23.1

The *S* co-operates with Others in obtaining and providing information which they need in connection with the *goods and services*.

SERVICES AND OTHER THINGS

SUPPLIER PROVIDES SUPPORT

23.2

The *P* and *S* provide services and other things in accordance with the GI.

PROVIDED?

23.2

Does the *S* provide services and other things as required?

NO →

YES →

COST PAID BY SUPPLIER

23.2

Any cost incurred by the *P* as a result of the *S* not providing the services and other things which he is to provide is assessed by the *SM* and paid by the *S*.

Finish

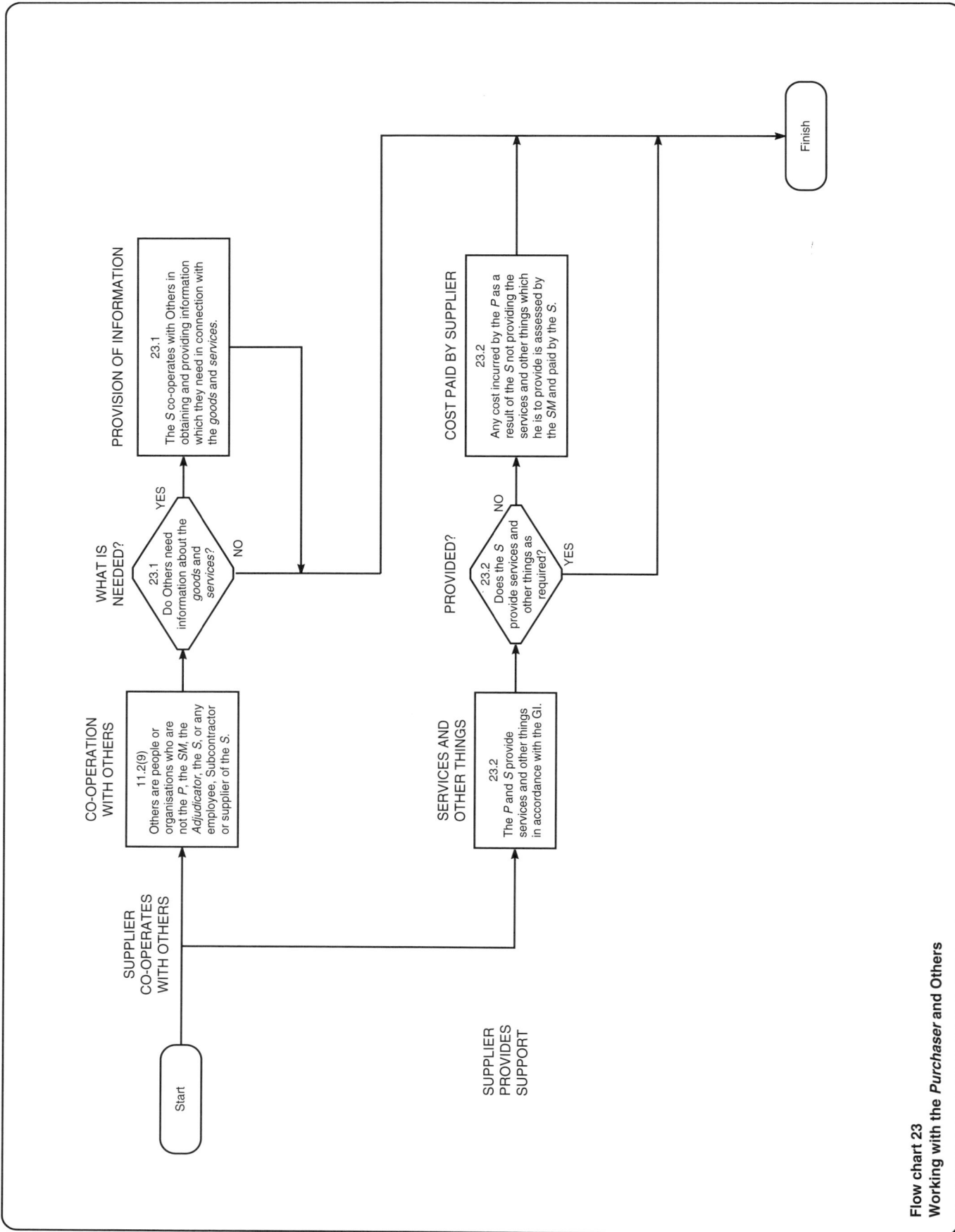

Flow chart 23
Working with the *Purchaser* and Others

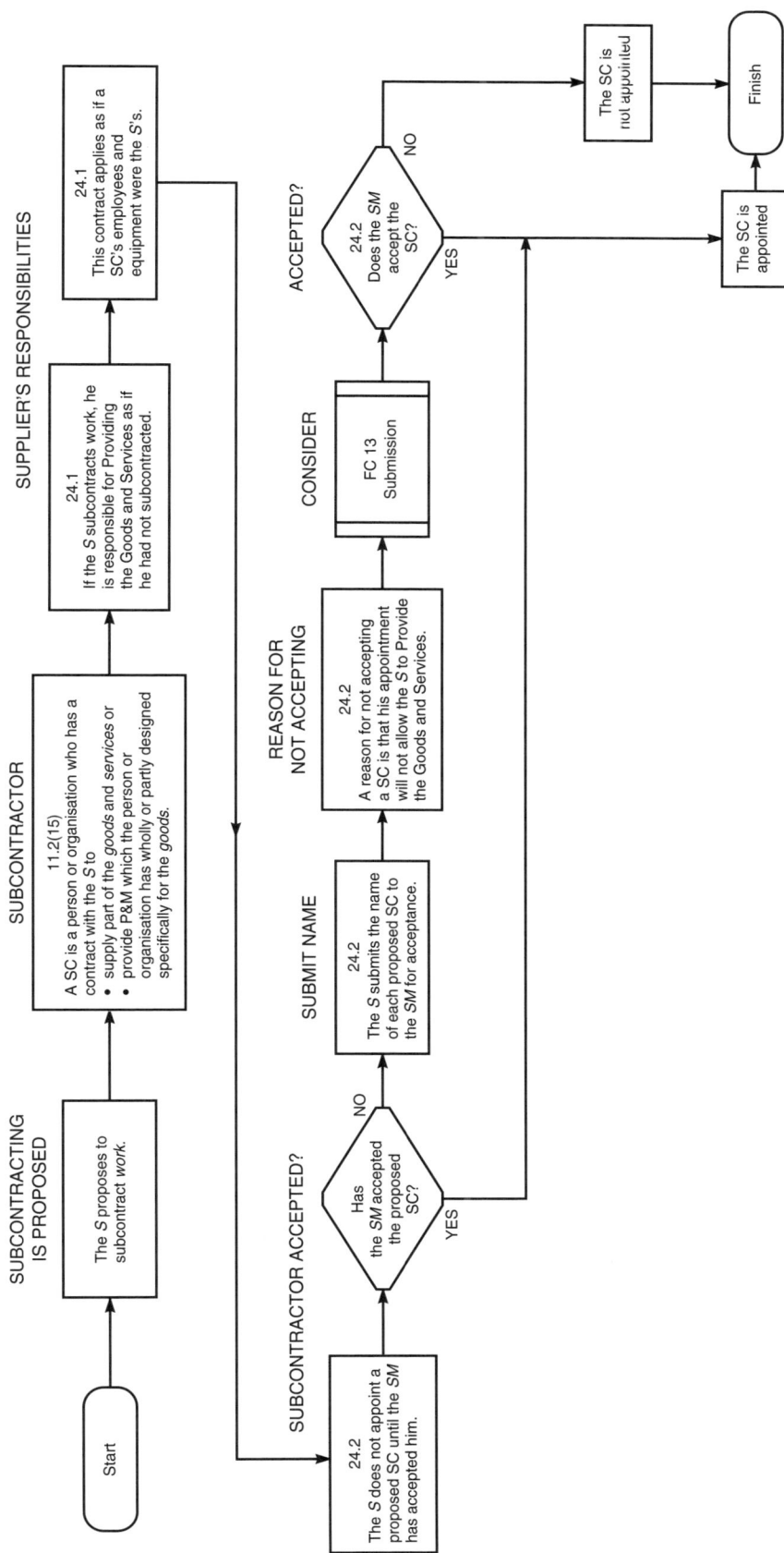

SUBCONTRACTING IS PROPOSED

Start

↓

The *S* proposes to subcontract *work*.

SUBCONTRACTOR

11.2(15)

A SC is a person or organisation who has a contract with the *S* to
- supply part of the *goods* and *services* or
- provide P&M which the person or organisation has wholly or partly designed specifically for the *goods*.

↓

SUPPLIER'S RESPONSIBILITIES

24.1

This contract applies as if a SC's employees and equipment were the *S*'s.

24.1

If the *S* subcontracts work, he is responsible for Providing the Goods and Services as if he had not subcontracted.

SUBCONTRACTOR ACCEPTED?

24.2

The *S* does not appoint a proposed SC until the *SM* has accepted him.

↓

Has the *SM* accepted the proposed SC? — NO →

YES ↓

SUBMIT NAME

24.2

The *S* submits the name of each proposed SC to the *SM* for acceptance.

REASON FOR NOT ACCEPTING

24.2

A reason for not accepting a SC is that his appointment will not allow the *S* to Provide the Goods and Services.

CONSIDER

FC 13
Submission

ACCEPTED?

24.2

Does the *SM* accept the SC?

NO → The SC is not appointed → **Finish**

YES ↓ The SC is appointed ↑

Start

SUPPLIER NEEDS DESIGN APROVAL

APPROVAL NEEDED

Approval of the S's design is necessary from Others.

OTHERS

11.2(9)
Others are people or organisations who are not the P, the SM, the Adjudicator, the S, or any employee, Subcontractor or supplier of the S.

DESIGN APPROVED

25.1
The S obtains approval of his design from Others where necessary.

APPROVAL OBTAINED?

Is the S successful in obtaining design approval from Others?

YES →

NO →

EARLY WARNING?

16.1
Does failure to get approval warrant early warning?

YES ↓

NO →

EARLY WARNING

FC 16
Early warning by the S to the SM

REVISE DESIGN AND RESUBMIT

The S revises his design (with the SM's acceptance) and resubmits.

Is the S being required to do something which is impossible or illegal?

IMPOSSIBLE/ILLEGAL REQUIREMENTS

FC 18
Illegal and impossible requirements

SUPPLIER PROVIDES ACCESS

ACCESS REQUIRED

The SM or Others require access to work.

NOTIFICATION OF OTHERS

25.2
The SM notifies the S of the Others who require access.

RIGHT TO WATCH TEST

25.2
The S may not restrict the SM's right to watch any test done by the S which is required by the GI or the applicable law.

Is such a test required?

NO →

YES →

25.1
The S provides access to work being done for this contract for
• the SM and
• Others notified to him by the SM subject to the restrictions stated in the CD.

RESTRICTION

Does the CD state restrictions to the access required?

YES →

NO →

The S does not provide access.

The S provides access.

Finish

A
Sheet 2

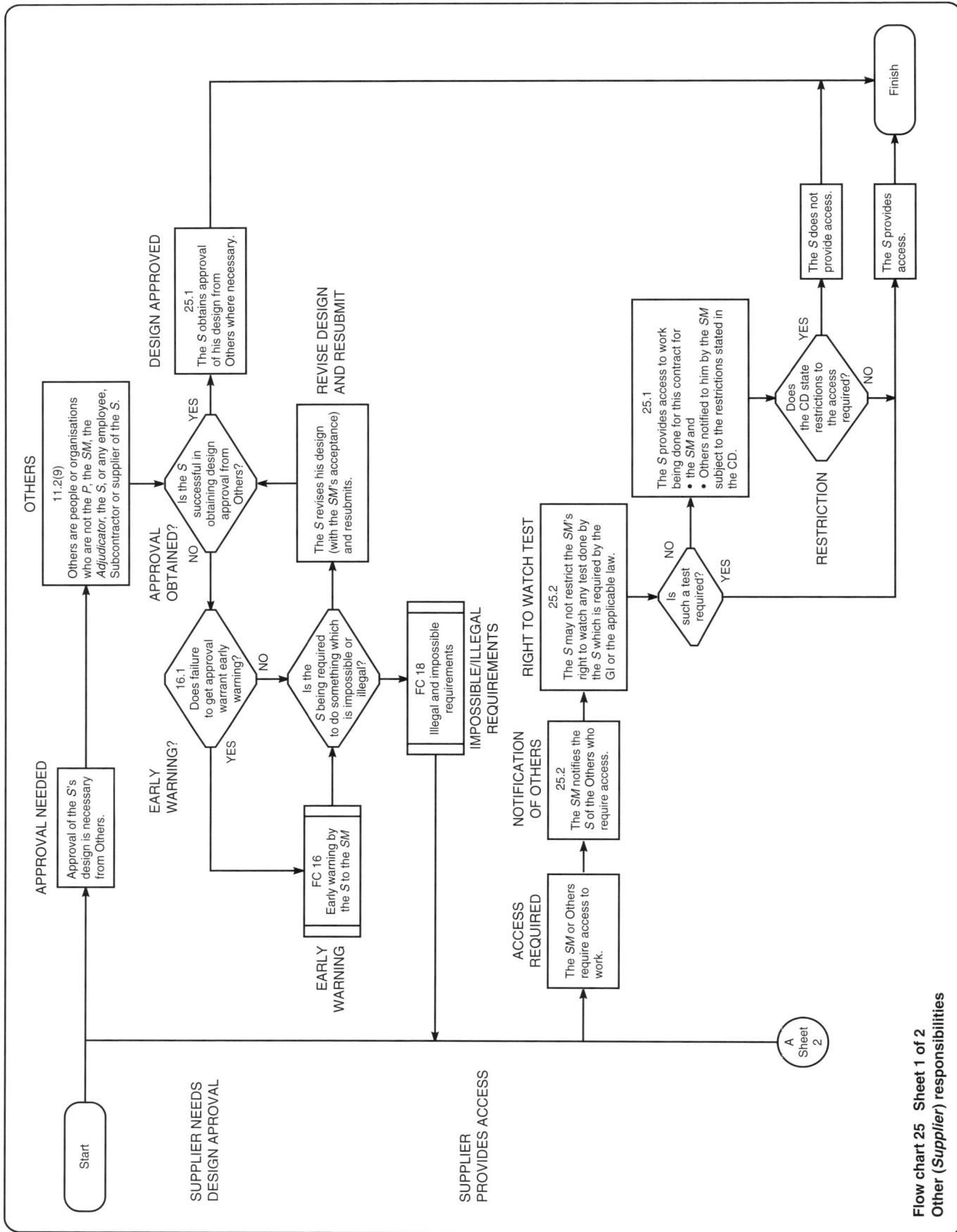

Flow chart 25 Sheet 1 of 2
Other (Supplier) responsibilities

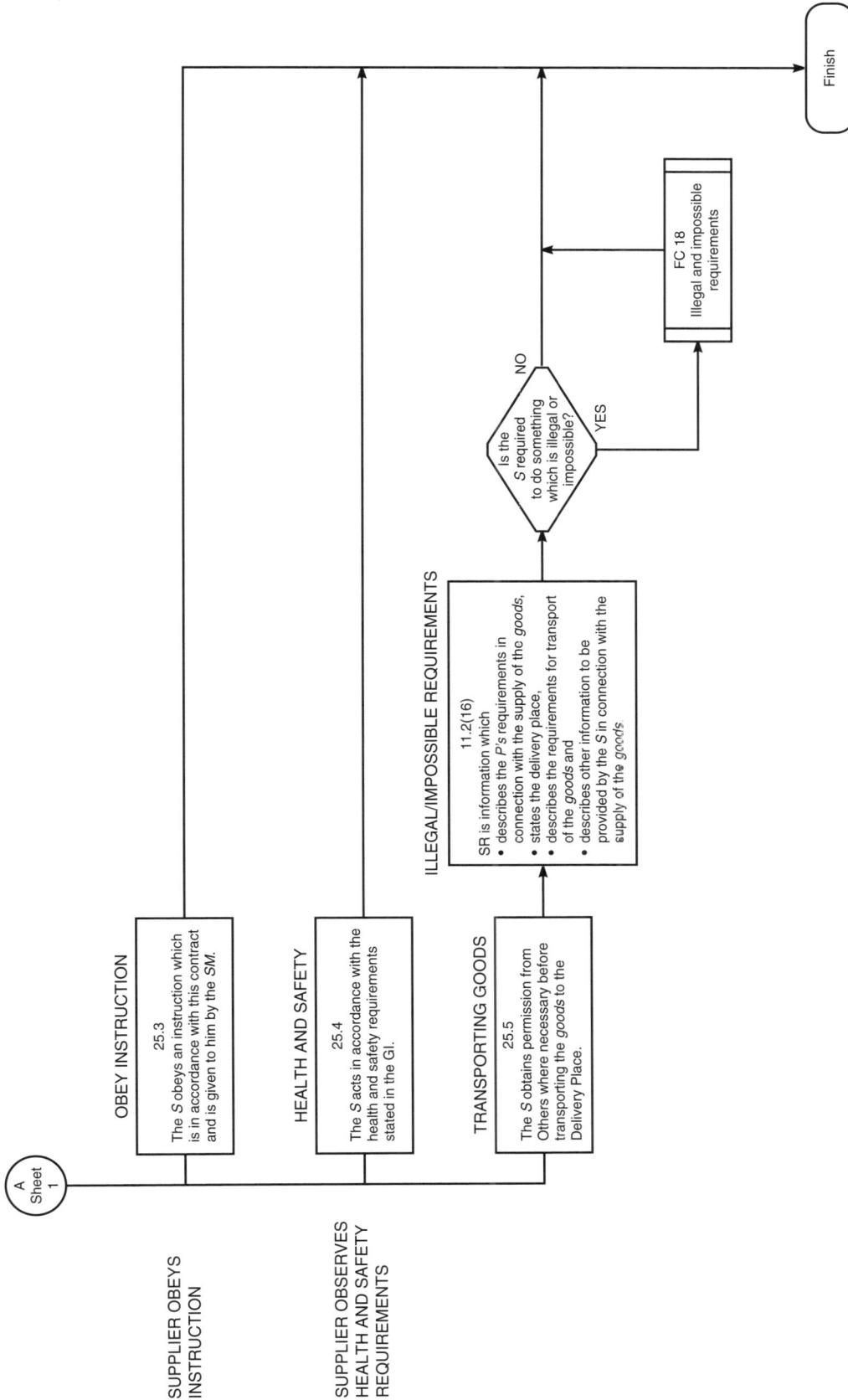

SUPPLIER OBEYS INSTRUCTION

A Sheet 1

OBEY INSTRUCTION

25.3

The *S* obeys an instruction which is in accordance with this contract and is given to him by the *SM*.

SUPPLIER OBSERVES HEALTH AND SAFETY REQUIREMENTS

HEALTH AND SAFETY

25.4

The *S* acts in accordance with the health and safety requirements stated in the GI.

TRANSPORTING GOODS

25.5

The *S* obtains permission from Others where necessary before transporting the *goods* to the Delivery Place.

ILLEGAL/IMPOSSIBLE REQUIREMENTS

11.2(16)

SR is information which
- describes the *P*'s requirements in connection with the supply of the *goods*,
- states the delivery place,
- describes the requirements for transport of the *goods* and
- describes other information to be provided by the *S* in connection with the supply of the *goods*

Is the *S* required to do something which is illegal or impossible?

NO

YES

FC 18
Illegal and impossible requirements

Finish

Start

30.1
The S does not start work until the *starting date*.

The *starting date* is stated in the CD.

Is it before the *starting date*?

YES → Work does not start. → Finish

NO

11.2(5)
Delivery is when the S has
• done all the work which the GI states he is to do by the Delivery Date and
• corrected Defects which would have prevented the P from using the *goods* or *services* or Others from doing their work.

30.1
The S does the work so that Delivery is on or before the Delivery Date.

11.2(6)
The Delivery Date is the *delivery date* unless later changed in accordance with this contract.

Is there more than one Delivery Date?

YES

12.5
In these *conditions of contract*, each reference and clause relevant to Delivery and the Delivery Date applies to each Delivery Date and its Delivery Date.

NO

Is it more than one week before the Delivery Date?

YES

Does the CD state that the S may not deliver more than one week before the Delivery Date?

YES

30.2
The S does not bring the *goods* to the Delivery Place more than one week before the Delivery Date if it is stated in the CD that he may not do so.

The S may not bring the *goods* early.

A sheet 2

NO

The S may bring the *goods* early.

FC25
Permission to transport goods

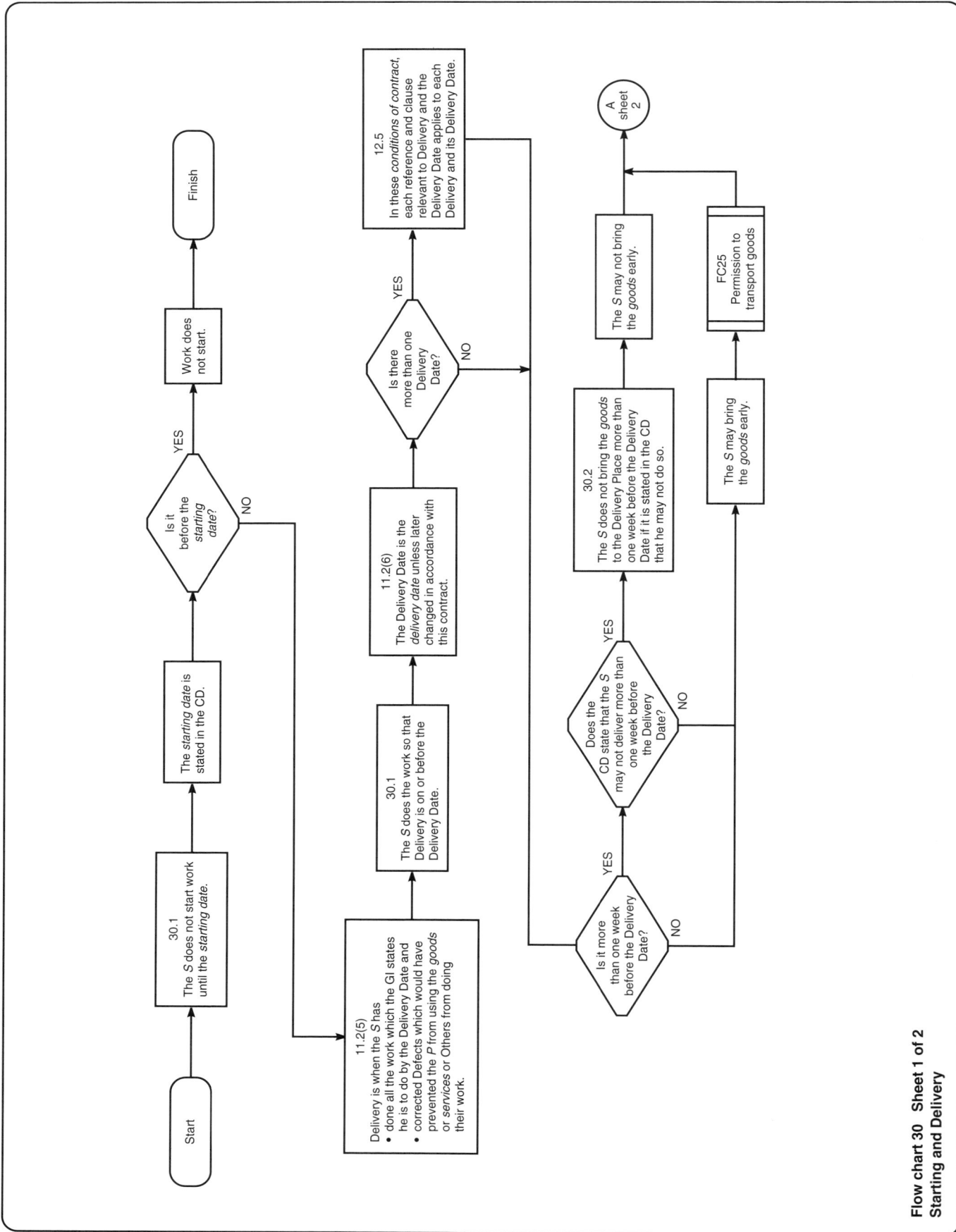

Flow chart 30   Sheet 1 of 2
Starting and Delivery

```
                                    ┌─────────┐
                                    │ Finish  │
                                    └─────────┘
                                     ▲       ▲
                              YES    │       │ NO
                        ◇ Does              ◇ Does
                        the S achieve        Option X7
                        Delivery on or       apply?
                        before the
                        Delivery Date?
                          ▲          NO ──────▶  YES
                        ( A                          │
                        sheet                        ▼
                          1 )                   ┌──────────┐
                                                │ FC X7    │
                                                │ Delay    │
                                                │ damages  │
                                                └──────────┘
                                                DELAY DAMAGES
```

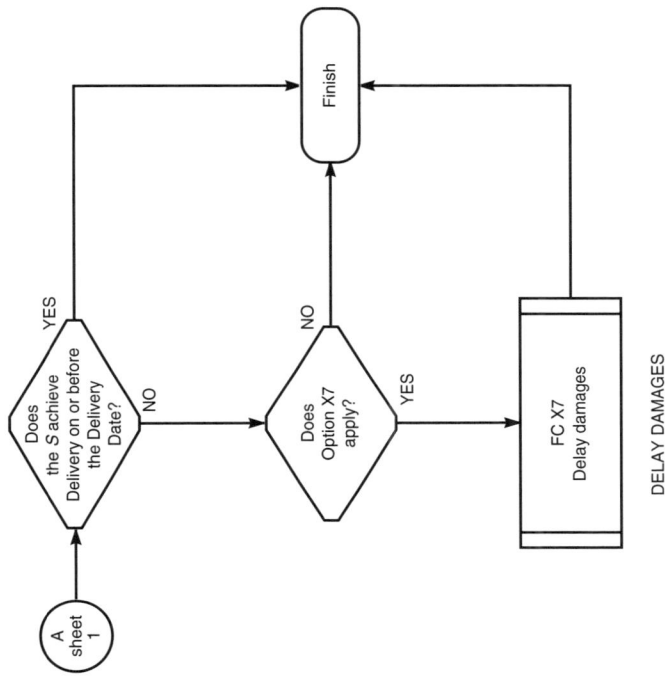

Flow chart 30   Sheet 2 of 2
Starting and Delivery

19

PROGRAMME IN CONTRACT DATA PART TWO?

Start

Is there an Accepted Programme? — NO

YES

31.1 Is a programme identified in the CD? — YES

NO

11.2(1) The Accepted Programme is the programme identified in the CD.

Finish

FIRST PROGRAMME

31.1 The S submits a first programme to the SM for acceptance within the period stated in the CD.

PERIOD FOR SUBMISSION OF A FIRST PROGRAMME

REVISED PROGRAMME

FC 32 Revising the programme

31.2 The S shows on each programme which he submits for acceptance
- the *starting date* and Delivery Date,
- planned Delivery,
- the dates, when in order to Provide the Goods and Services the S will need
  - access to the P's premises,
  - acceptances and
  - P&M and other things to be provided by the P,
- the dates when the S plans to conduct factory acceptance tests or inspections and
- other information which the GI requires the S to show on a programme.

INFORMATION TO BE SHOWN ON A PROGRAMME SUBMITTED FOR ACCEPTANCE

FC 13 Submission for Acceptance

PROGRAMME SUBMITTED

A sheet 2

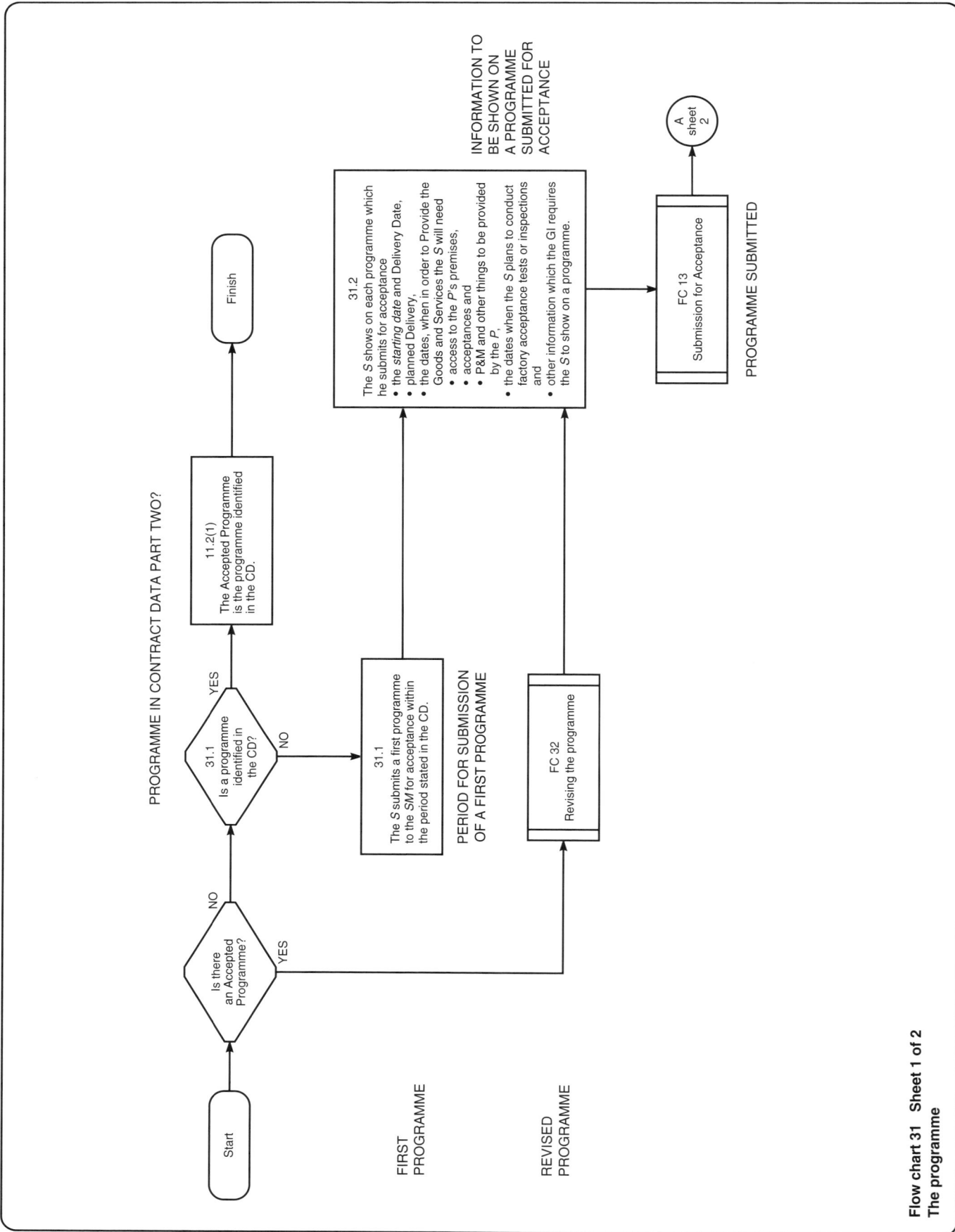

Flow chart 31   Sheet 1 of 2
The programme

TIMELY SUBMISSION?

A sheet 1

Does the S submit a programme for acceptance on time?
- NO → EARLY WARNING
- YES →

EARLY WARNING

FC 15
Early warning given by SM to S

REASONS FOR NOT ACCEPTING THE PROGRAMME

31.3
A reason for not accepting a programme is that
- the S's plans which it shows are not practicable,
- it does not show the information which this contract requires,
- it does not represent the S's plans realistically or
- it does not comply with the GI.

The GI includes the SR

TIMELY REPLY?

31.3
Does the SM reply within two weeks of the submission?
- NO → LATE REPLY
- YES →

LATE REPLY

FC 61
Notify CE 60.1(6)

PROGRAMME ACCEPTED?

31.3
Does the SM accept the programme submitted?
- YES → NEW ACCEPTED PROGRAMME
- NO → REASONS NOT ACCEPTED

NEW ACCEPTED PROGRAMME

11.2(1)
The Accepted Programme is the latest programme accepted by the SM and it supersedes previous Accepted Programmes.

→ Finish

REASONS NOT ACCEPTED

31.3
The SM notifies the S of his reasons for not accepting the programme.

→ Finish

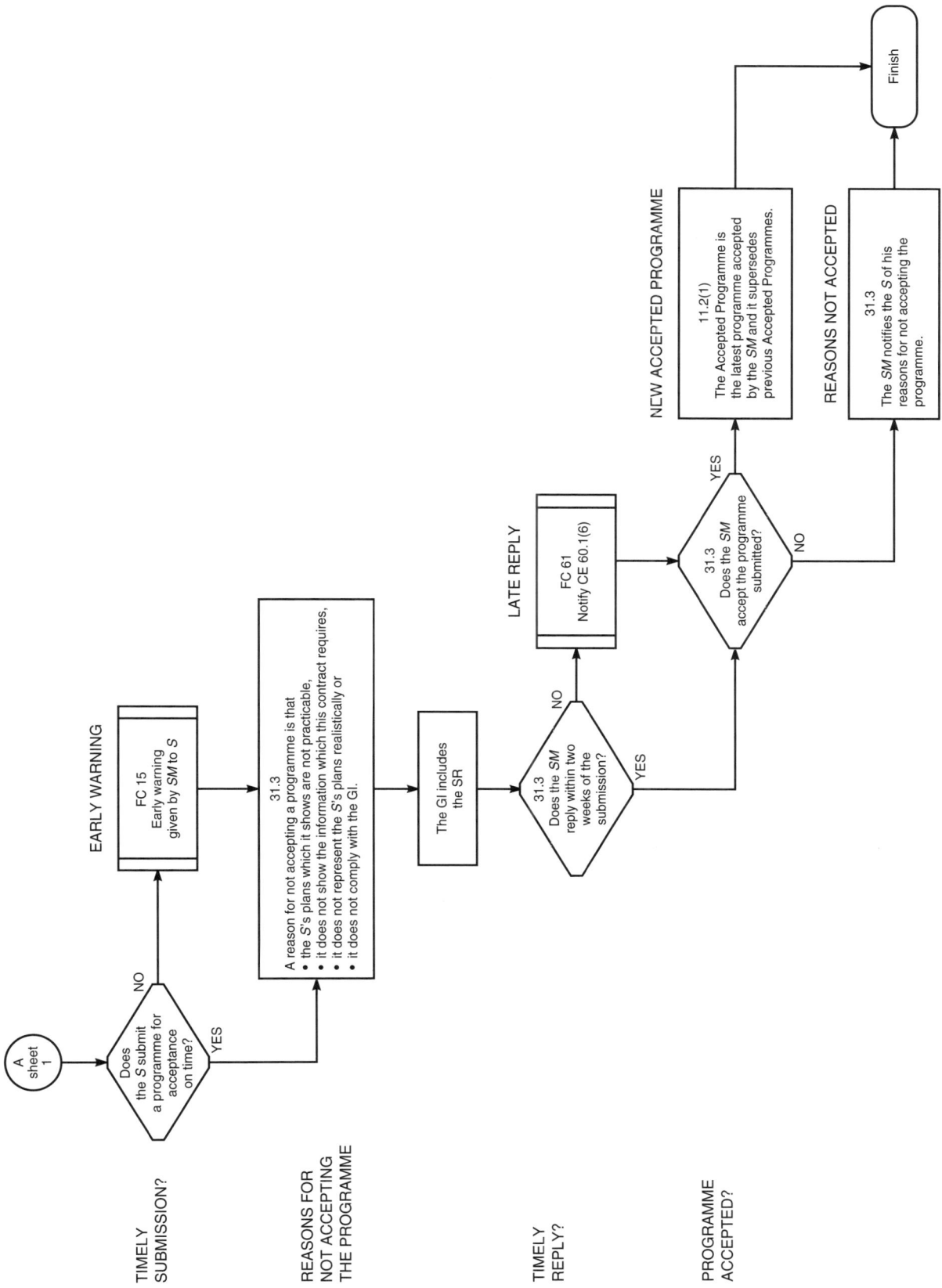

Flow chart 31   Sheet 2 of 2
The programme

REVISED PROGRAMME

Start

A revised programme is to be submitted for acceptance.

REVISION FREQUENCY

32.2
The S submits a revised programme to the SM for acceptance at no longer interval than the interval stated in the CD from the *starting date* until Delivery of the whole of the *goods* and *services*.

SUPPLY MANAGER INSTRUCTS THAT A REVISED PROGRAMME BE SUBMITTED?

32.2
Does the *SM* instruct the S to submit a revised programme?

YES →

32.2
The S submits a revised programme to the *SM* for acceptance within the *period for reply* after the *SM* has instructed him to.

NO

SUPPLIER CHOOSES TO SUBMIT HIS REVISED PROGRAMME?

32.2
Does the S choose to submit a revised programme?

YES

NO

IN ANY CASE, IS A REGULAR REVISED PROGRAMME DUE TO BE SUBMITTED?

32.2
In any case, is a revised programme due to be submitted?

YES

NO

INFORMATION TO BE SHOWN ON A REVISED PROGRAMME

32.1
The S shows on each revised programme
- the actual progress achieved on each operation and its effect upon the timing of the remaining work,
- the effects of implemented compensation events,
- how the S plans to deal with any delays and to correct notified Defects and
- any other changes which the S proposes to make to the Accepted Programme.

Finish

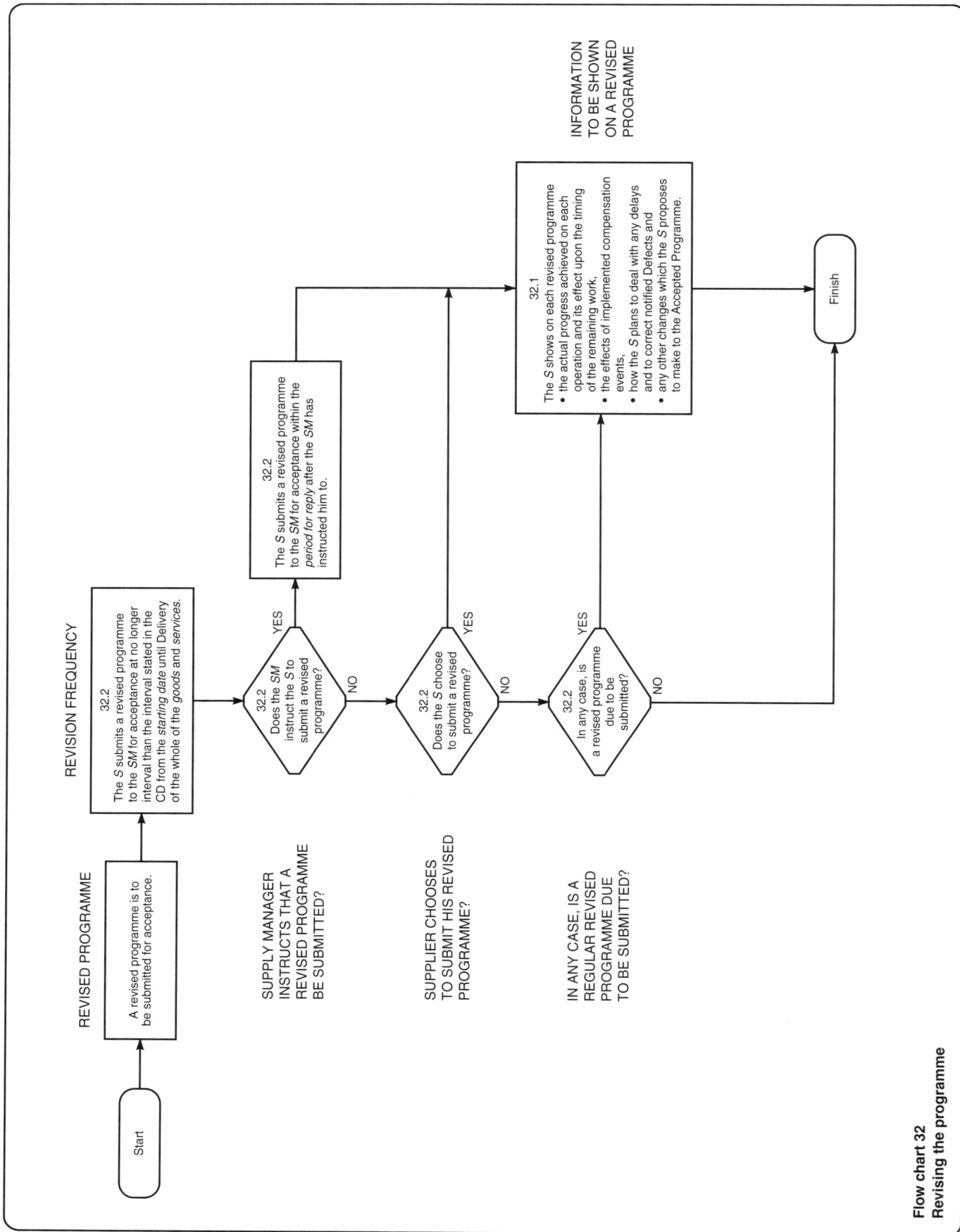

Flow chart 32
Revising the programme

```
Start → The S needs access to and use of the P's premises → 33.1 The P allows access to and use of his premises to the S as necessary for the work included in this contract.

Is the access required for work in this contract?
  NO → The P does not provide access → Finish
  YES → Does the P allow access to the S as necessary?
          NO → FC 16 Possible CE 60.1(2) → Finish
          YES → Finish
```

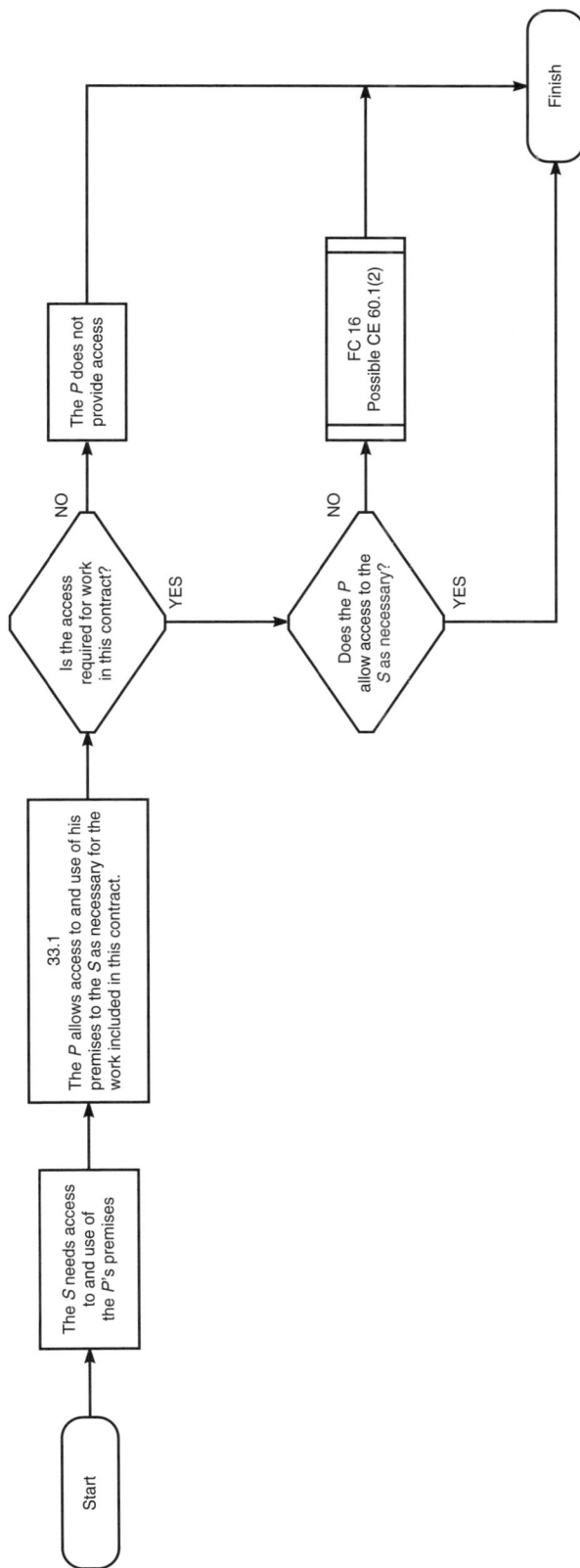

Flow chart 33
Access

23

Start

The *SM* may instruct the *S* to stop or not to start any work.

34.1
Does the *SM* issue such an instruction?

— YES →

INSTRUCTION TO STOP OR NOT START WORK

FC 13
Instruction

COMPENSATION EVENT

FC 61
Notify CE 60.1(4)

OBEY INSTRUCTION

25.3
The *S* obeys an instruction which is in accordance with this contract and is given to him by the *SM*.

— NO →

RE-START OR START WORK

34.1
The *SM* may later instruct the *S* to re-start or start it.

34.1
Does the *SM* issue such an instruction?

— YES →

INSTRUCTION TO RE-START OR TO START WORK

FC 13
Instruction

OBEY INSTRUCTION

25.3
The *S* obeys an instruction which is in accordance with this contract and is given to him by the *SM*.

→ **Finish**

— NO →

REASON FOR TERMINATION?

91.6
Is substantial work affected?

— YES →

Have 13 weeks elapsed since the instruction stopping work?

— YES →

TERMINATION

FC 90
Possible termination (R18 to R20)

— NO →

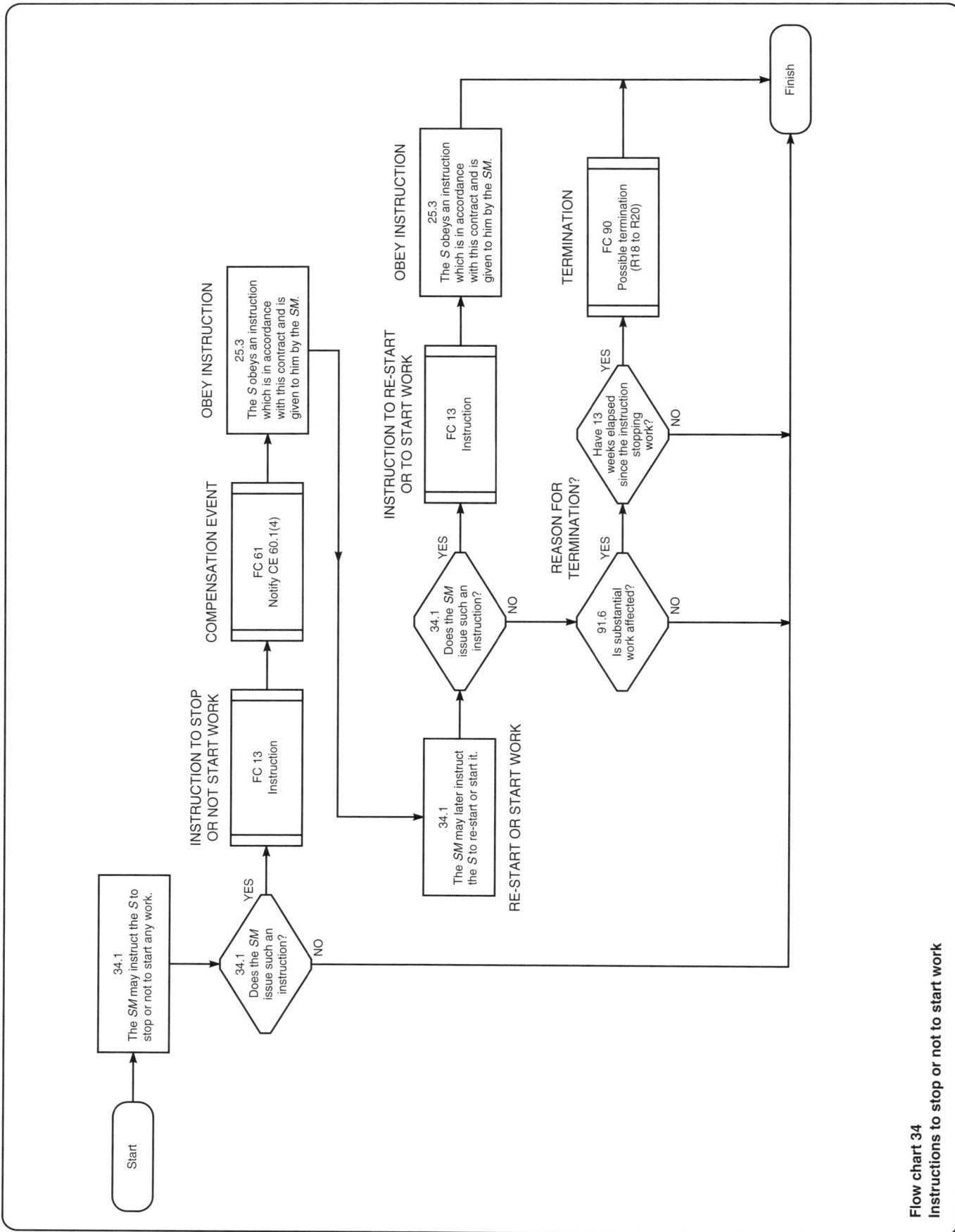

Flow chart 34
Instructions to stop or not to start work

Start

ACCEPTED PROGRAMME

11.2(1)
The Accepted Programme is the programme identified in the CD or is the latest programme accepted by the *SM*. The latest programme accepted by the *SM* supersedes previous Accepted Programmes

DELIVERY

11.2(5)
Delivery is when the *S* has
- done all the work which the GI states he is to do by the Delivery Date and
- corrected Defects which would have prevented the *P* from using the *goods* or *services* and Others from doing their work.

DELIVERY DATE

11.2(6)
The Delivery Date is the *delivery date* (stated in the CD) unless later changed in accordance with this contract

12.5
In these *conditions of contract*, each reference and clause relevant to Delivery and the Delivery Date applies to each Delivery and its Delivery Date

FORM OF QUOTATION

35.1
A quotation for an acceleration comprises proposed changes to the Prices and the Delivery Date. The *S* submits details of his assessment with each quotation

INSTRUCTION TO QUOTE?

35.1
Does the *SM* instruct the *S* to submit such quotations? — NO / YES

QUOTATION FOR ACCEPTANCE

35.1
The *SM* may instruct the *S* to submit a quotation for an acceleration to achieve Delivery before the Delivery Date.

INSTRUCTION TO QUOTE

FC 13
SM's instruction

SUPPLIER REPLIES

35.2
The *S* submits a quotation or gives his reasons for not doing so within the *period for reply*

35.2
Does the *S* submit a quotation? — NO / YES

QUOTATION SUBMITTED

35.2
The *S* gives his reason for not doing so within the *period for reply*

FC 13
S's reply

QUOTATION SUBMITTED

35.2
The *S* submits his quotation for acceleration

FC 13
Submission for acceptance

ACCEPTED?

35.2
Does the *SM* accept the quotation? — NO / YES

QUOTATION ACCEPTED

IMPLEMENT ACCELERATION

35.2
When the *SM* accepts a quotation for an acceleration, he changes the Prices and the Delivery Date accordingly

25.3
The *S* obeys an instruction which is in accordance with this contract and is given by him by the *SM*

FC 13
SM's instruction

SUPPLIER PROVIDES THE GOODS AND SERVICES

FC 20
Providing the Goods and Services

Finish

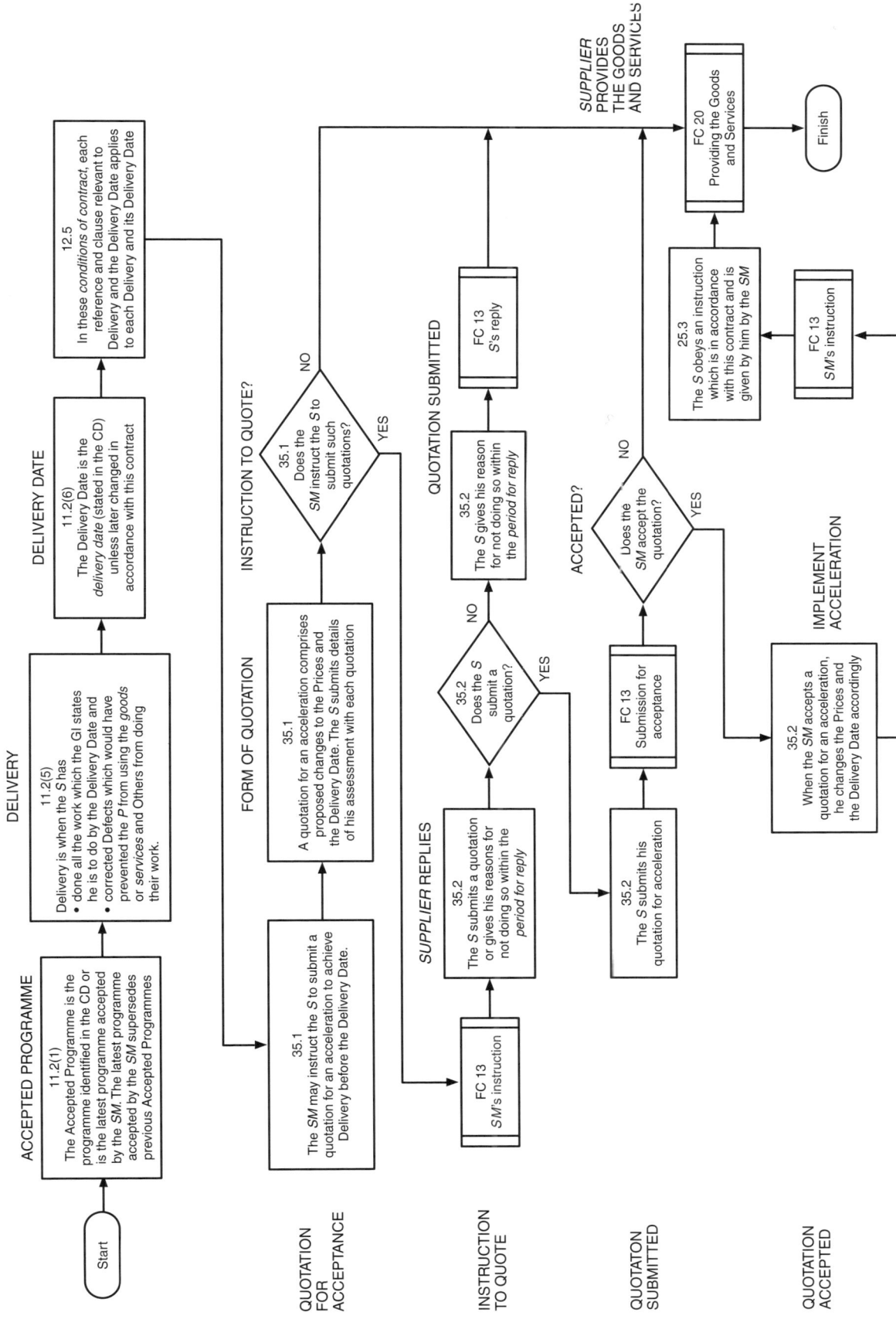

Flow chart 35
Acceleration

SUPPLIER TESTS

The test or inspection is done by the S.

ANY DEFECT?

Does the test or inspection reveal a Defect?

NO → Finish

YES → FC 42 Notifying Defects

DOES THIS CLAUSE APPLY?

40.1 This clause does not apply.

40.1 Is this test or inspection required by the applicable law?

NO

YES

TEST TO BE DONE

Start

A test or inspection is to be done.

40.1 Is this test or inspection required by the GI?

NO

YES

RECORDS DATA SHEETS, MATERIALS, FACILITIES & SAMPLES

40.2 The S and SM provide records, data sheets, materials, facilities and samples for tests and inspections as stated in the GI.

40.2 Are these requirements provided as stated?

NO → FC 16 Early warning and possible CE 60.1(11)

YES

NOTIFICATION OF TEST OR INSPECTION

40.3 The S and the SM each notifies the other of each of his tests and inspections before it starts and afterwards notifies the other of its results.

40.3 The S notifies the SM in time for a test or inspection to be arranged and done before doing work which would obstruct the test or inspection.

FC 13 Notification

SUPPLY MANAGER MAY WATCH TEST

40.3 The SM may watch any test done by the S.

Does the S need to give access?

YES → FC 25 Other responsibilities

NO

40.3 Do the SM and the S act accordingly?

NO → FC 16 Early warning

YES

SUPPLY MANAGER ACTS PROMPTLY

40.5 The SM does his tests and inspections without causing unnecessary delay to the work or to a payment which is conditional upon a test or inspection being successful.

40.3 Does the SM act accordingly?

NO → FC 16 Early warning and possible CE 60.1(10)

YES

A sheet 2

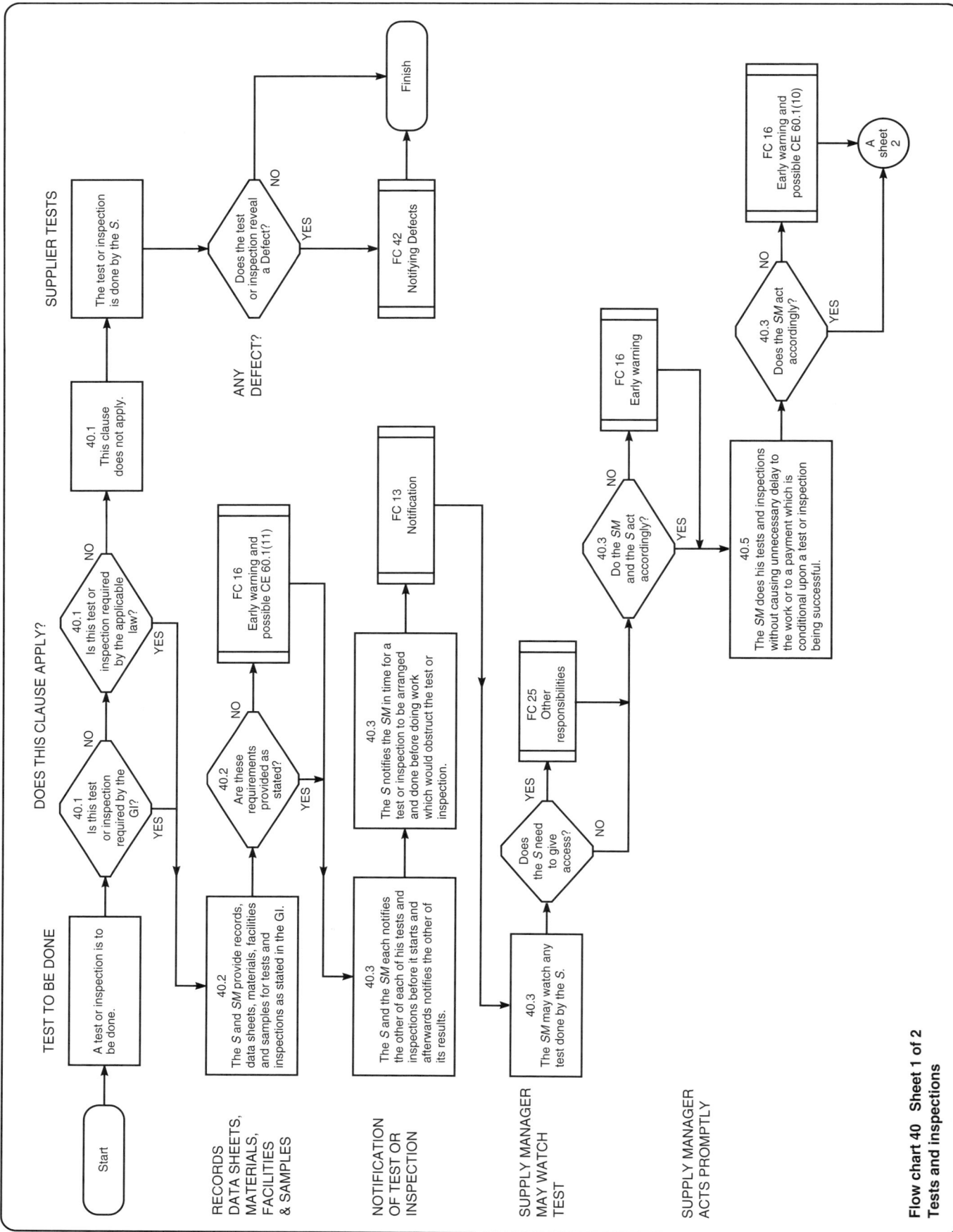

Flow chart 40   Sheet 1 of 2
Tests and inspections

A DEFECT

11.2(3)

A Defect is
- a part of the *goods and services* which is not in accordance with the GI or
- a part of the *goods* designed by the *S* which is not in accordance with the applicable law or the *S*'s design which the *SM* has accepted.

GOODS INFORMATION

11.2(8)

GI is information which
- specifies and describes the *goods* and *services* and
- states any constraints on how the *S* Provides the Goods and Services

and is in
- the documents which the CD states it is in,
- the SR or
- an instruction given in accordance with this contract.

SUPPLY REQUIREMENTS

11.2(16)

SR is information which
- describes the *P*'s requirements in connection with the supply of the *goods*,
- states the delivery place,
- describes the requirements for the transport of the *goods* and
- describes other information to be provided by the *S* in connection with the supply of the *goods*.

DEFECTS DATE

The *defects date* is stated in the CD as a date occuring a number of weeks after Delivery.

DEFECT CORRECTION PERIODS

The *defect correction period* and any specific *defect correction periods* for parts of the *goods* and *services* are stated in the CD.

PAYMENT NOT DUE

A payment may not be due because of an unsuccessful test or inspection.

ASSESSMENT

FC 50

Assessing the amount due.

SUPPLIER PAYS

40.6

The *SM* assesses the cost incurred by the *P* when a test or inspection is repeated after a Defect is found. The *S* pays the amount assessed.

REPEAT TEST

40.4

The *S* corrects the Defect and the test or inspection is repeated.

DEFECT NOTIFIED AND CORRECTED

FC 42 and FC 43

Notifying and Correcting Defects

ANY DEFECT?

40.4 Does a test or inspection show that any work has a Defect?

YES / NO

Finish

A sheet 1

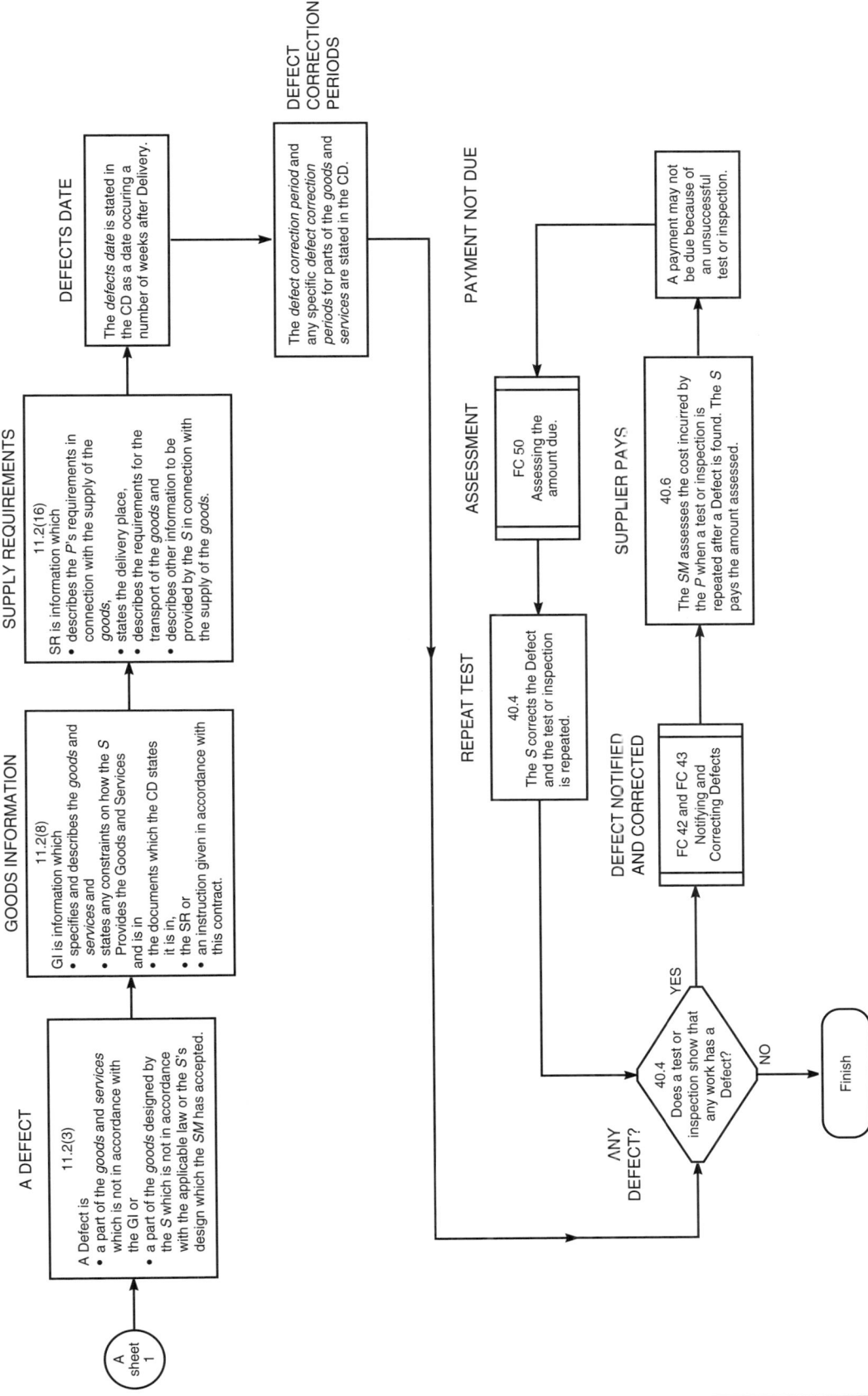

Flow chart 40   Sheet 2 of 2
Tests and inspections

GOODS INFORMATION

11.2(8)

Goods Information is information which
- specifies and describes the *goods and services* and
- states any constraints on how the *S* Provides the Goods and Services

and is in
- the documents which the CD states it is in,
- the SR or
- an instruction given is accordance with the contract.

DELIVERY PLACE

11.2(7)

The Delivery Place is the delivery place stated in the SR.

Start

TEST OR INSPECTION

41.1

The *S* does not bring to the Delivery Place those *goods* which the GI states are to be tested or inspected before being brought to the Delivery Place until
- the *SM* has notified the *S* that they have passed the test or inspection which the *SM* is to do and
- the *S* has notified the *SM* that they have passed the test or inspection which the *S* is to do.

TEST OR INSPECTION REQUIRED PRIOR TO DELIVERY?

41.1
Does the *S* wish to bring to the Delivery Place goods which the GI states is to be tested or inspected before being brought to the Delivery Place?

— YES →

— NO →

FC 40
Tests and inspections

FC 20
S Provides the Goods and Services

FC 61
Notifying compensation events 60.1(10)

LATE TEST OR INSPECTION?

Is notification withheld because the *SM* has not done the test or inspection which he is to do in time?

— YES →

— NO →

FC 16
Possible early warning

FAILED TEST OR INSPECTION?

Is notification withheld because the *SM* or *S* has notified the other the *goods* have not passed the test or inspection?

— YES →

— NO →

FC 42
Notifying Defects

NOTIFICATION OF PASSING

41.1
Does the *SM* or *S* notify the other that *goods* have passed the test or inspection?

— YES →

— NO →

Is notification withheld because the *SM* or the *S* notify the other of a Defect?

— YES →

— NO →

NO DEFECTS?

FC 20
S Provides the Goods and Services

The *S* may bring the *goods* to the Delivery Place.

DELIVERY

Finish

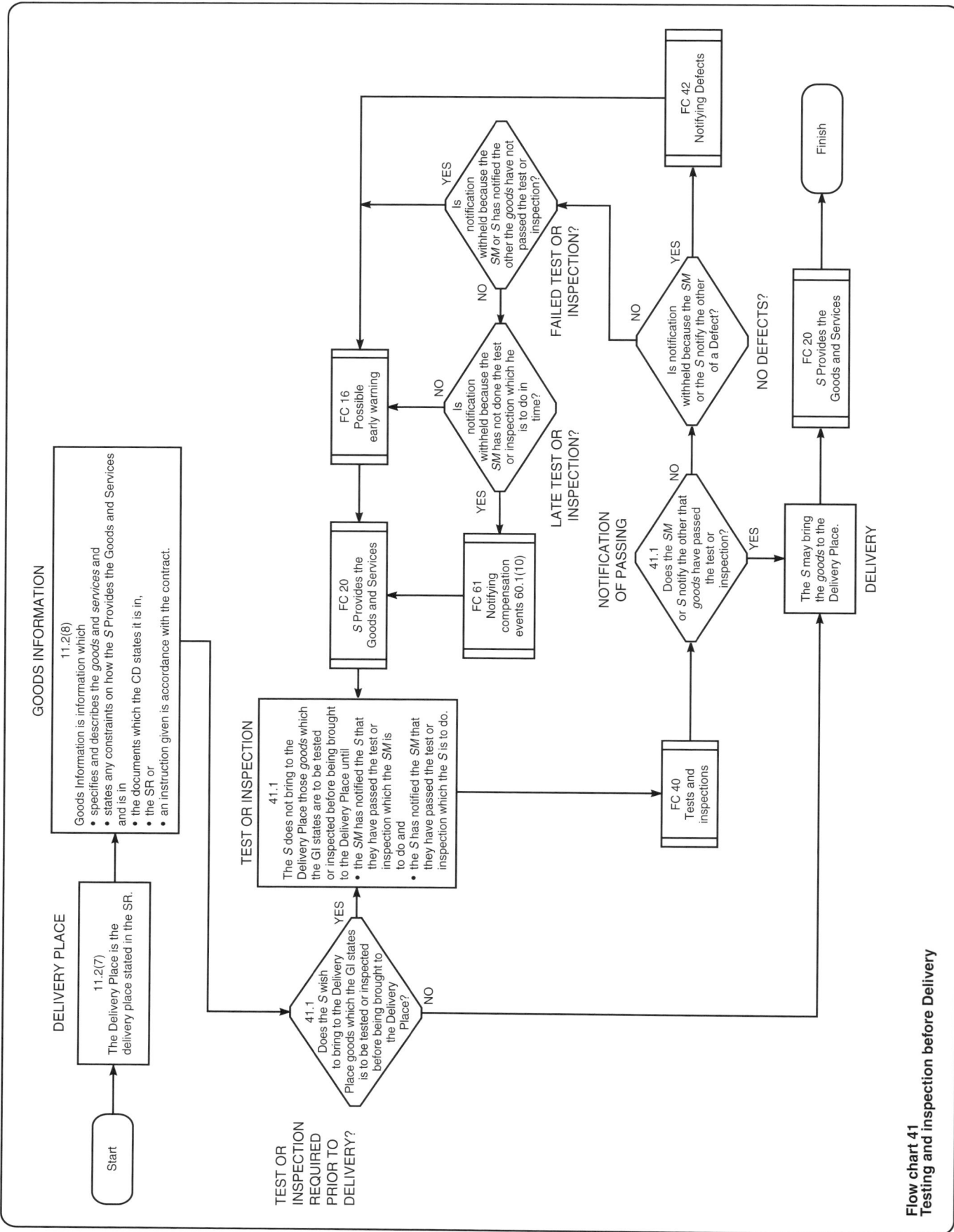

Flow chart 41
Testing and inspection before Delivery

A DEFECT

11.2(3)

A Defect is
- a part of the *goods and services* which is not in accordance with the GI or
- a part of the *goods* designed by the *S* which is not in accordance with the applicable law or the *S*'s design which the *SM* has accepted.

GOODS INFORMATION

11.2(8)

Goods Information is information which either
- specifies and describes the *goods and services* and
- states any constraints on how the *S* Provides the Goods and Services and is in
  - the documents which the CD states it is in
  - the Delivery Requirements or
  - an instruction given in accordance with this contract.

SUPPLY REQUIREMENTS

11.2(16)

SR is information which
- describes the *P*'s requirements in connection with the supply of the *goods*
- states the delivery place
- describes the requirements for transport of the *goods* and
- describes other information to be provided by the *S* in connection with the supply of the *goods*.

The *defects date* for the *goods and services* and included in Delivery is stated in the CD.

COMPENSATION EVENT?

60.1(9)

A CE has occurred unless the search was only needed because the *S* gave insufficient notice of doing work obstructing a required test or inspection.

Did the *S* give insufficient notice?
— NO → FC 61 Notify CE 60.1(9) → Finish
— YES →

DEFECT?

Is a Defect found?
— NO →
— YES → **42.2** Until the *defects date* for the *goods and services* included in Delivery, the *SM* notifies the *S* of each Defect as soon as he becomes aware of it and the *S* notifies the *SM* of each Defect as soon as he becomes aware of it. → FC 13 Notification → FC 43 Correcting Defects

REASON

42.1

The *SM* gives his reason for the search with his instruction.

SEARCH?

42.1

Does the *SM* instruct the *S* to search for a Defect?
— YES →
— NO → Is a Defect found?
  — YES →
  — NO →

42.1

Until the *defects date* for the *goods and services* included in Delivery, the *SM* may instruct the *S* to search for a Defect in the *goods and services* included in the Delivery.

Start

SEARCH UNTIL DEFECTS DATE

42.1

Has the *defects date* for the *goods and services* stated in the Delivery occurred?
— NO →
— YES →

DEFECTS NOTIFIED UNTIL DEFECTS DATE

DEFECT NOTIFIED

DEFECT CORRECTED

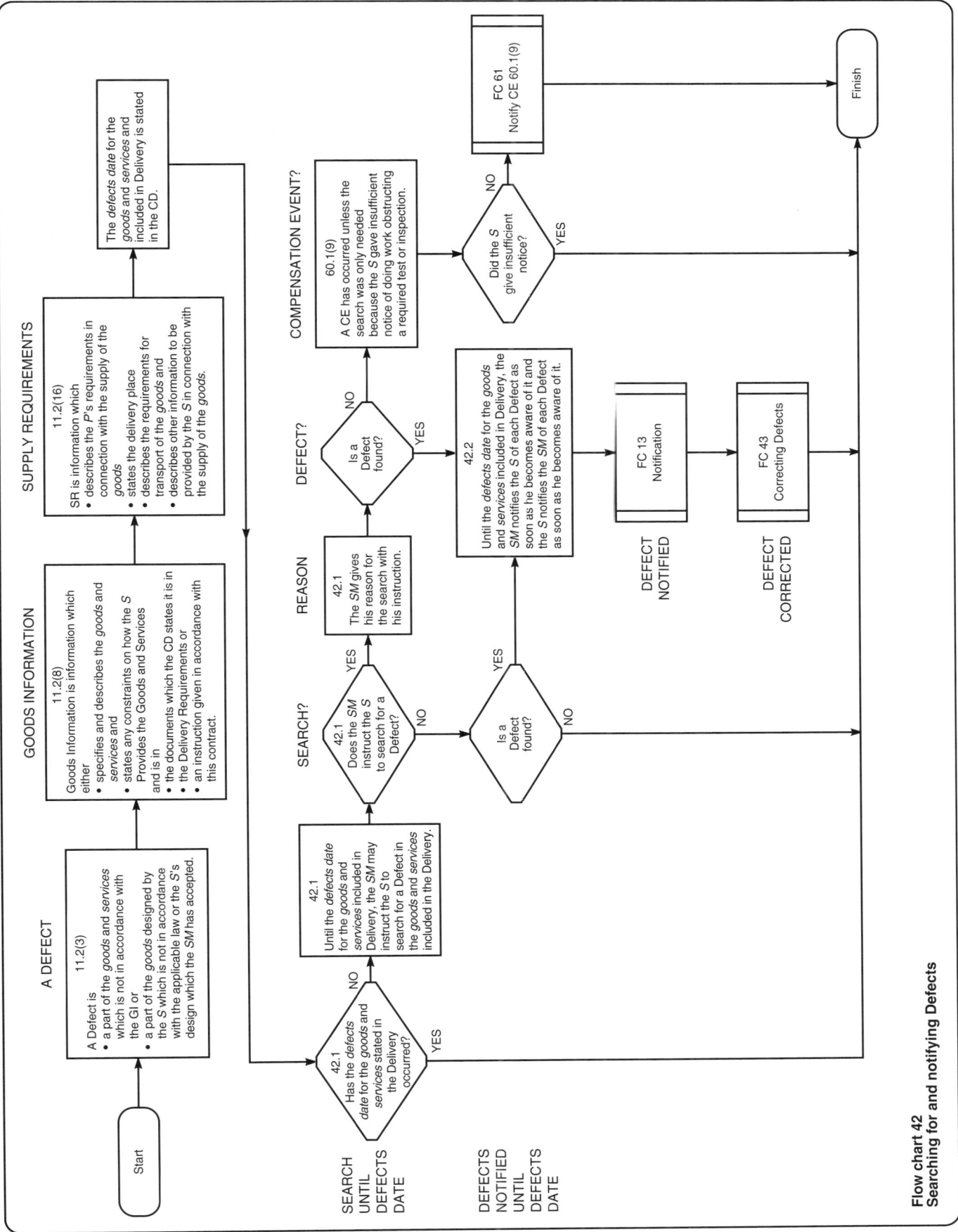

Flow chart 42
Searching for and notifying Defects

DEFECT FOUND?

Start

Has a Defect been found before the end of the defects date?
— YES →
— NO →

A DEFECT

11.2(3)

A Defect is
• a part of the goods and services which is not in accordance with the GI or
• a part of the goods designed by the S which is not in accordance with the applicable law or the S's design which the SM has accepted.

DELIVERY

11.2(5)

Delivery is when the S has
• done all the work which the GI states he is to do by the Completion Date and
• corrected Defects which would have prevented the P from using the goods or services and Others from doing their work.

12.5

In these conditions of contract, each reference and clause relevant to Delivery and the Delivery Date applies to each Delivery and its Delivery Date.

DEFECT NOTIFIED?

43.2 Has the Defect been notified?
— YES
— NO →

43.1 The S corrects a Defect whether or not the SM notifies him of it.

CORRECT DEFECT

The defect correction period and specific defect correction periods are stated in the CD.

START DATE FOR CORRECTION PERIOD

43.2 Was the Defect notified before Delivery?
— YES → 11.2(5) The S corrects the Defect before Delivery if it would prevent the P from using the goods or services and Others from doing their work.
43.2 The defect correction period begins at Delivery.
— NO → 43.2 The defect correction period begins when the SM has arranged the access necessary for the S to correct the Defect.

LIMIT OF LIABILITY

43.3 Was access given to the S to correct a Defect within the defect access period following notification?
— NO → 43.3 After Delivery, the P allows access to correct a notified Defect within the defect access period following notification. The S is not liable for any damage to the goods or services resulting from a failure by the P to provide access to correct a notified Defect later than the end of the defect access period following notification.
— YES →

DEFECT ACCEPTED

Does the C or SM propose the notified Defect be accepted?
— YES → FC 44 Accepting Defects
— NO →

DEFECT UNCORRECTED

Is the notified Defect uncorrected after the defect correction period?
— YES → FC 45 Uncorrected Defects
— NO →

NOTIFIED DEFECT IS CORRECTED

43.2 After Delivery the S corrects a notified Defect before the end of the (relevant) defect correction period.

Finish

NOTIFIED DEFECT TO BE CORRECTED

LIMIT OF LIABILITY IF NO ACCESS

DEFECT ACCEPTED OR UNCORRECTED?

Flow chart 43 Correcting Defects

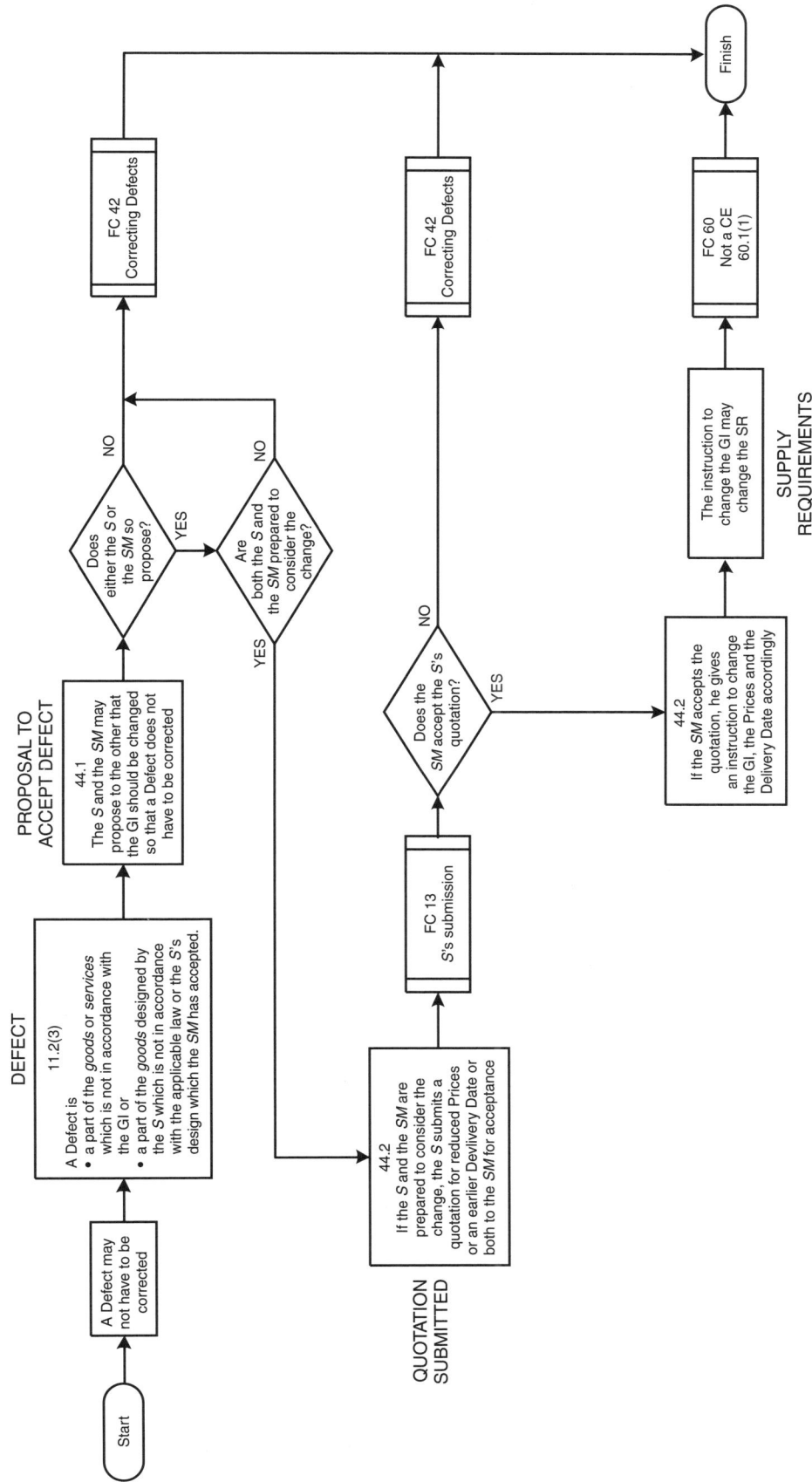

Flow chart 44
Accepting Defects

Start

↓

A Defect may not have to be corrected

↓

DEFECT

11.2(3)

A Defect is
- a part of the *goods* or *services* which is not in accordance with the GI or
- a part of the *goods* designed by the *S* which is not in accordance with the applicable law or the *S*'s design which the *SM* has accepted.

↓

PROPOSAL TO ACCEPT DEFECT

44.1

The *S* and the *SM* may propose to the other that the GI should be changed so that a Defect does not have to be corrected

↓

Does either the *S* or the *SM* so propose?

— NO → **FC 42 Correcting Defects**

YES
↓

Are both the *S* and the *SM* prepared to consider the change?

— NO → **FC 42 Correcting Defects**

YES
↓

QUOTATION SUBMITTED

44.2

If the *S* and the *SM* are prepared to consider the change, the *S* submits a quotation for reduced Prices or an earlier Delivery Date or both to the *SM* for acceptance

↓

FC 13 *S*'s submission

↓

Does the *SM* accept the *S*'s quotation?

— NO → **FC 42 Correcting Defects**

YES
↓

44.2

If the *SM* accepts the quotation, he gives an instruction to change the GI, the Prices and the Delivery Date accordingly

↓

SUPPLY REQUIREMENTS

The instruction to change the GI may change the SR

↓

FC 60 Not a CE 60.1(1)

↓

Finish

Start

DEFECT

11.2(3)

A Defect is
- a part of the *goods or services* which is not in accordance with the GI or
- a part of the *goods* designed by the *S* which is not in accordance with the applicable law or the *S's* design which the *SM* has accepted.

DEFECTS DATE

The *defects date* is stated in the CD.

UNCORRECTED DEFECT

A notified Defect has not been corrected by the *S*.

SUPPLIER GIVEN ACCESS?

45.1 and 45.2 Has the *S* been given access in order to correct a notified Defect? — YES

EXPIRED?

45.1 Has the *S* corrected it within the *defect correction period*? — YES / NO

SUPPLIER CORRECTS

The *S* corrects this Defect

ASSESS COST

45.1 The *SM* assesses the cost to the *P* of having the Defect corrected by other people.

NO (from SUPPLIER GIVEN ACCESS?)

DEFECTS DATE PASSED?

45.2 Has the *defects date* passed? — YES / NO

ASSESS COST

45.2 The *SM* assesses the cost to the *S* of correcting the Defect at the time it was notified.

SUPPLIER PAYS

45.1 and 45.2 The *S* pays this amount.

GOODS INFORMATION CHANGED ACCORDINGLY

45.1 and 45.2 The GI is treated as having been changed to accept the Defect.

SUPPLIER CORRECTS

The *S* corrects this Defect

Finish

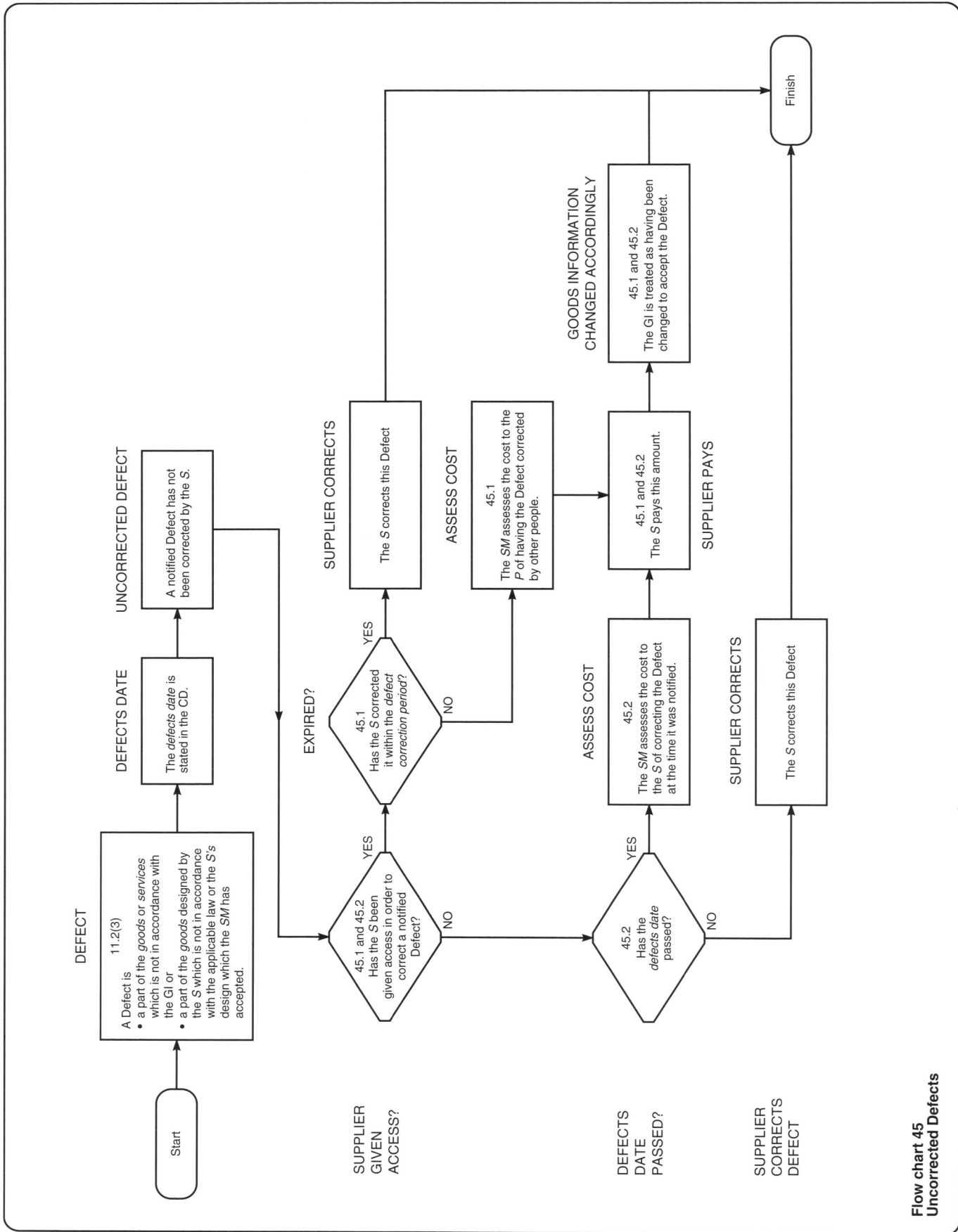

**Flow chart 45
Uncorrected Defects**

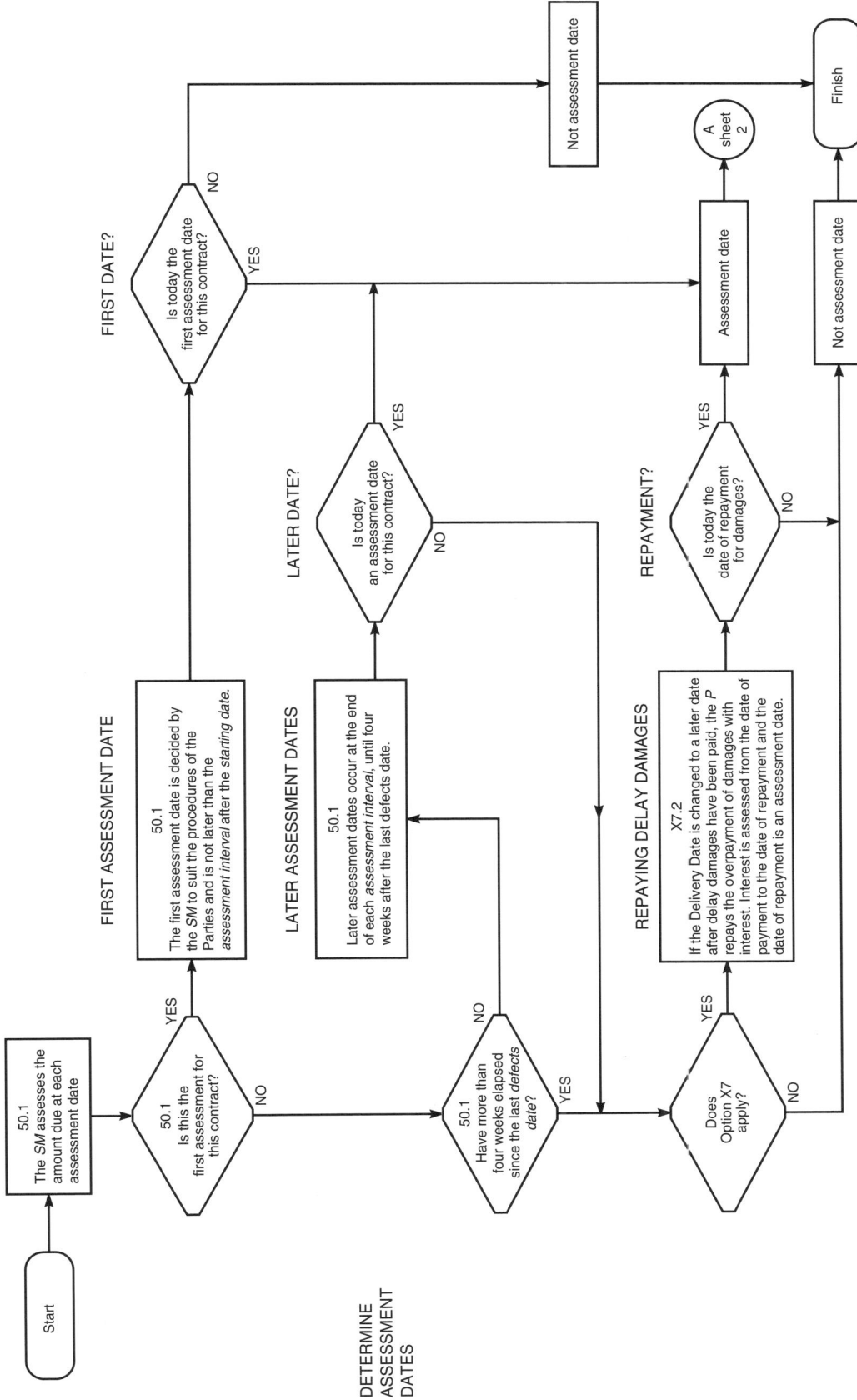

Flow chart 50 — Sheet 1 of 4
Assessing the amount due

Start

↓

50.1
The *SM* assesses the amount due at each assessment date

↓

50.1
Is this the first assessment for this contract?

— **YES** →

FIRST ASSESSMENT DATE

50.1
The first assessment date is decided by the *SM* to suit the procedures of the Parties and is not later than the *assessment interval* after the *starting date*.

↓

FIRST DATE?

Is today the first assessment date for this contract?

— **NO** → **Not assessment date** → **Finish**

— **YES** → **Assessment date**

50.1 — NO →

50.1
Have more than four weeks elapsed since the last *defects date*?

— **NO** →

LATER ASSESSMENT DATES

50.1
Later assessment dates occur at the end of each *assessment interval*, until four weeks after the last defects date.

↓

LATER DATE?

Is today an assessment date for this contract?

— **YES** → **Assessment date**

— **NO** →

Have more than four weeks elapsed since the last defects date? — YES →

Does Option X7 apply?

— **YES** →

REPAYING DELAY DAMAGES

X7.2
If the Delivery Date is changed to a later date after delay damages have been paid, the *P* repays the overpayment of damages with interest. Interest is assessed from the date of payment to the date of repayment and the date of repayment is an assessment date.

↓

REPAYMENT?

Is today the date of repayment for damages?

— **YES** → **Assessment date** → **A sheet 2**

— **NO** → **Not assessment date** → **Finish**

Does Option X7 apply? — NO → **Not assessment date**

DETERMINE ASSESSMENT DATES

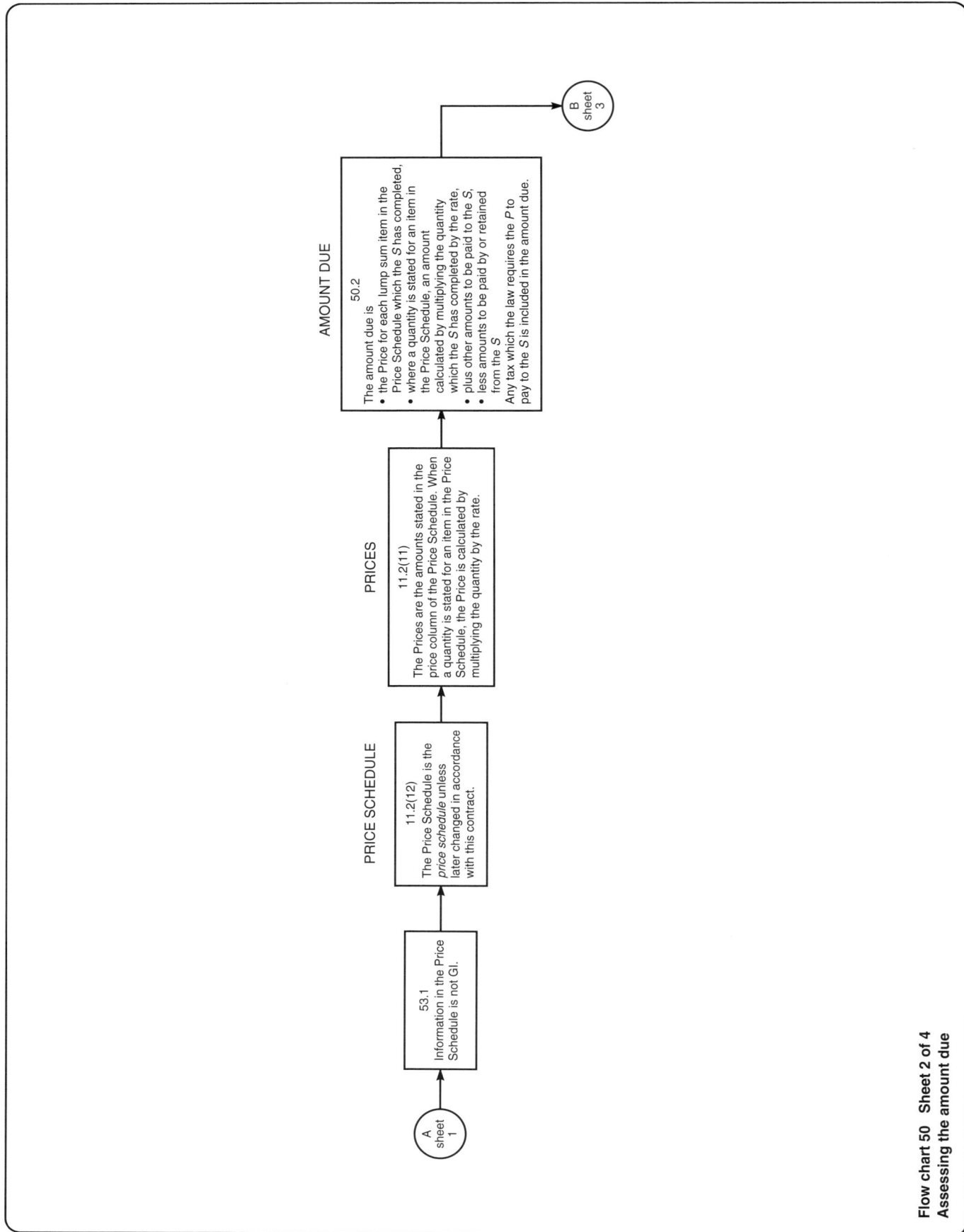

A sheet 1

53.1
Information in the Price Schedule is not GI.

PRICE SCHEDULE

11.2(12)
The Price Schedule is the *price schedule* unless later changed in accordance with this contract.

PRICES

11.2(11)
The Prices are the amounts stated in the price column of the Price Schedule. When a quantity is stated for an item in the Price Schedule, the Price is calculated by multiplying the quantity by the rate.

AMOUNT DUE

50.2
The amount due is
• the Price for each lump sum item in the Price Schedule which the *S* has completed,
• where a quantity is stated for an item in the Price Schedule, an amount calculated by multiplying the quantity which the *S* has completed by the rate,
• plus other amounts to be paid to the *S*,
• less amounts to be paid by or retained from the *S*

Any tax which the law requires the *P* to pay to the *S* is included in the amount due.

B sheet 3

DETERMINE
OTHER
AMOUNTS

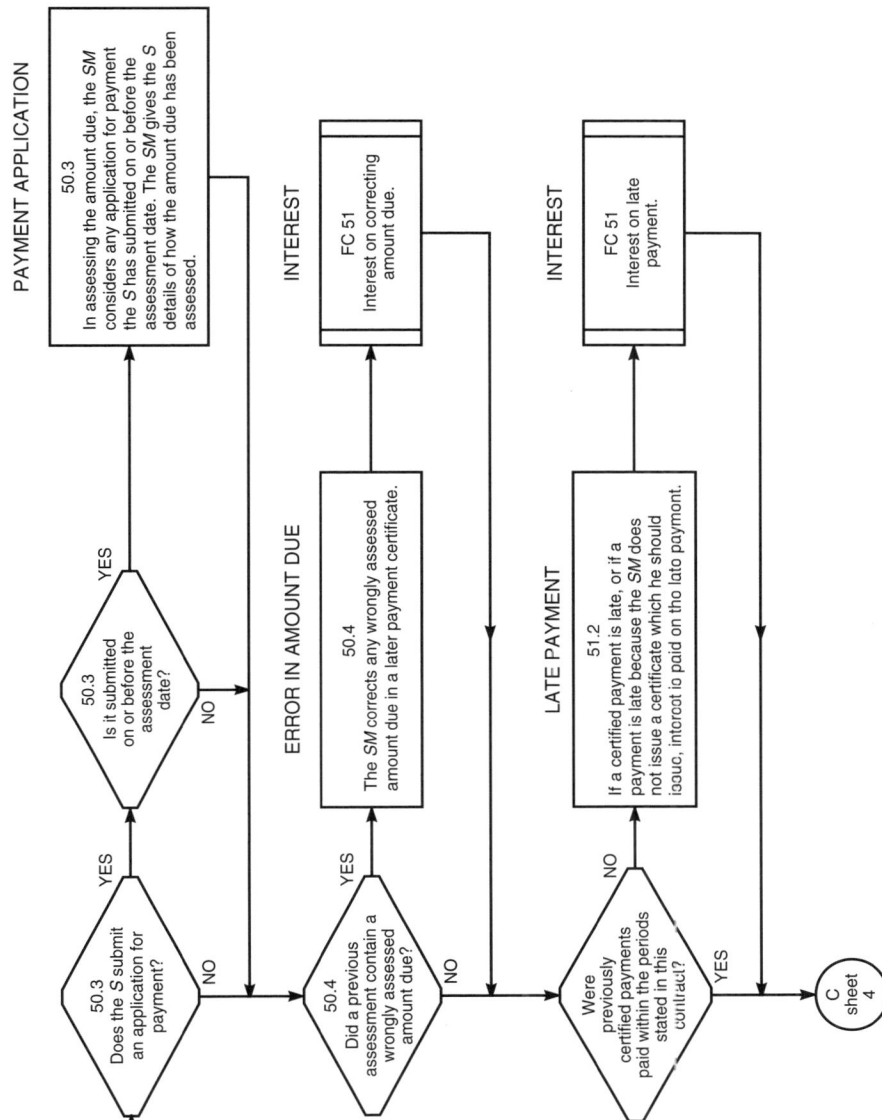

(B
sheet
2)

PAYMENT APPLICATION

50.3
Does the *S* submit
an application for
payment?

— YES →

50.3
Is it submitted
on or before the
assessment
date?

— YES →

50.3
In assessing the amount due, the *SM*
considers any application for payment
the *S* has submitted on or before the
assessment date. The *SM* gives the *S*
details of how the amount due has been
assessed.

NO

NO

ERROR IN AMOUNT DUE

50.4
Did a previous
assessment contain a
wrongly assessed
amount due?

— YES →

50.4
The *SM* corrects any wrongly assessed
amount due in a later payment certificate.

INTEREST

FC 51
Interest on correcting
amount due.

NO

LATE PAYMENT

Were
previously
certified payments
paid within the periods
stated in this
contract?

— NO →

51.2
If a certified payment is late, or if a
payment is late because the *SM* does
not issue a certificate which he should
issue, interest is paid on the late payment.

INTEREST

FC 51
Interest on late
payment.

YES

(C
sheet
4)

Flow chart 50   Sheet 3 of 4
Assessing the amount due

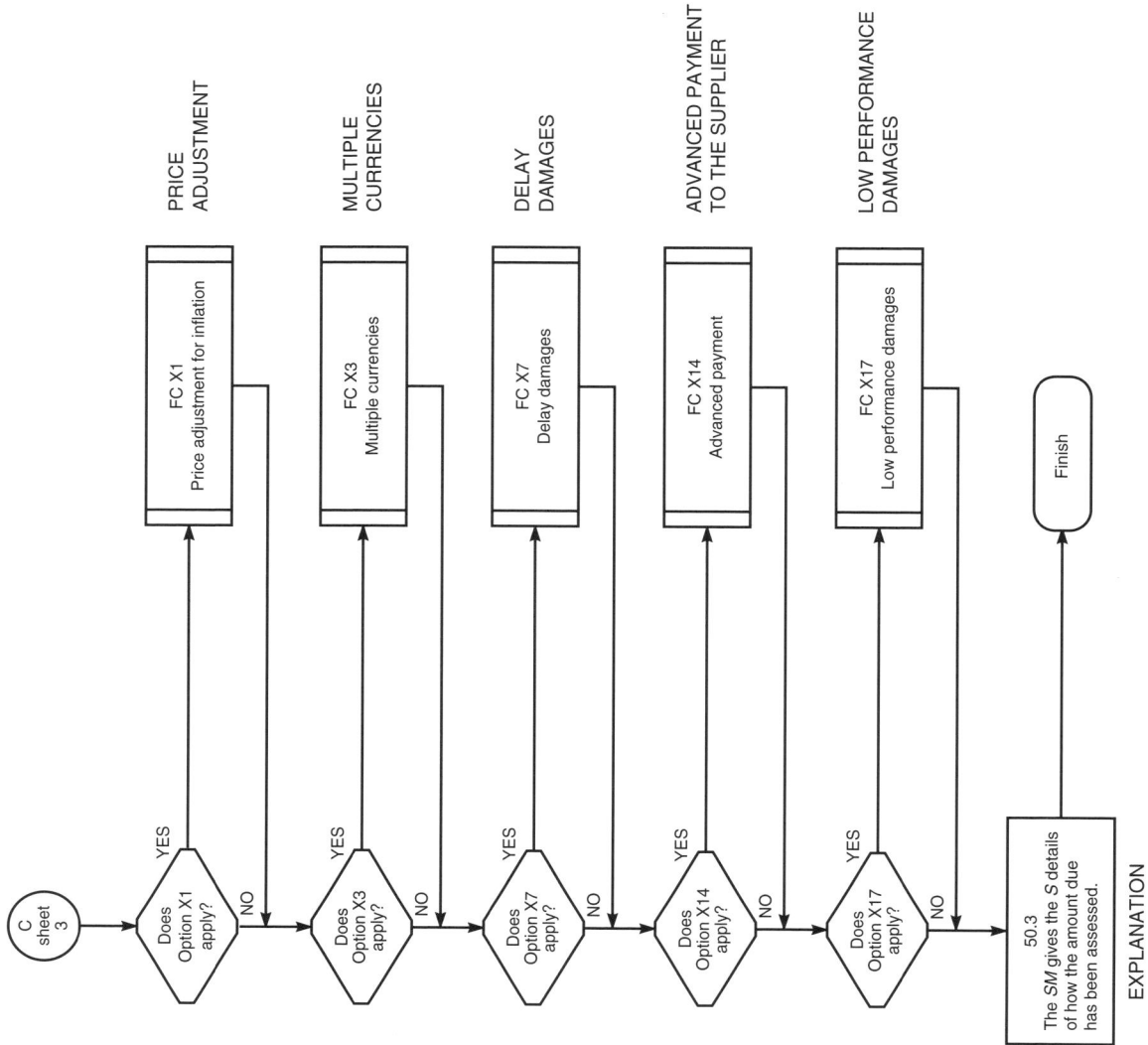

DETERMINE
OTHER
AMOUNTS
(CONTINUED)

```
      ┌────────┐
      │   C    │
      │ sheet  │
      │   3    │
      └────────┘
          │
          ▼
     ╱─────────╲        YES
    ╱ Does       ╲──────────────►  ┌──────────────────────┐
    ╲ Option X1  ╱                 │ FC X1                 │   PRICE
     ╲ apply?  ╱                   │                       │   ADJUSTMENT
      ╲──────╱                     │ Price adjustment      │
          │ NO                     │ for inflation         │
          │                        └──────────────────────┘
          ▼
     ╱─────────╲        YES
    ╱ Does       ╲──────────────►  ┌──────────────────────┐
    ╲ Option X3  ╱                 │ FC X3                 │   MULTIPLE
     ╲ apply?  ╱                   │                       │   CURRENCIES
      ╲──────╱                     │ Multiple currencies   │
          │ NO                     └──────────────────────┘
          ▼
     ╱─────────╲        YES
    ╱ Does       ╲──────────────►  ┌──────────────────────┐
    ╲ Option X7  ╱                 │ FC X7                 │   DELAY
     ╲ apply?  ╱                   │                       │   DAMAGES
      ╲──────╱                     │ Delay damages         │
          │ NO                     └──────────────────────┘
          ▼
     ╱─────────╲        YES
    ╱ Does       ╲──────────────►  ┌──────────────────────┐
    ╲ Option X14 ╱                 │ FC X14                │   ADVANCED PAYMENT
     ╲ apply?  ╱                   │                       │   TO THE SUPPLIER
      ╲──────╱                     │ Advanced payment      │
          │ NO                     └──────────────────────┘
          ▼
     ╱─────────╲        YES
    ╱ Does       ╲──────────────►  ┌──────────────────────┐
    ╲ Option X17 ╱                 │ FC X17                │   LOW PERFORMANCE
     ╲ apply?  ╱                   │                       │   DAMAGES
      ╲──────╱                     │ Low performance       │
          │ NO                     │ damages               │
          │                        └──────────────────────┘
          ▼
  ┌──────────────────┐
  │ 50.3             │
  │ The SM gives the │            ┌──────────┐
  │ S details of how │            │  Finish  │
  │ the amount due   │            └──────────┘
  │ has been         │
  │ assessed.        │
  └──────────────────┘
```

EXPLANATION

**Flow chart 50   Sheet 4 of 4
Assessing the amount due**

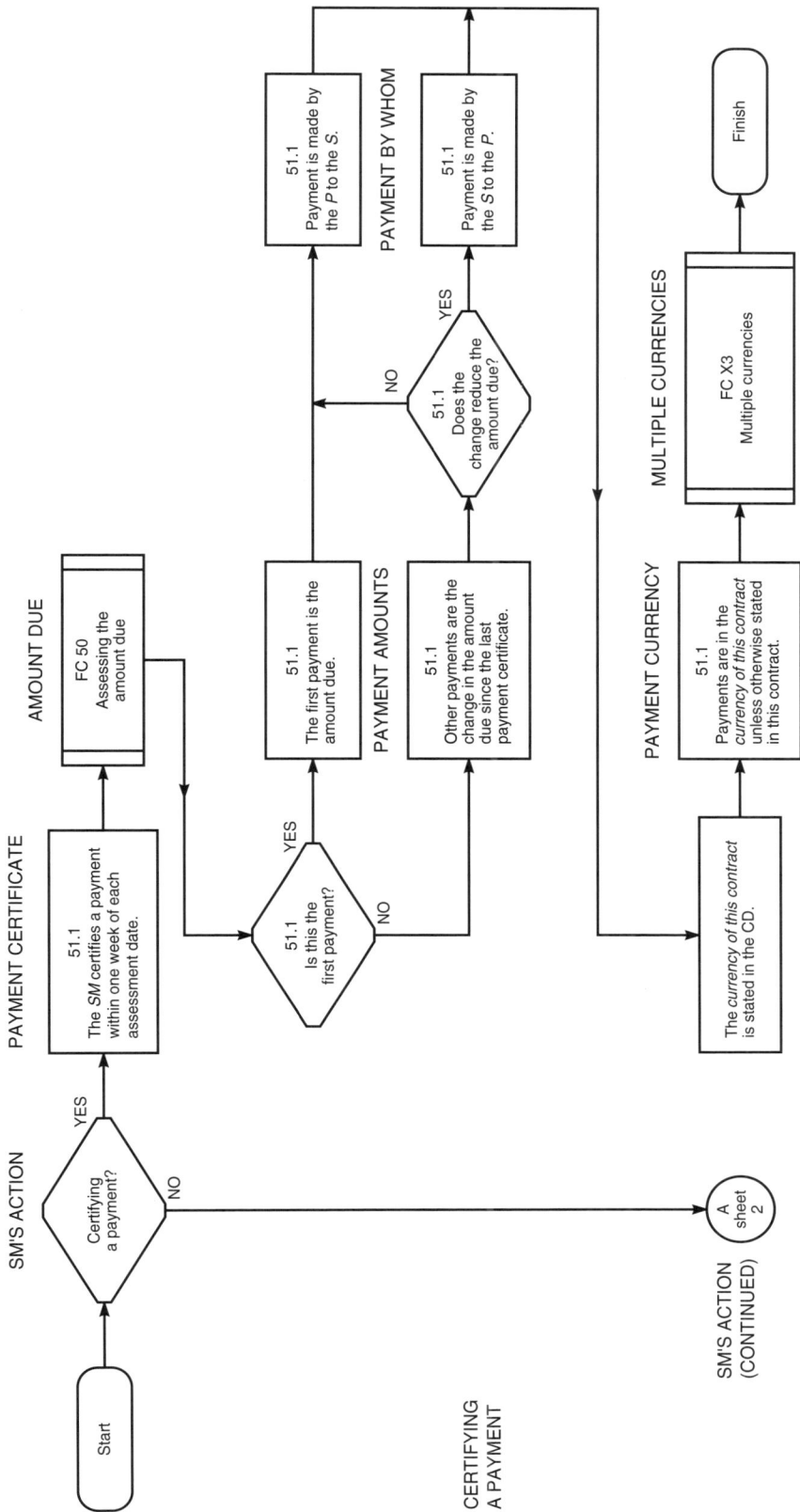

CERTIFYING A PAYMENT

SM'S ACTION

Start

Certifying a payment?

— YES →

— NO →

PAYMENT CERTIFICATE

51.1
The *SM* certifies a payment within one week of each assessment date.

AMOUNT DUE

FC 50
Assessing the amount due

51.1
Is this the first payment?

— YES →

— NO →

51.1
The first payment is the amount due.

PAYMENT AMOUNTS

51.1
Other payments are the change in the amount due since the last payment certificate.

51.1
Does the change reduce the amount due?

— NO →

— YES →

PAYMENT BY WHOM

51.1
Payment is made by the *P* to the *S*.

51.1
Payment is made by the *S* to the *P*.

SM'S ACTION (CONTINUED)

A sheet 2

The *currency of this contract* is stated in the CD.

PAYMENT CURRENCY

51.1
Payments are in the *currency of this contract* unless otherwise stated in this contract.

MULTIPLE CURRENCIES

FC X3
Multiple currencies

Finish

Flow chart 51   Sheet 1 of 2
Payment

SM'S ACTION

MAKING A PAYMENT

A sheet 1

Making a payment?
- YES
- NO

CERTIFIED PAYMENT

51.2
Each certified payment is made within three weeks of the assessment date or, if a different period is stated in the CD, within the period stated.

LATE PAYMENT?

CALCULATING INTEREST ON A LATE PAYMENT

Calculating interest on a late payment?
- YES
- NO

51.2
Is a certified payment late?
- YES
- NO

51.2
Is a payment late because the *SM* does not issue a certificate which he should issue?
- YES
- NO

INTEREST RATE

The *interest rate* is stated in the CD.

INTEREST CALCULATION

51.4
Interest is calculated on a daily basis at the *interest rate* and is compounded annually.

INTEREST AMOUNT

51.2
Interest is paid on the late payment. Interest is assessed from the date by which the late payment should have been made until the date when late payment is made, and is included in the first assessment after the late payment is made.

CORRECTING AMOUNT

CORRECTING AN AMOUNT DUE

Correcting an amount due?
- YES
- NO

51.3
If an amount due is corrected in a later certificate either
• by the *SM* in relation to a mistake or a CE or
• following a decision of the *Adjudicator* or the *tribunal*, interest on the correcting amount is paid.

CORRECTION?

Does the amount due include a correcting amount?
- YES
- NO

INTEREST CALCULATION

51.4
Interest is calculated on a daily basis at the *interest rate* and is compounded annually.

INTEREST AMOUNT

51.3
Interest is assessed from the date when the incorrect amount was certified until the date when the correcting amount is certified and is included in the assessment which includes the correcting amount.

Finish

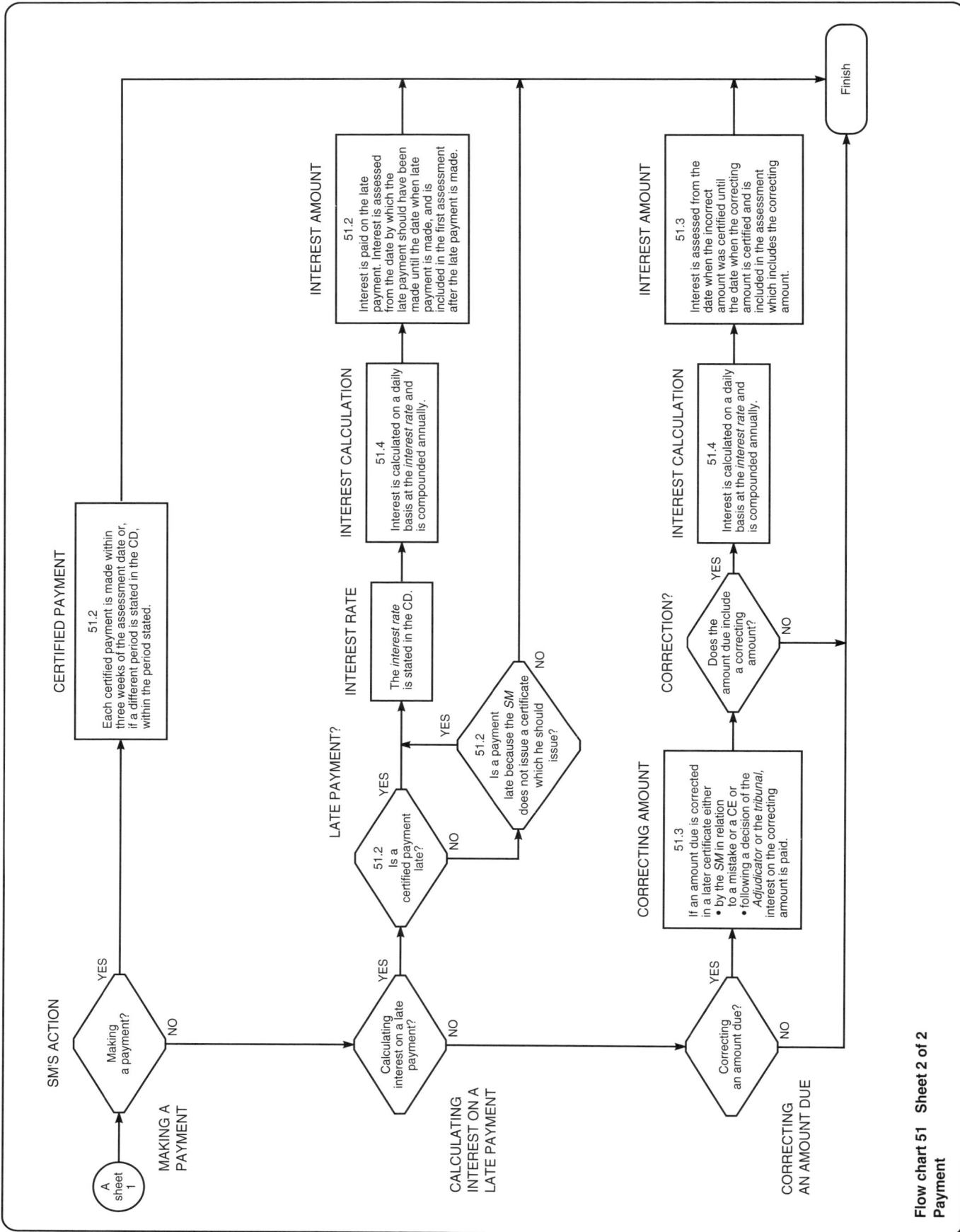

Flow chart 51 Sheet 2 of 2
Payment

Start

11.2(4)

Defined Cost is an amount paid by the S in Providing the Goods and Services (excluding any tax which the S can recover) for

- people,
- equipment,
- P&M to be included in the *goods* and
- transport

whether work is subcontacted or not excluding the cost of preparing quotations for CEs.

COSTS NOT INCLUDED IN DEFINED COST

52.1

All the S's costs which are not included in the Defined Cost are treated as included in the *percentage for overheads and profit*.

The *percentage for overheads and profit* is stated in the CD

DEFINED COST

52.1

Defined Cost includes only amounts calculated at open market or competitively tendered prices with deductions for all discounts, rebates and taxes which can be recovered.

Finish

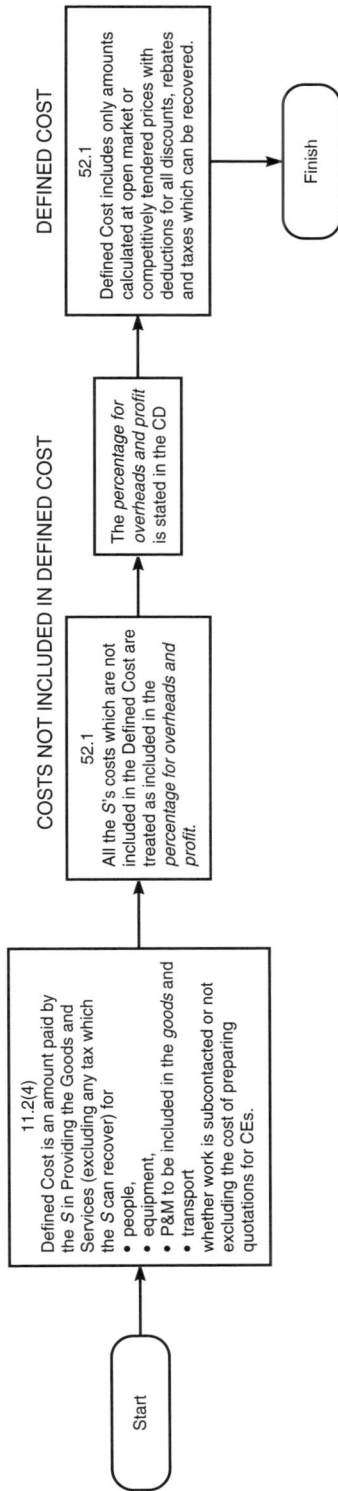

Flow chart 52
Defined Cost

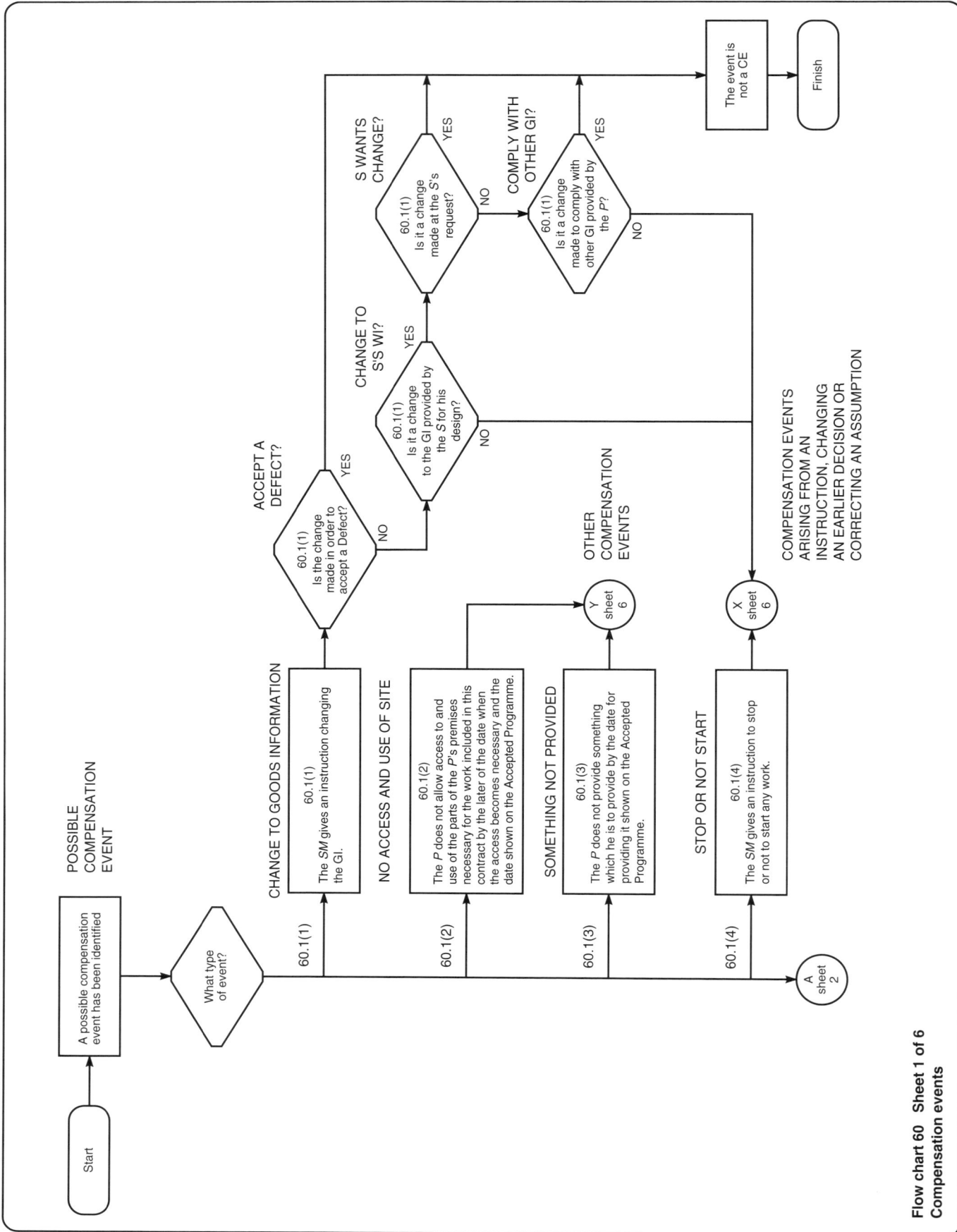
Start

POSSIBLE COMPENSATION EVENT

A possible compensation event has been identified

↓

What type of event?

CHANGE TO GOODS INFORMATION

60.1(1) → The *SM* gives an instruction changing the GI.

NO ACCESS AND USE OF SITE

60.1(2) → The *P* does not allow access to and use of the parts of the *P*'s premises necessary for the work included in this contract by the later of the date when the access becomes necessary and the date shown on the Accepted Programme.

SOMETHING NOT PROVIDED

60.1(3) → The *P* does not provide something which he is to provide by the date for providing it shown on the Accepted Programme.

→ (Y sheet 6)

STOP OR NOT START

60.1(4) → The *SM* gives an instruction to stop or not to start any work.

→ (X sheet 6)

(A sheet 2)

ACCEPT A DEFECT?

60.1(1) Is the change made in order to accept a Defect? — YES →

NO ↓

CHANGE TO S'S WI?

60.1(1) Is it a change to the GI provided by the *S* for his design? — YES →

NO →

S WANTS CHANGE?

60.1(1) Is it a change made at the *S*'s request? — YES →

NO →

COMPLY WITH OTHER GI?

60.1(1) Is it a change made to comply with other GI provided by the *P*? — YES →

NO →

The event is not a CE → Finish

COMPENSATION EVENTS ARISING FROM AN INSTRUCTION, CHANGING AN EARLIER DECISION OR CORRECTING AN ASSUMPTION

Flow chart 60   Sheet 1 of 6
Compensation events

www.neccontract.com

TYPE OF CE (CONTINUED)

WORK BY PURCHASER OR OTHERS

60.1(5)

60.1(5)
The *P* or people acting on behalf of the *P* do not work within the conditions stated in the GI

LATE REPLY TO COMMUNICATION

60.1(6)

60.1(6)
The *SM* does not reply to a communication from the *S* within the period required by this contract.

PREVIOUS DECISION CHANGED

60.1(7)

60.1(7)
The *SM* changes a decision which he has previously communicated to the *S*.

X sheet 6

ACCEPTANCE WITHHELD

60.1(8)

60.1(8)
The *SM* withholds an acceptance (other than acceptance of a quotation for an acceleration or for not correcting a Defect) for a reason not stated in this contract.

COMPENSATION EVENTS ARISING FROM AN INSTRUCTION, CHANGING AN EARLIER DECISION OR CORRECTING AN ASSUMPTION

Y sheet 6

OTHER COMPENSATION EVENTS

A sheet 1

B sheet 3

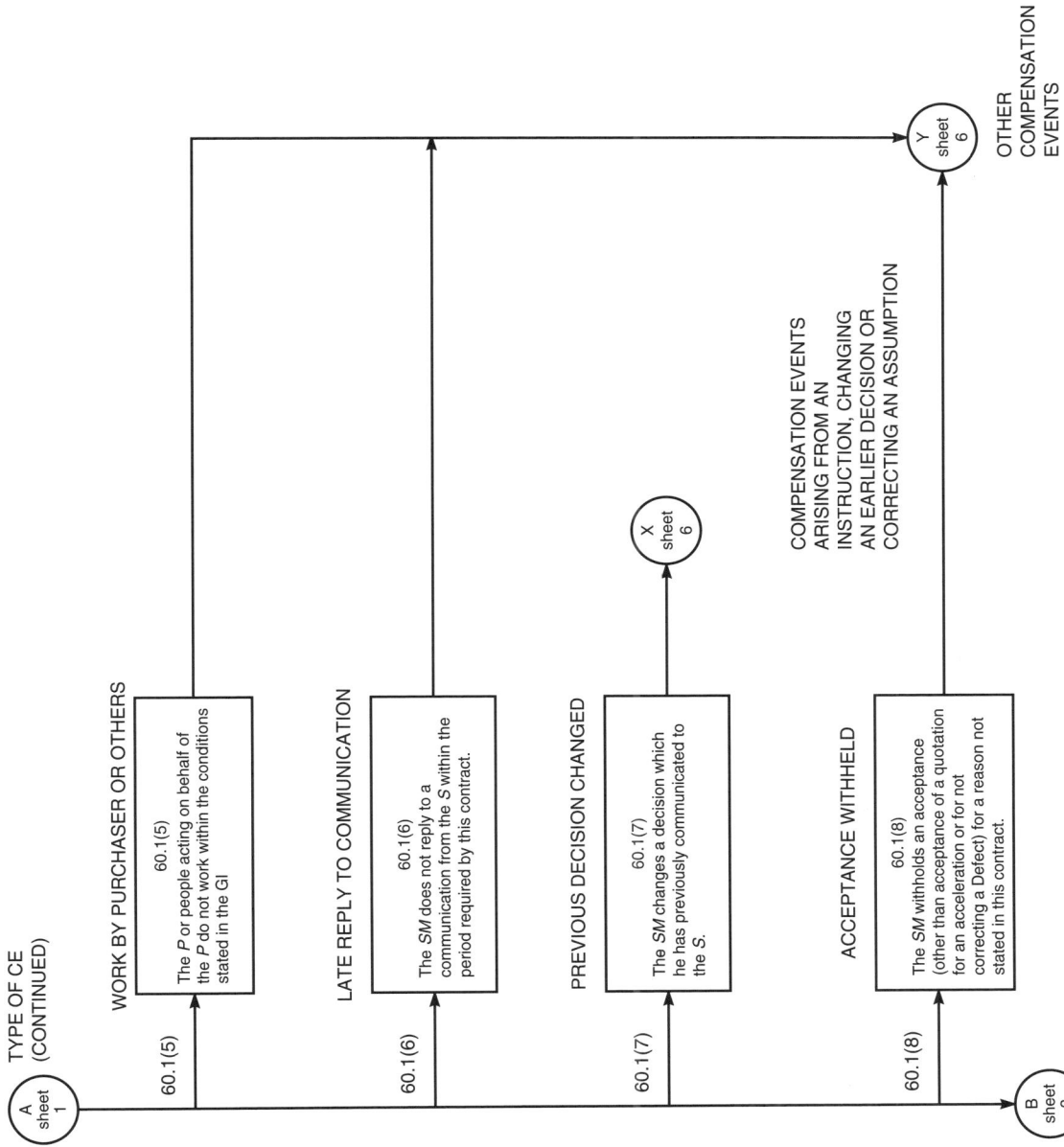

Flow chart 60   Sheet 2 of 6
Compensation events

TYPE OF CE
(CONTINUED)

B
sheet
2

SEARCH BUT NO DEFECT

60.1(9)

60.1(9)

The *SM* instructs the *S* to search for a Defect and no Defect is found.

SUPPLIER GIVES NOTICE

60.1(9)

The *S* gives sufficient notice of doing work obstructing a required test or inspection.

60.1(9)

Is the search needed only because the *S* gave insufficient notice?

NO → X sheet 6

COMPENSATION EVENTS ARISING FROM AN INSTRUCTION, CHANGING AN EARLIER DECISION OR CORRECTING AN ASSUMPTION

YES

The event is not a CE

Finish

TEST CAUSES A DELAY

60.1(10)

60.1(10)

A test or inspection done by the *SM* causes unnecessary delay.

Y
sheet
6

OTHER
COMPENSATION
EVENTS

C
sheet
4

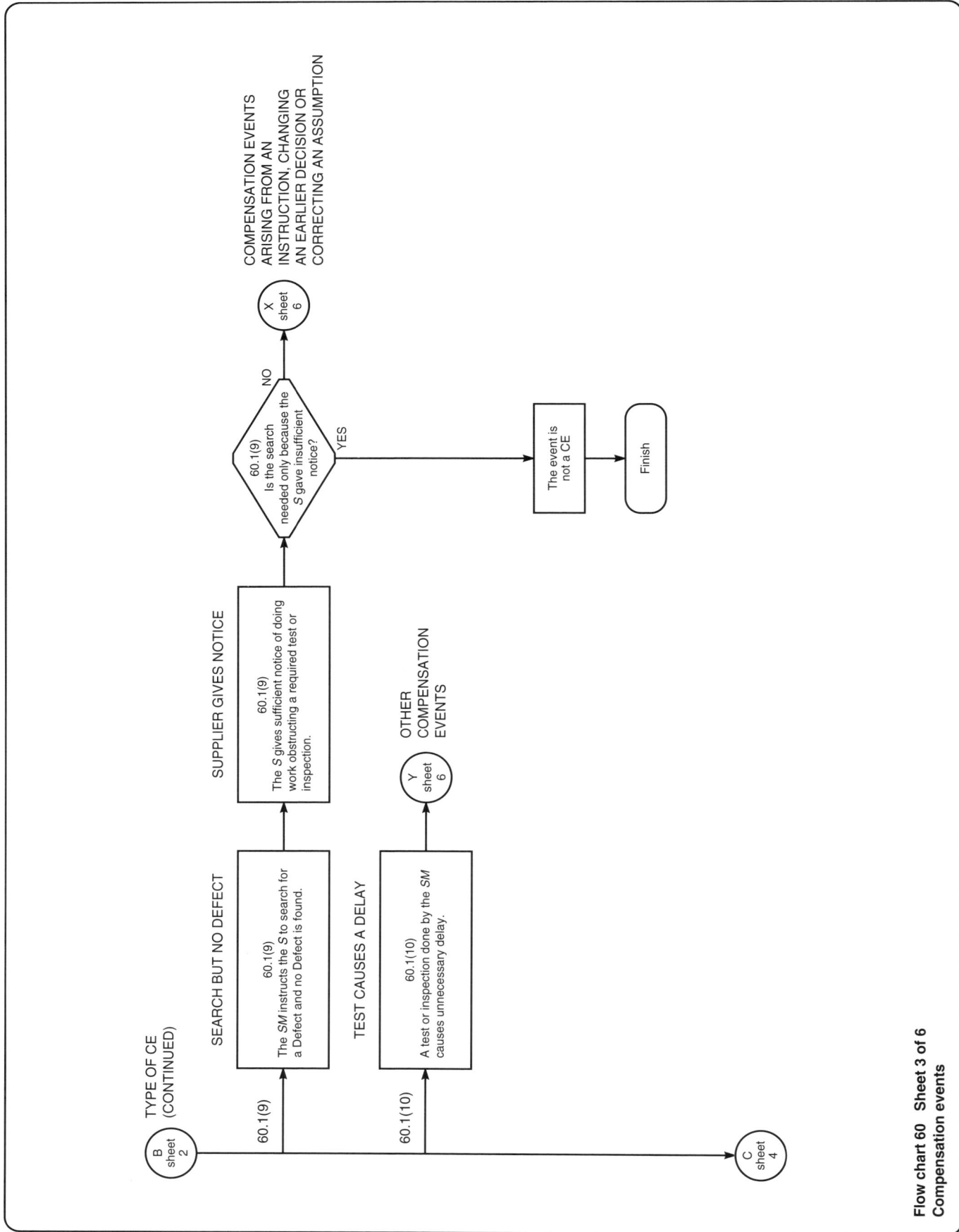

Flow chart 60   Sheet 3 of 6
Compensation events

TYPE OF CE (CONTINUED)

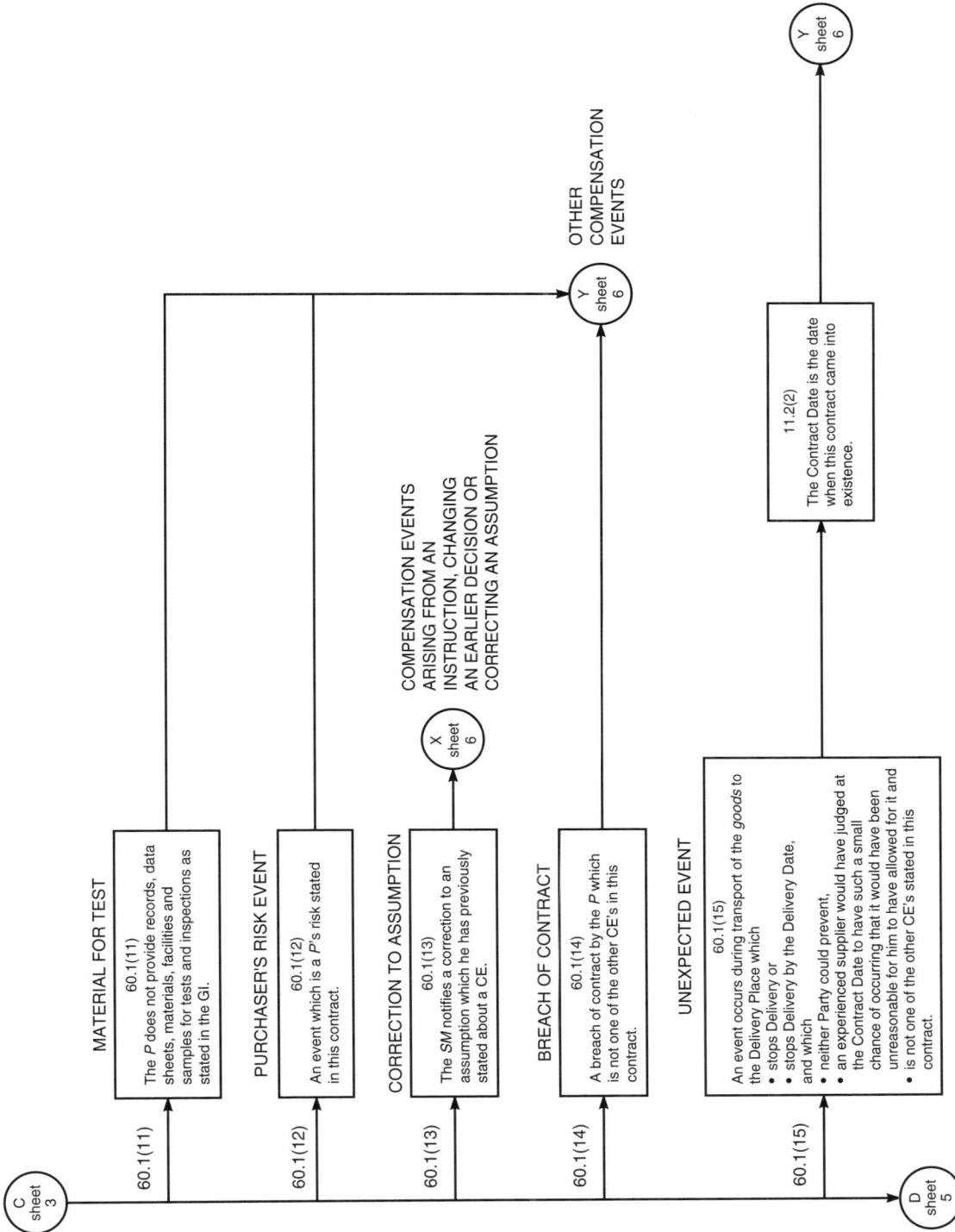

C
sheet
3

MATERIAL FOR TEST

60.1(11)

60.1(11)
The *P* does not provide records, data sheets, materials, facilities and samples for tests and inspections as stated in the GI.

PURCHASER'S RISK EVENT

60.1(12)

60.1(12)
An event which is a *P*'s risk stated in this contract.

CORRECTION TO ASSUMPTION

60.1(13)

60.1(13)
The *SM* notifies a correction to an assumption which he has previously stated about a CE.

X
sheet
6

COMPENSATION EVENTS ARISING FROM AN INSTRUCTION, CHANGING AN EARLIER DECISION OR CORRECTING AN ASSUMPTION

BREACH OF CONTRACT

60.1(14)

60.1(14)
A breach of contract by the *P* which is not one of the other CE's in this contract.

Y
sheet
6

OTHER COMPENSATION EVENTS

UNEXPECTED EVENT

60.1(15)

60.1(15)
An event occurs during transport of the *goods* to the Delivery Place which
- stops Delivery or
- stops Delivery by the Delivery Date,

and which
- neither Party could prevent,
- an experienced supplier would have judged at the Contract Date to have such a small chance of occurring that it would have been unreasonable for him to have allowed for it and
- is not one of the other CE's stated in this contract.

D
sheet
5

11.2(2)
The Contract Date is the date when this contract came into existence.

Y
sheet
6

**Flow chart 60 Sheet 4 of 6
Compensation events**

TYPE OF CE (CONTINUED)

CHANGE IN LAW OF COUNTRY

X2 CHANGES IN THE LAW

X2.1

Does Option X2 apply? — YES →

X2.1 A change in the law of the country stated in the Contract Data is a CE if it occurs after the Contract Date.

NO

CHANGE TO PARTNERING INFORMATION

X12 PARTNERING

X12.3(6)

Does Option X12 apply? — YES →

X12.3(6) Each change to the Partnering Information is a CE which may lead to reduced Prices.

NO

CHANGE TO PARTNERS' TIMETABLE

X12 PARTNERING

X12.3(7)

Does Option X12 apply? — YES →

X12.3(7) Each change to the S's programme to comply with the Partners' revised timetable is a CE which may lead to reduced Prices.

NO

DELAYED ADVANCED PAYMENT

X14 ADVANCED PAYMENT

X14.2

Does Option X14 apply? — YES →

X14.2 Delay in making the advanced payment to the S is a CE.

NO

COMPENSATION EVENTS ARISING FROM AN INSTRUCTION, CHANGING AN EARLIER DECISION OR CORRECTING AN ASSUMPTION

X sheet 6

Y sheet 6 — OTHER COMPENSATION EVENTS

D sheet 4

E sheet 6

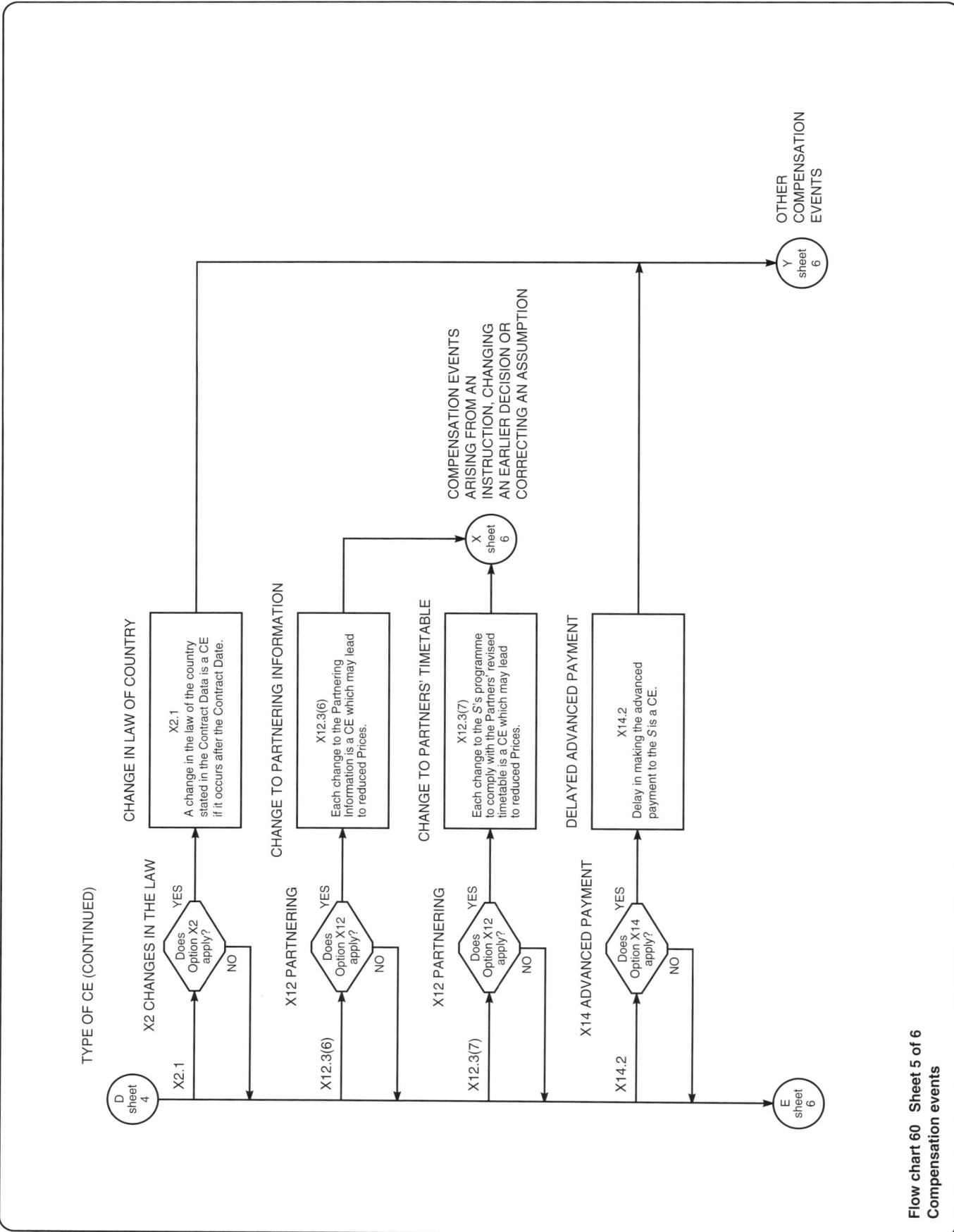

Flow chart 60   Sheet 5 of 6
Compensation events

    www.neccontract.com

TYPE OF CE (CONTINUED)

E
sheet
5

OTHER COMPENSATION EVENTS

21.1
Other CE's may be defined by the *P* as *additional conditions of contract* in the Contract Data Part 1.

Z

61.1
Does the CE arise from the *SM* giving an instruction, changing an earlier decision or correcting an assumption?

NO → Y
sheets
1–5

OTHER COMPENSATION EVENTS

YES

COMPENSATION EVENTS ARISING FROM AN INSTRUCTION, CHANGING AN EARLIER DECISION OR CORRECTING AN ASSUMPTION

X
sheets
1–5

61.1
The CE arises from the *SM* giving an instruction, changing an earlier decision or correcting an assumption.

61.1
The CE does not arise from the *SM* giving an instruction, changing an earlier decision or correcting an assumption.

FC 61
Notifying CEs

The event is not a CE

Finish

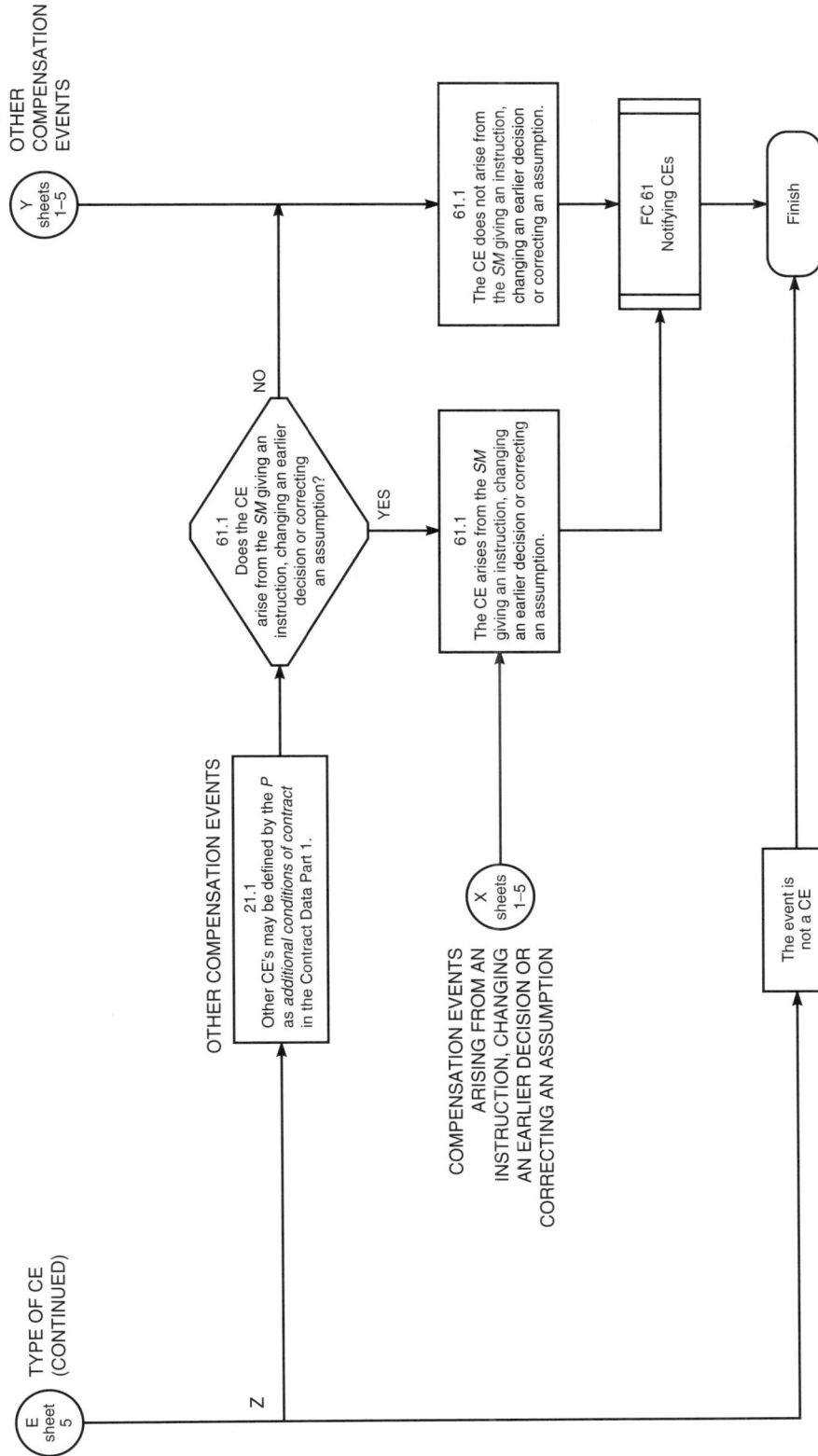

Flow chart 60   Sheet 6 of 6
Compensation events

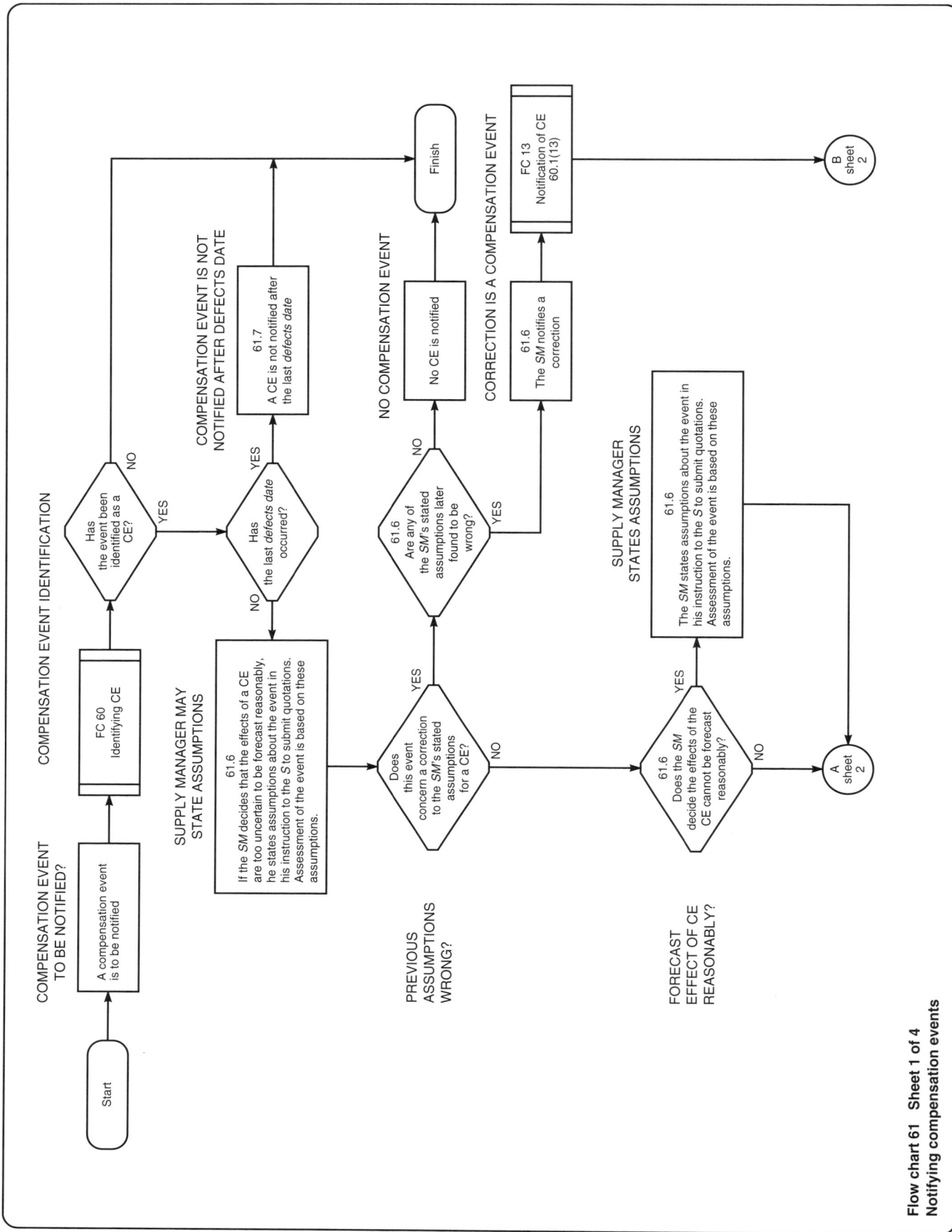

COMPENSATION EVENT TO BE NOTIFIED?

Start

A compensation event is to be notified

COMPENSATION EVENT IDENTIFICATION

FC 60
Identifying CE

Has the event been identified as a CE?

— NO →

— YES →

COMPENSATION EVENT IS NOT NOTIFIED AFTER DEFECTS DATE

Has the last *defects date* occurred?

— YES →

61.7
A CE is not notified after the last *defects date*

— NO →

SUPPLY MANAGER MAY STATE ASSUMPTIONS

61.6
If the *SM* decides that the effects of a CE are too uncertain to be forecast reasonably, he states assumptions about the event in his instruction to the *S* to submit quotations. Assessment of the event is based on these assumptions.

PREVIOUS ASSUMPTIONS WRONG?

Does this event concern a correction to the *SM*'s stated assumptions for a CE?

— YES →

61.6
Are any of the *SM*'s stated assumptions later found to be wrong?

— NO →

No CE is notified

Finish

NO COMPENSATION EVENT

— YES →

61.6
The *SM* notifies a correction

FC 13
Notification of CE 60.1(13)

CORRECTION IS A COMPENSATION EVENT

— NO →

FORECAST EFFECT OF CE REASONABLY?

61.6
Does the *SM* decide the effects of the CE cannot be forecast reasonably?

— YES →

61.6
The *SM* states assumptions about the event in his instruction to the *S* to submit quotations. Assessment of the event is based on these assumptions.

SUPPLY MANAGER STATES ASSUMPTIONS

— NO →

A
sheet 2

B
sheet 2

Flow chart 61   Sheet 1 of 4
Notifying compensation events

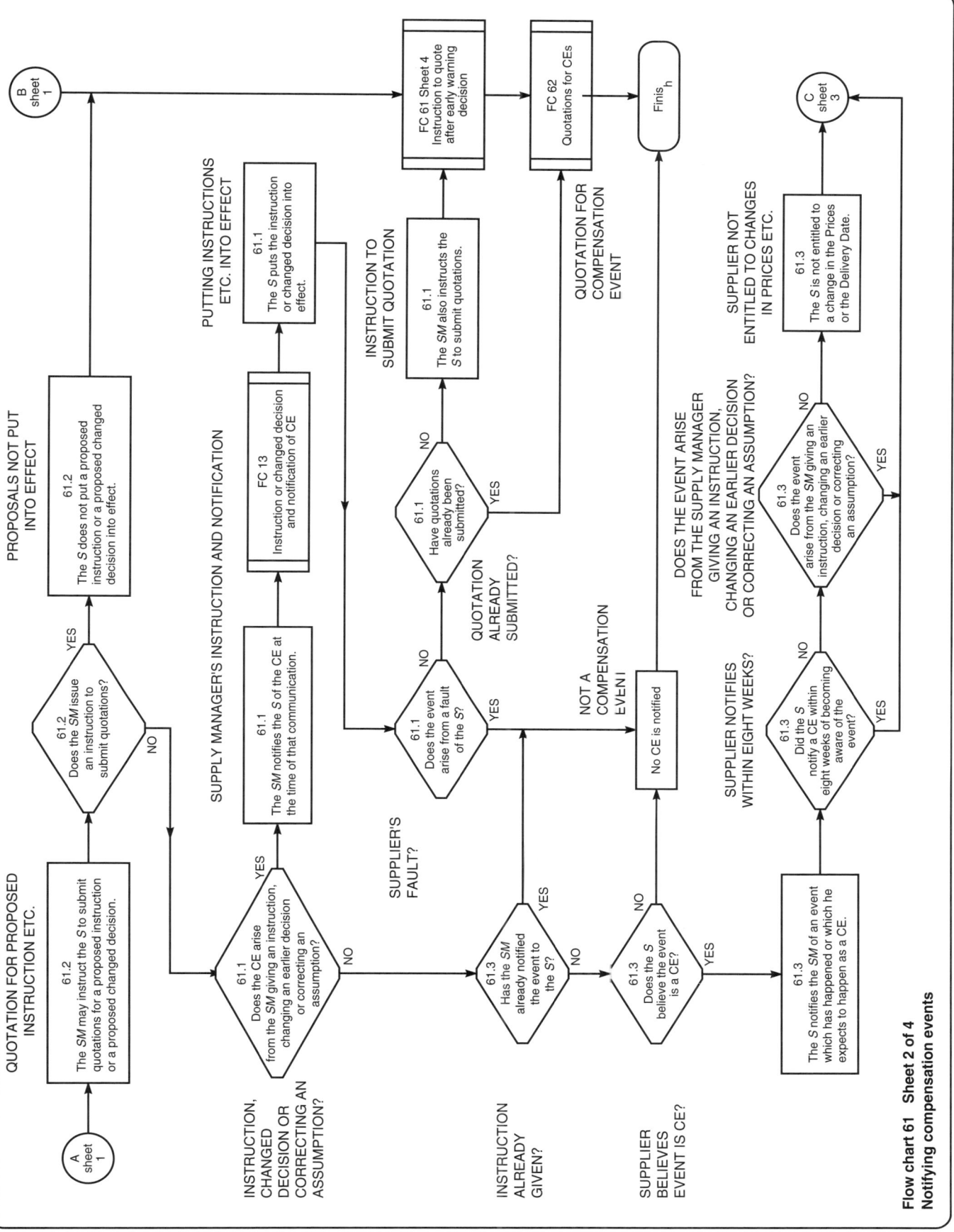

Flow chart 61 Sheet 2 of 4
Notifying compensation events

QUOTATION FOR PROPOSED INSTRUCTION ETC.

A sheet 1

61.2
The *SM* may instruct the *S* to submit quotations for a proposed instruction or a proposed changed decision.

PROPOSALS NOT PUT INTO EFFECT

61.2
Does the *SM* issue an instruction to submit quotations?

— YES → 61.2 The *S* does not put a proposed instruction or a proposed changed decision into effect.

— NO →

B sheet 1

PUTTING INSTRUCTIONS ETC. INTO EFFECT

61.1
The *S* puts the instruction or changed decision into effect.

INSTRUCTION, CHANGED DECISION OR CORRECTING AN ASSUMPTION?

61.1
Does the CE arise from the *SM* giving an instruction, changing an earlier decision or correcting an assumption?

— YES →

FC 13
Instruction or changed decision and notification of CE

SUPPLY MANAGER'S INSTRUCTION AND NOTIFICATION

61.1
The *SM* notifies the *S* of the CE at the time of that communication.

— NO →

SUPPLIER'S FAULT?

61.1
Does the event arise from a fault of the *S*?

— YES →

— NO →

QUOTATION ALREADY SUBMITTED?

61.1
Have quotations already been submitted?

— NO →

FC 61 Sheet 4
Instruction to quote after early warning decision

— YES →

INSTRUCTION TO SUBMIT QUOTATION

61.1
The *SM* also instructs the *S* to submit quotations.

FC 62
Quotations for CEs

Finish

QUOTATION FOR COMPENSATION EVENT

INSTRUCTION ALREADY GIVEN?

61.3
Has the *SM* already notified the event to the *S*?

— YES →

— NO →

SUPPLIER BELIEVES EVENT IS CE?

61.3
Does the *S* believe the event is a CE?

— NO →

NOT A COMPENSATION EVENT

No CE is notified

— YES →

61.3
The *S* notifies the *SM* of an event which has happened or which he expects to happen as a CE.

DOES THE EVENT ARISE FROM THE SUPPLY MANAGER GIVING AN INSTRUCTION, CHANGING AN EARLIER DECISION OR CORRECTING AN ASSUMPTION?

61.3
Does the event arise from the *SM* giving an instruction, changing an earlier decision or correcting an assumption?

— NO →

61.3
Does the event arise from the *SM* giving an instruction, changing an earlier decision or correcting an assumption?

— YES →

SUPPLIER NOTIFIES WITHIN EIGHT WEEKS?

61.3
Did the *S* notify a CE within eight weeks of becoming aware of the event?

— NO →

SUPPLIER NOT ENTITLED TO CHANGES IN PRICES ETC.

61.3
The *S* is not entitled to a change in the Prices or the Delivery Date.

— YES →

C sheet 3

Flow chart 61   Sheet 3 of 4
Notifying compensation events

EARLY WARNING

Start

61.5
If the *SM* decides that the *S* did not give an early warning of the event which an experienced supplier could have given, he notifies this decision to the *S* when he instructs him to submit quotations.

61.5
Does the *SM* decide the *S* did not give such an early warning?

NO

YES

EARLY WARNING DECISION

61.5
The *SM* notifies this decision to the *S* when he instructs him to submit quotations.

FC 13
Notification of decision

FC 13
Instruction to submit quotations

Finish

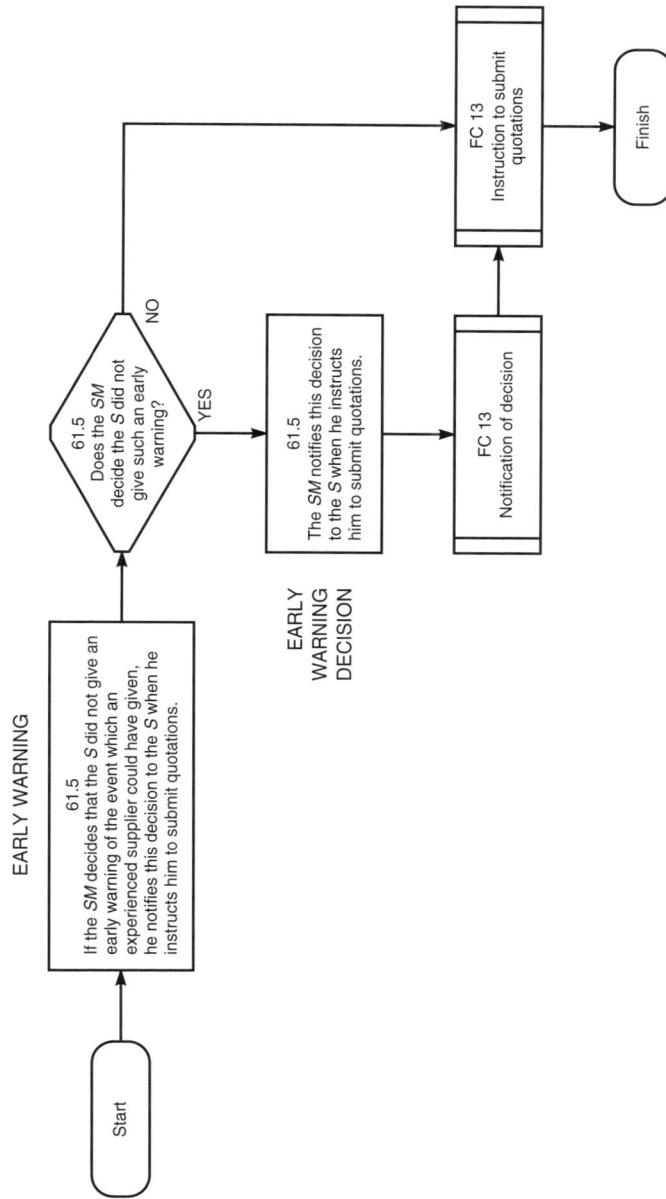

Flow chart 61   Sheet 4 of 4
Notifying compensation events

NEW QUOTATION?

Start

Has the *SM* instructed the *S* to submit quotations for a CE?
- YES →
- NO →

PURCHASER'S ALTERNATIVES

62.1
After discussing with the CE the *S* different ways of dealing with the CE which are practicable, the *SM* may instruct the *S* to submit alternative quotations.

SUPPLIER'S ALTERNATIVES

62.1
The *S* submits the required quotations to the *SM* and may submit quotations for other methods of dealing with the CE which he considers practicable.

FORM OF QUOTATION

62.2
Quotations for CE comprise proposed changes to the Prices and any delay to the Delivery Date assessed by the *S*.

SUPPLIER'S SUBMISSION

62.2
The *S* submits details of his assessment with each quotation.

62.2
Is the programme for remaining work altered by the CE?
- YES →
- NO →

PROGRAMME ALTERATIONS

62.2
The *S* includes the alterations to the Accepted Programme in his quotation.

SUPPLIER'S ASSESSMENT

FC 63
Assessment of CE by *S*

PERIOD FOR SUBMISSION

62.3
The *S* submits quotations within three weeks of being instructed to do so by the *SM*.

EXTENSION OF PERIOD

62.5
The *SM* extends the time allowed for the *S* to submit quotations for a CE if the *SM* and the *S* agree to the extension before the submission is due.

62.5
Do the *SM* and the *S* agree to extend the time allowed?
- YES →
- NO →

62.5
The *SM* notifies the extension that has been agreed to the *S*.

FC 13
Notification

62.3
Does the *S* submit quotations within the period for submission?
- NO → B sheet 2
- YES →

FC 13
S's submission

REVISED QUOTATION

C sheet 2

QUOTATION SUBMITTED?

Has the *S* submitted a quotation to the *SM*?
- YES →
- NO → **Finish**

REVIEW QUOTATION

FC 63
SM reviews *S*'s assessment of CE

SUPPLY MANAGER ASSESSES

B sheet 2

EXTENSION OF PERIOD

62.5
The *SM* extends the time allowed for the *SM* to reply to a quotation if the *SM* and the *S* agree to the extension before the reply is due.

62.5
Do the *SM* and the *S* agree to extend the time allowed?
- YES →
- NO →

62.5
The *SM* notifies the extension that has been agreed to the *S*.

FC 13
Notification

A sheet 2

SUPPLY MANAGER REPLIES

SUPPLY MANAGER'S REPLY

62.3
The *SM* replies within two weeks of the submission.

Flow chart 62 Sheet 1 of 2
Quotations for compensation events

TIMELY REPLY

SUPPLY MANAGER REPLIES

A sheet 1

62.3 — Does the *SM* reply within the period for reply to the *S*'s submission?

NO → **LATE OR NO REPLY**

62.6 — If the *SM* does not reply to a quotation within the time allowed, the *S* may notify the *SM* of his failure.

NOTIFY?

62.6 — Does the *S* notify the *SM* to this effect?

YES → **DESIGNATED QUOTE**

62.6 — If the *S* submitted more than one quotation for the CE, he states in his notification which quotation is to be accepted.

→ **SUPPLIER NOTIFIES QUOTE**

FC 13 — *S*'s Notification

NO → **LATE REPLY CE**

FC 61 — Late reply CE 60.1(6)

→ **DEFAULTED?**

62.6 — Is the *S*'s notification treated as acceptance by the *SM*?

NO (up to FC 61)

YES → **TREATED AS ACCEPTED**

62.6 — If the *SM* does not reply to the notification within two weeks, and unless the quotation is for a proposed instruction or a proposed changed decision, the *S*'s notification is treated as acceptance of the quotation by the *SM*.

YES (from TIMELY REPLY 62.3) →

How does the *SM* reply?

SUPPLY MANAGER'S REPLY

ACCEPTANCE OF QUOTATION

62.3 — The *SM*'s reply is an acceptance of a quotation.

→ **IMPLEMENT COMPENSATION EVENT**

FC 65 — Implementing CE's

→ Finish

SUPPLY MANAGER'S ASSESSMENT

62.3 — The *SM*'s reply is a notification that he will be making his own assessment.

FC 13 — *SM*'s Notification

→ **SUPPLY MANAGER ASSESSES**

B sheet 1

FC 64 — *SM* assesses CE

→ FC 65

PROPOSAL NOT ACCEPTABLE

62.3 — The *SM*'s reply is a notification that a proposed instruction will not be given or a proposed changed decision will not be made.

FC 13 — *SM*'s Notification

→ Finish

REVISED QUOTATION

62.3 — The *SM*'s reply is an instruction to submit a revised quotation.

→ **REASON GIVEN**

62.4 — The *SM* instructs the *S* to submit a revised quotation only after explaining his reason for doing so to the *S*.

→ **RE-SUBMIT**

FC 13 — *SM*'s Instruction

→ **RE-SUBMISSION PERIOD**

62.4 — The *S* submits the revised quotation within three weeks of being instructed to do so.

→ C sheet 1 — **REVISE QUOTATION**

EXTENSION OF PERIOD FOR RE-SUBMISSION

62.5 — The *SM* extends the time allowed for the *S* to submit quotations for a CE if the *S* and the *SM* agree to the extension before the submission is due.

62.5 — Does the *SM* and the *S* agree to extend the time allowed?

YES → **62.5** — The *SM* notifies the extension that has been agreed to the *S*.

FC 13 — *SM*'s Notification

→ **62.5** — The *S* revises his quotation.

→ C sheet 1 — **REVISE QUOTATION**

NO →

Flow chart 62   Sheet 2 of 2
Quotations for compensation events

COMPENSATION EVENT IS TO BE ASSESSED

Start

11.2(4)
Defined Cost is an amount paid by the *S* in Providing the Goods and Services (excluding any tax which the *S* can recover) for
- people,
- equipment,
- P&M to be included in the *goods* and
- transport
whether work is subcontracted or not excluding the cost of preparing quotations for CE's.

RIGHTS TO CHANGE PRICE ETC

12.5
In these *conditions of contract*, each reference and clause relevant to Delivery and the Delivery Date applies to each Delivery and its Delivery Date

RISK ALLOWANCES

63.7
Assessment of the effect of a CE includes risk allowances for cost and time for matters which have a significant chance of occurring and are at the *S*'s risk under this contract

63.5
The rights of the *P* and the *S* to make changes to the Prices and the Delivery Date are their only rights in respect of a CE

61.5 and 63.6
The *SM* notifies the *S* of his decision that the *S* did not give an early warning of the CE which an experienced supplier could have given

EARLY WARNING

WARNING GIVEN?

A CE is to be assessed

63.6
Has the *SM* notified the *S* that that the *S* did not give such early warning?

YES → **63.6**
The CE is assessed as if the *S* had given early warning

NO → **53.1**
Information in the Price Schedule is not GI

CHANGES TO THE PRICES

63.1
Does the CE only affect the quantities of *goods* and *services* shown in the Price Schedule?

YES → **63.1**
If the *SM* and the *S* agree, for a CE which only affects the quantities of *goods* and *services* shown in the Price Schedule, the change to the Prices is assessed by multiplying the changed quantities by the appropriate rates in the Price Schedule

Do the *SM* and the *S* agree?

YES → **63.1**
Appropriate rates in the Price Schedule are used → **B Sheet 2**

NO ↓

NO ↓

CHANGES TO THE PRICES

AGREEMENT TO USE RATES AND LUMP SUMS

63.12
If the *SM* and the *S* agree, rates and lump sums may be used to assess a CE instead of Defined Cost

Do the *SM* and the *S* agree?

YES → **63.12**
Rates and lump sums are used → **B Sheet 2**

NO ↓

CALCULATION FOR QUOTATION

63.2
Effects on Defined Cost are assessed separately for
- people,
- equipment,
- P&M included in the *goods*,
- work subcontracted by the *S* and
- transport

63.2
The *S* shows how each of these effects is built up in each quotation for a CE → **FC 62 Quotation for CE** → **A Sheet 2**

COMPETENT REACTION

63.8
Assessments are based upon the assumptions that the *S* reacts competently and promptly to the CE, that any Defined Cost and time due to the event are reasonably incurred and that the *S*'s Accepted Programme can be changed

WORK DONE DEFINED

63.2
If the CE arose from the *SM* giving an instruction, changing an earlier decision or correcting an assumption, the date which divides the work already done from the work not yet done is the date of that communication

63.2
In all other cases, the date is the date of the notification of the CE

CHANGES TO THE PRICES

63.2
For other CE's, the changes to the Prices are assessed as the effect of the CE upon
- the actual Defined Cost of the work already done,
- the forecast Defined Cost of the work not yet done and
- the resulting amount calculated by applying the *percentage for overheads and profit* to the Defined Cost of the work

Are any tax charges for customs clearance, export or import included in the effect on Defined Cost?

NO ↑

YES → **63.2**
The *percentage for overheads and profit* is applied to the assessed effect of the event on Defined Cost except that it is not applied to any tax charges for
- customs clearance and
- export and import

Flow chart 63 Sheet 1 of 2
Assessing compensation events

REDUCED PRICES?

63.3
If the effect of a CE is to reduce the total Defined Cost, the Prices are not reduced except as stated in this contract

63.10
Is the effect of a CE to reduce the total Defined Cost? — YES / NO

QUALIFYING EVENT?

63.10
Is the event a change to the GI? — YES / NO

63.10
Is the event a correction of an assumption stated by the *SM* for assessing an earlier CE? — YES / NO

63.10
The Prices are reduced

63.10
The Prices are not reduced

ASSESSMENT OF DELAY

63.4
A delay to the Delivery Date is assessed on the length of time that, due to the CE, planned Delivery is later than planned Delivery as shown on the Accepted Programme

CHANGE TO GOODS INFORMATION

63.9
Does the CE include an instruction to change the GI in order to resolve an ambiguity or inconsistency? — YES / NO

INTERPRETATION DEPENDS ON PROVISION OF GOODS INFORMATION

63.9
The effect of the CE assessed as if the Prices and the Delivery Date were for the interpretation most favourable to the Party which did not provide the GI

PRICE SCHEDULE

63.11
Assessments for changed Prices for CE's are in the form of changes to the Price Schedule

Finish

A Sheet 1

B Sheet 1

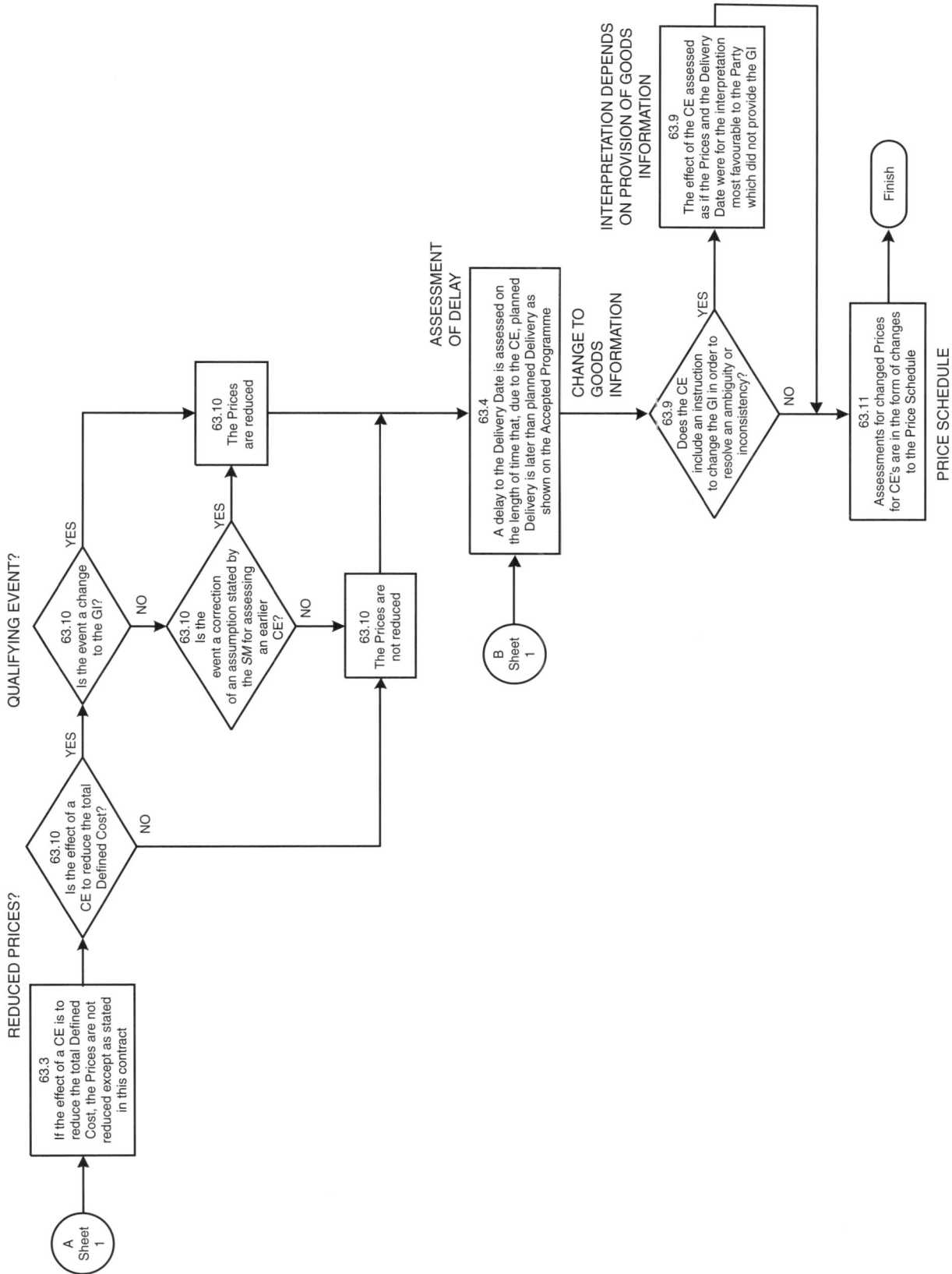

Flow chart 63 Sheet 2 of 2
Assessing compensation events

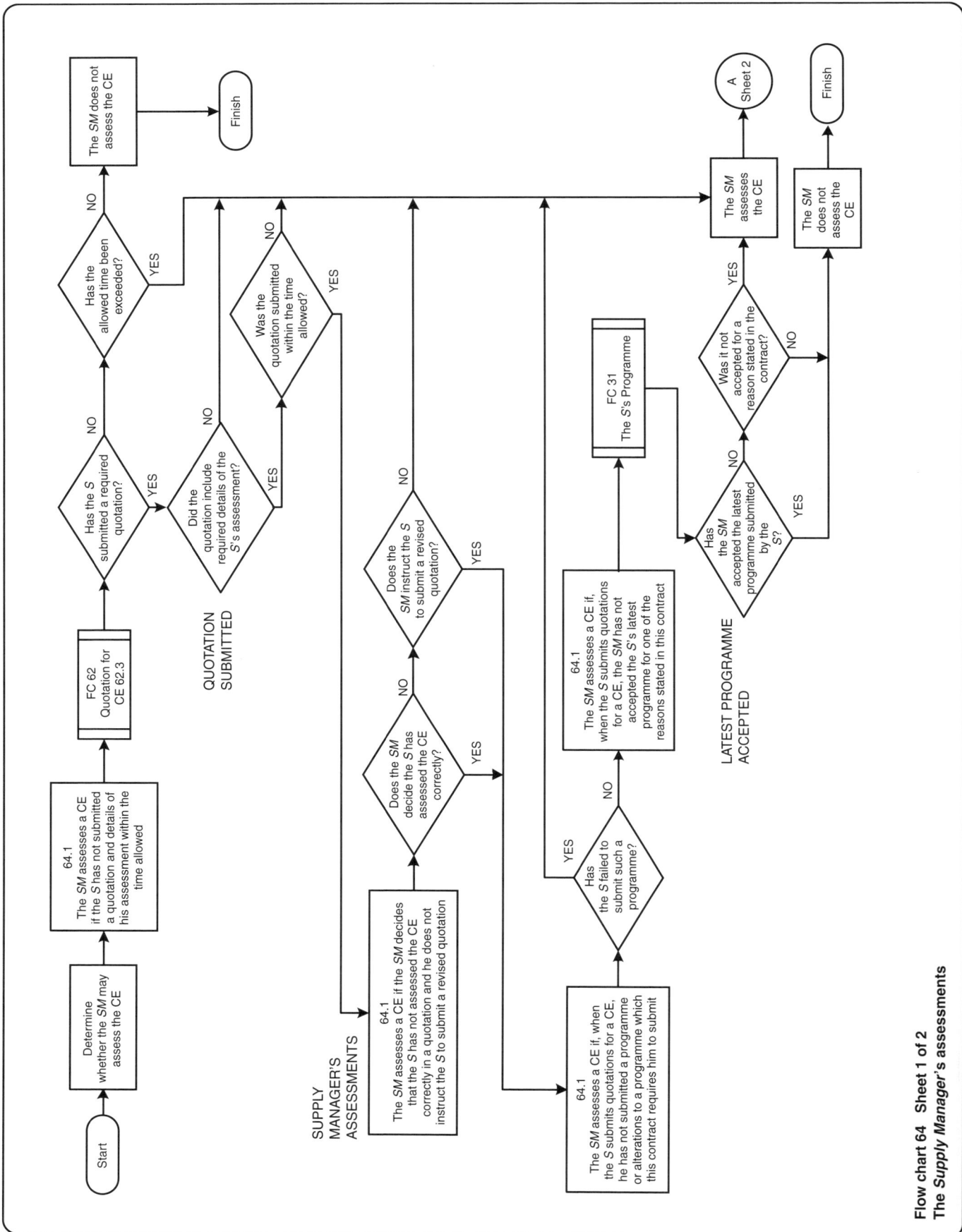

SUPPLY MANAGER'S ASSESSMENTS

Start

Determine whether the *SM* may assess the CE

64.1
The *SM* assesses a CE if the *S* has not submitted a quotation and details of his assessment within the time allowed

FC 62
Quotation for CE 62.3

Has the *S* submitted a required quotation? — NO

Has the allowed time been exceeded? — NO → The *SM* does not assess the CE → Finish
— YES

YES → Did the quotation include required details of the *S*'s assessment? — NO → Was the quotation submitted within the time allowed? — NO
— YES →

QUOTATION SUBMITTED

64.1
The *SM* assesses a CE if the *SM* decides that the *S* has not assessed the CE correctly in a quotation and he does not instruct the *S* to submit a revised quotation

Does the *SM* decide the *S* has assessed the CE correctly? — NO → Does the *SM* instruct the *S* to submit a revised quotation? — NO
— YES

64.1
The *SM* assesses a CE if, when the *S* submits quotations for a CE, he has not submitted a programme or alterations to a programme which this contract requires him to submit

Has the *S* failed to submit such a programme? — YES — NO

64.1
The *SM* assesses a CE if, when the *S* submits quotations for a CE, the *SM* has not accepted the *S*'s latest programme for one of the reasons stated in this contract

FC 31
The *S*'s Programme

LATEST PROGRAMME ACCEPTED

Has the *SM* accepted the latest programme submitted by the *S*? — NO → Was it not accepted for a reason stated in the contract? — YES → The *SM* assesses the CE → A Sheet 2
— YES — NO → The *SM* does not assess the CE → Finish

Flow chart 64   Sheet 1 of 2
The *Supply Manager*'s assessments

ASSESSMENT BY SUPPLY MANAGER

A Sheet 1

SUPPLIER'S PROGRAMME?

64.2 Is there an Accepted Programme?

— NO →

64.2 Has the S submitted a programme or alterations to a programme as required by this contract?

SUPPLY MANAGER USES HIS OWN PROGRAMME

64.2 The SM assesses a CE using his own assessment of the programme for the remaining work.

— YES →

FC 63 Assessment by SM

SUPPLY MANAGER NOTIFIES ASSESSMENT

64.3 The SM notifies the S of his assessment of a CE and gives him details of it within the period allowed for the S's submission of his quotation for the same event. This period starts when the need for the SM's assessment becomes apparent.

TIMELY ASSESSMENT?

64.4 Does the SM assess the CE within the time allowed?

LATE OR NO REPLY

64.4 If the SM does not assess a CE within the time allowed, the S may notify the SM of his failure.

NOTIFY?

64.4 Does the S notify the SM to this effect?

DESIGNATED QUOTE

64.4 If the S submitted more than one quotation for the CE, he states in his notification which way of dealing with the CE he proposes be accepted.

SUPPLIER NOTIFIES QUOTE

FC 13 S's notification

64.4 If the SM does not reply within two weeks of this notification, the notification is treated as acceptance of the S's quotation by the SM.

SUPPLIER'S QUOTATION TREATED AS ACCEPTED

DEFAULTED?

64.4 Is the S's notification treated as acceptance by the SM?

LATE REPLY CE

FC 61 Late reply CE 60.1(6)

Finish

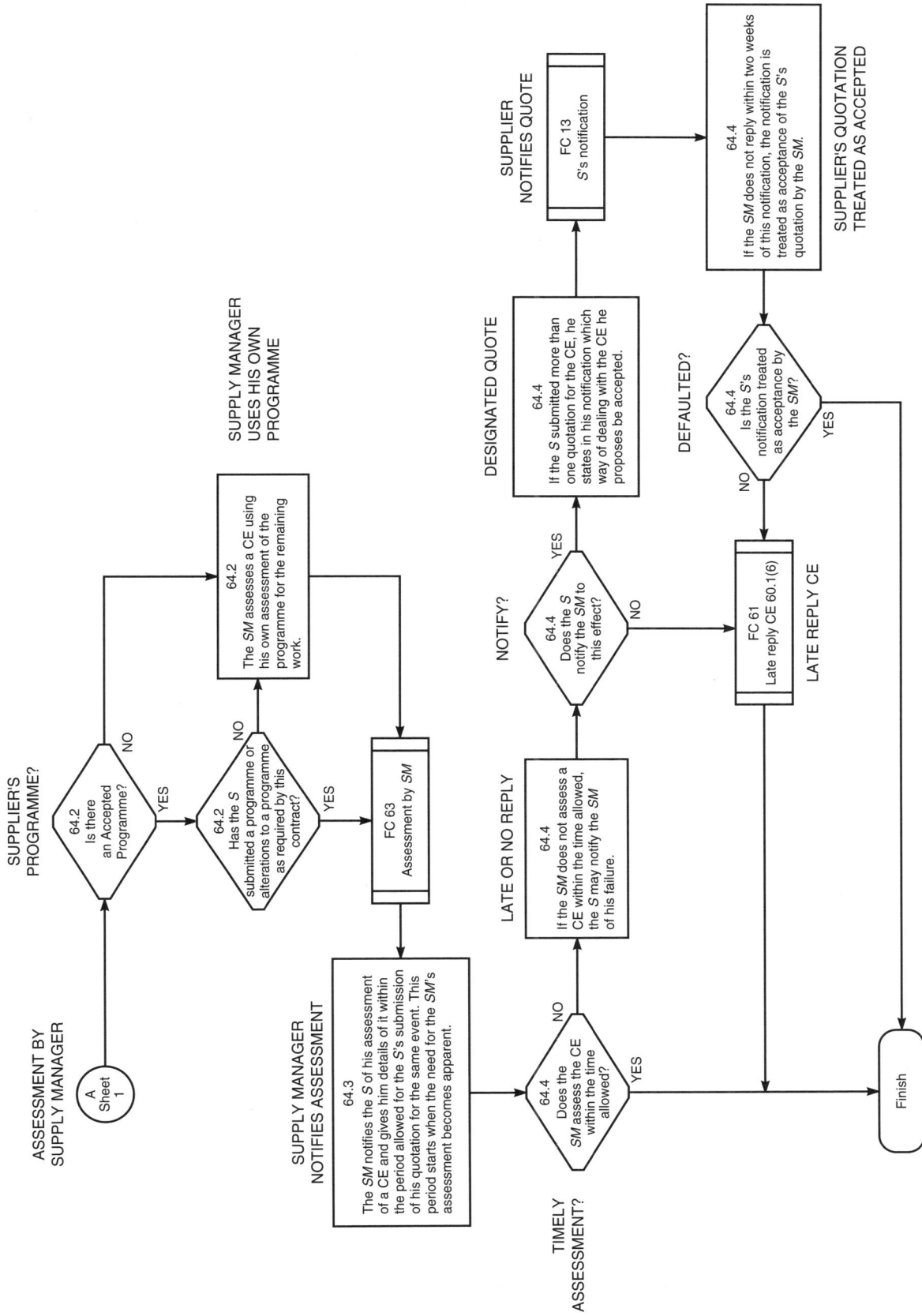

Flow chart 64 Sheet 2 of 2
The Supply Manager's assessments

Start

↓

A CE is to be implemented

↓

NOTIFICATION OF SUPPLIER'S QUOTATION ACCEPTED

65.1
Has the *SM* notified his acceptance of the *S*'s quotation?

— YES →

65.1
The *SM* implements the CE by notifying his acceptance of the *S*'s quotation.

NO
↓

NOTIFICATION OF SUPPLY MANAGER'S OWN ASSESSMENT

65.1
Has the *SM* notified the *S* of his own assessment?

— YES →

65.1
The *SM* implements the CE by notifying the *S* of his own assessment.

NO
↓

SUPPLIER'S QUOTATION TREATED AS ACCEPTED

65.1
Is a *S*'s quotation treated as having been accepted by the *SM*?

— YES →

65.1
A CE is implemented when a *S*'s quotation is treated as having been accepted by the *SM*.

NO
↓

ASSESSMENT NOT REVISED

65.2
The assessment of a CE is not revised if a forecast upon which it is based is shown by later recorded information to have been wrong.

↓

CHANGES TO PRICES AND DELIVERY DATE

65.3
The changes to the Prices and the Delivery Date are included in the notification implementing a CE.

↓

12.5
In these *conditions of contract*, each reference and clause relevant to Delivery and Delivery Date applies to each Delivery and its Delivery Date.

↓

SUPPLIER NOTIFIED

FC 13
Notification to *S*

↓

Finish

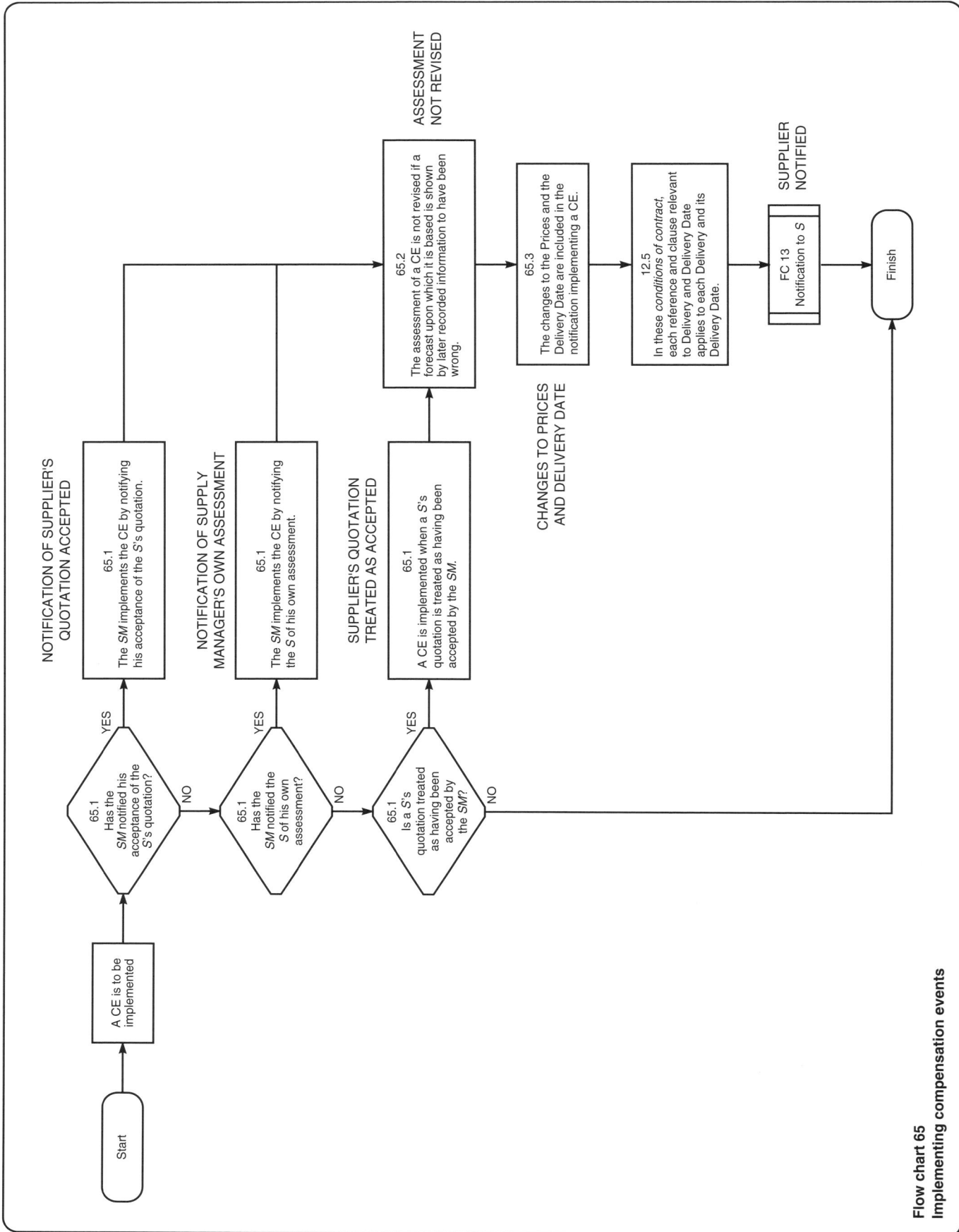

**Flow chart 65
Implementing compensation events**

GOODS FOR CONTRACT?

Start → The P requires title to goods → Are these goods required for the contract?

Are these goods required for the contract? — NO → Title does not pass → Finish

Are these goods required for the contract? — YES → 70.2 Before payment for the goods is made, the S provides information to the P to show that he is able to pass title to the goods

SUPPLIER HAS TITLE?

Can the S pass title? — NO → Payment is not made → Title does not pass

Can the S pass title? — YES → Has the P made payment?

Has the P made payment? — NO → Title does not pass

Has the P made payment? — YES → 70.1 Title to the goods passes to the P when payment for the goods which this contract requires has been made.

Title passes → Finish

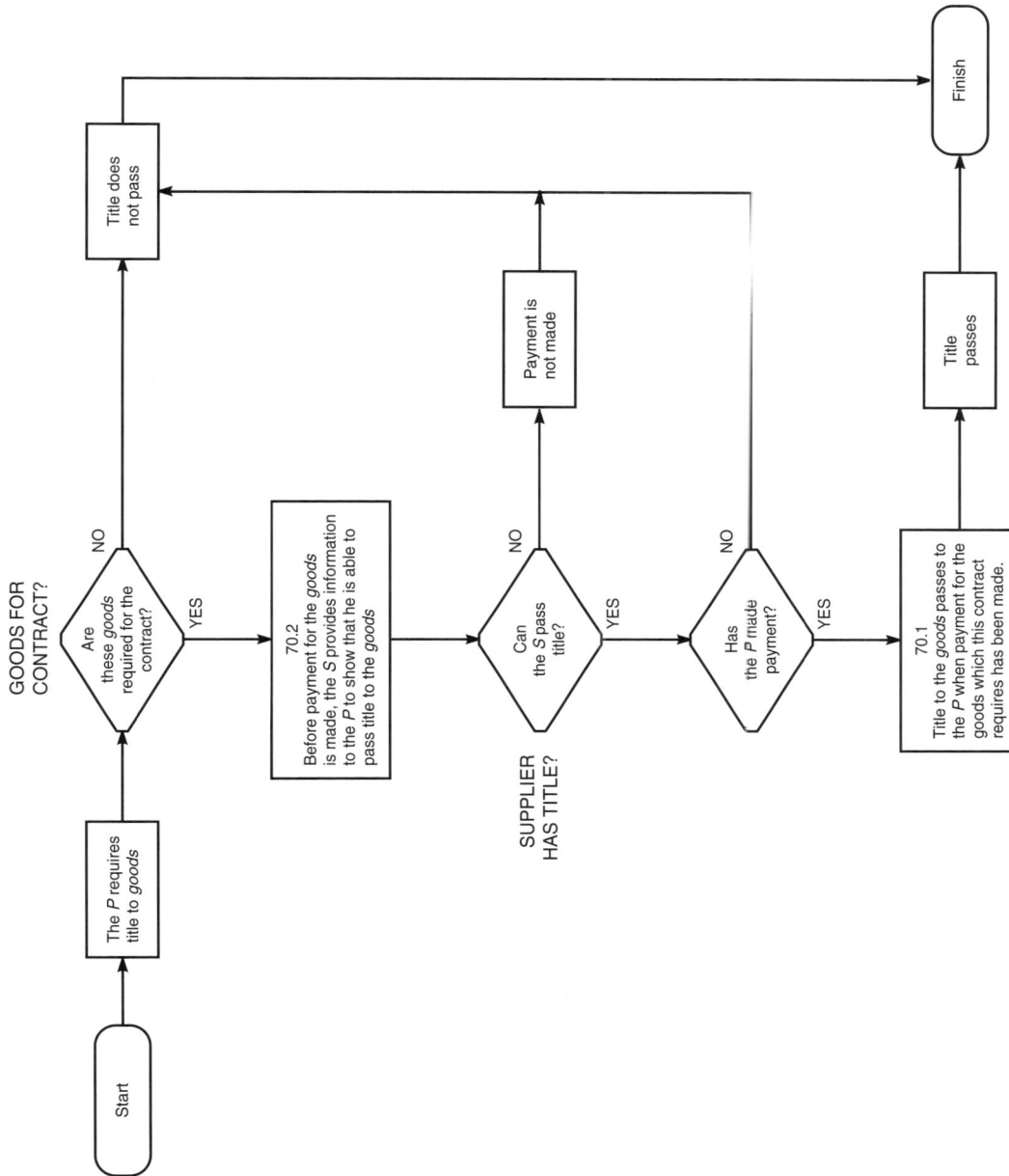

Flow chart 70
The Purchaser's title to the goods

GOODS IDENTIFIED FOR MARKING?

Start

Does the contract identify the *goods* for payment before they are brought to the Delivery Place?

NO

YES

71.1
The *S* marks the *goods* as the GI requires if this contract identifies them for payment before they are brought within the Delivery Place

FC50
Assessing the amount due

PAYMENT

Finish

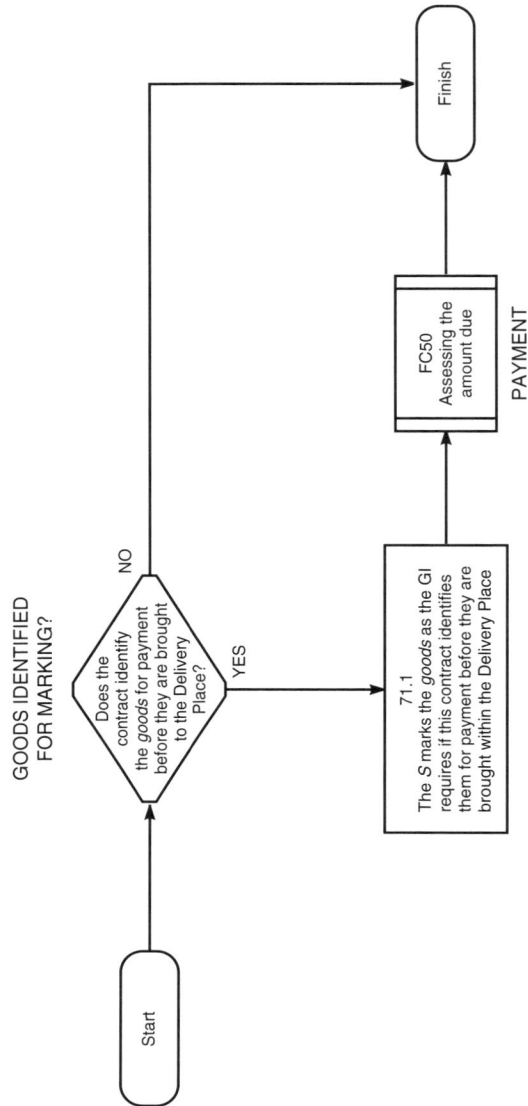

Flow chart 71
Marking *goods* before Delivery

Start

Determine whether the *P* bears the risk of an event

What type of event?

CLAIMS, PROCEEDINGS, ETC.

80.1
Claims, proceedings, compensation and costs payable which are

due to?

DUE TO PROVIDING THE GOODS AND SERVICES

80.1
the unavoidable result of the supply of the *goods* and *services*

DUE TO NEGLIGENCE ETC.

80.1
negligence, breach of statutory duty or interference with any legal right by the *P* or by any person employed or contracted to him except the *S*.

DUE TO PURCHASER'S FAULT

80.1
a fault of the *P* or a fault in his design

DUE TO ANOTHER REASON

PURCHASER'S RISK

The event is at *P*'s risk

Finish

NOT PURCHASER'S RISK

The event is not at *P*'s risk

A
Sheet 2

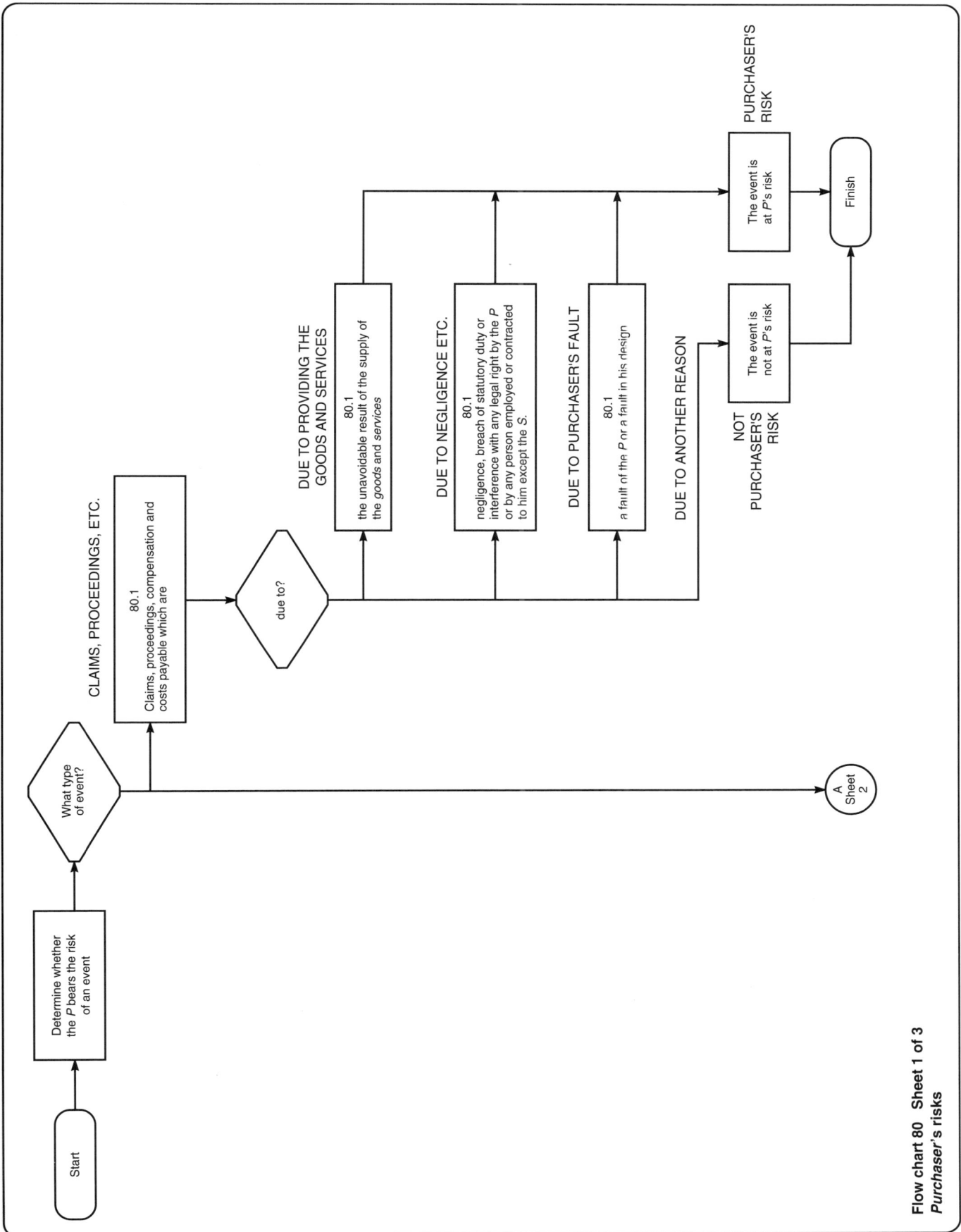

Flow chart 80   Sheet 1 of 3
Purchaser's risks

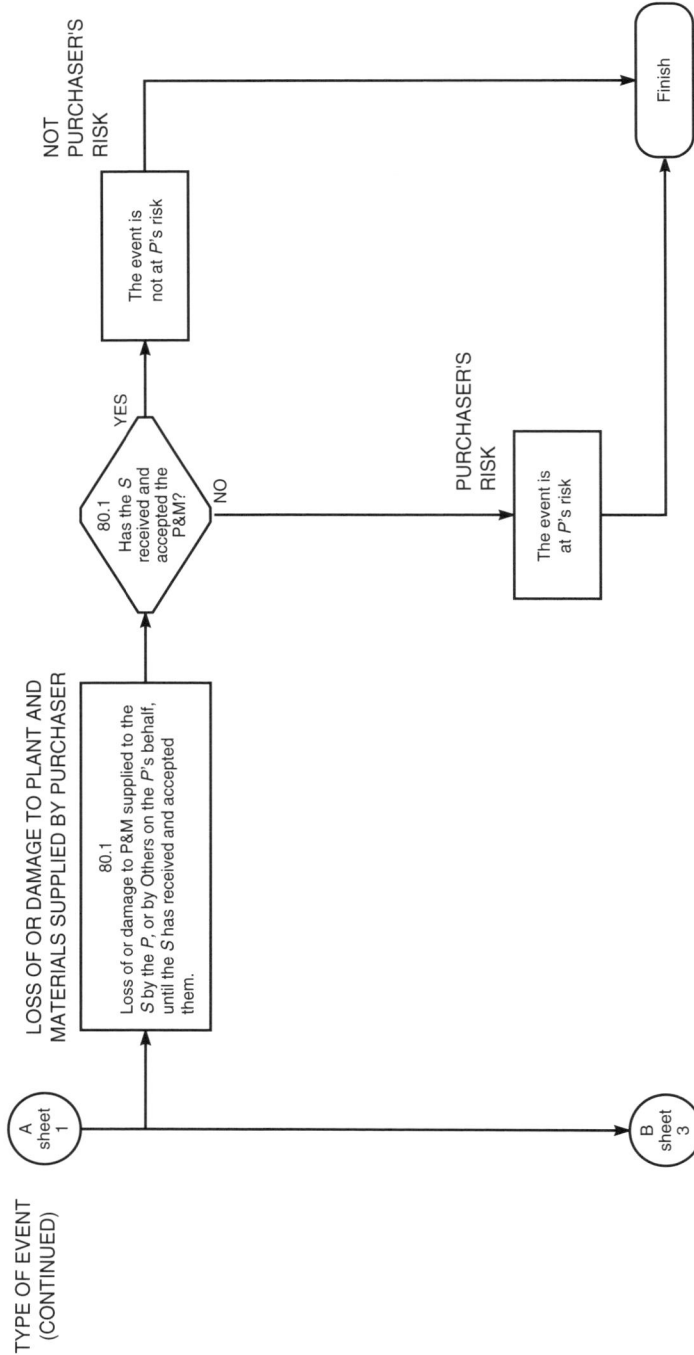

TYPE OF EVENT
(CONTINUED)

LOSS OF OR DAMAGE TO PLANT AND
MATERIALS SUPPLIED BY PURCHASER

A
sheet
1

80.1

Loss of or damage to P&M supplied to the
S by the P, or by Others on the P's behalf,
until the S has received and accepted
them.

80.1
Has the S
received and
accepted the
P&M?

YES

The event is
not at P's risk

NOT
PURCHASER'S
RISK

NO

PURCHASER'S
RISK

The event is
at P's risk

Finish

B
sheet
3

Flow chart 80   Sheet 2 of 3
Purchaser's risks

TYPE OF EVENT
(CONTINUED)

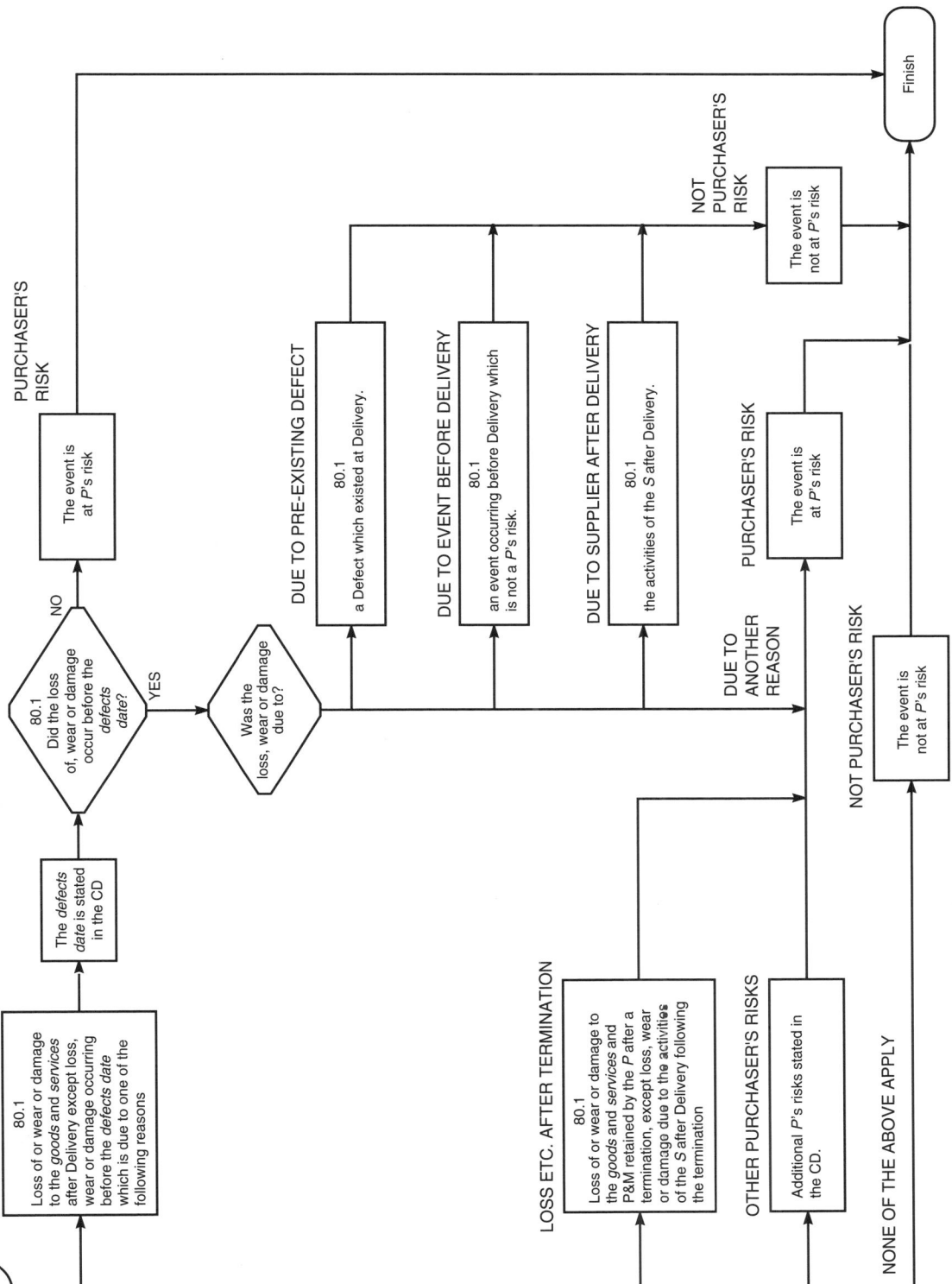

(B sheet 2)

LOSS ETC. AFTER DELIVERY

80.1
Loss of or wear or damage to the *goods* and *services* after Delivery except loss, wear or damage occurring before the *defects date* which is due to one of the following reasons

The *defects date* is stated in the CD

80.1
Did the loss of, wear or damage occur before the *defects date?*

NO → PURCHASER'S RISK

The event is at *P*'s risk

YES → Was the loss, wear or damage due to?

DUE TO PRE-EXISTING DEFECT

80.1
a Defect which existed at Delivery.

DUE TO EVENT BEFORE DELIVERY

80.1
an event occurring before Delivery which is not a *P*'s risk.

DUE TO SUPPLIER AFTER DELIVERY

80.1
the activities of the *S* after Delivery.

NOT PURCHASER'S RISK

The event is not at *P*'s risk

Finish

DUE TO ANOTHER REASON

PURCHASER'S RISK

The event is at *P*'s risk

LOSS ETC. AFTER TERMINATION

80.1
Loss of or wear or damage to the *goods* and *services* and P&M retained by the *P* after a termination, except loss, wear or damage due to the activities of the *S* after Delivery following the termination

OTHER PURCHASER'S RISKS

Additional *P*'s risks stated in the CD.

NONE OF THE ABOVE APPLY

NOT PURCHASER'S RISK

The event is not at *P*'s risk

Flow chart 80   Sheet 3 of 3
Purchaser's risks

Start

Determine whether the *S* bears the risks of an event

The *starting date* is stated in the CD

BEFORE STARTING DATE

81.1
Did the event occur before the *starting date?*

YES →

NO ↓

The *defects date* is stated in the CD

BEFORE THE END OF LAST DEFECTS DATE?

81.1
Did the event occur before the last *defects date* has ended?

YES →

NO ↑

PURCHASER'S RISK?

FC 80
P's risks

81.1
Is the event a risk carried by the *P?*

YES →

NO ↓

SUPPLIER'S RISK

81.1
From the *starting date* until the last *defects date* the risks which are not carried by the *P* are carried by the *S*

Event is a *S's* risk

NOT A SUPPLIER'S RISK

Event is not a *S's* risk

Finish

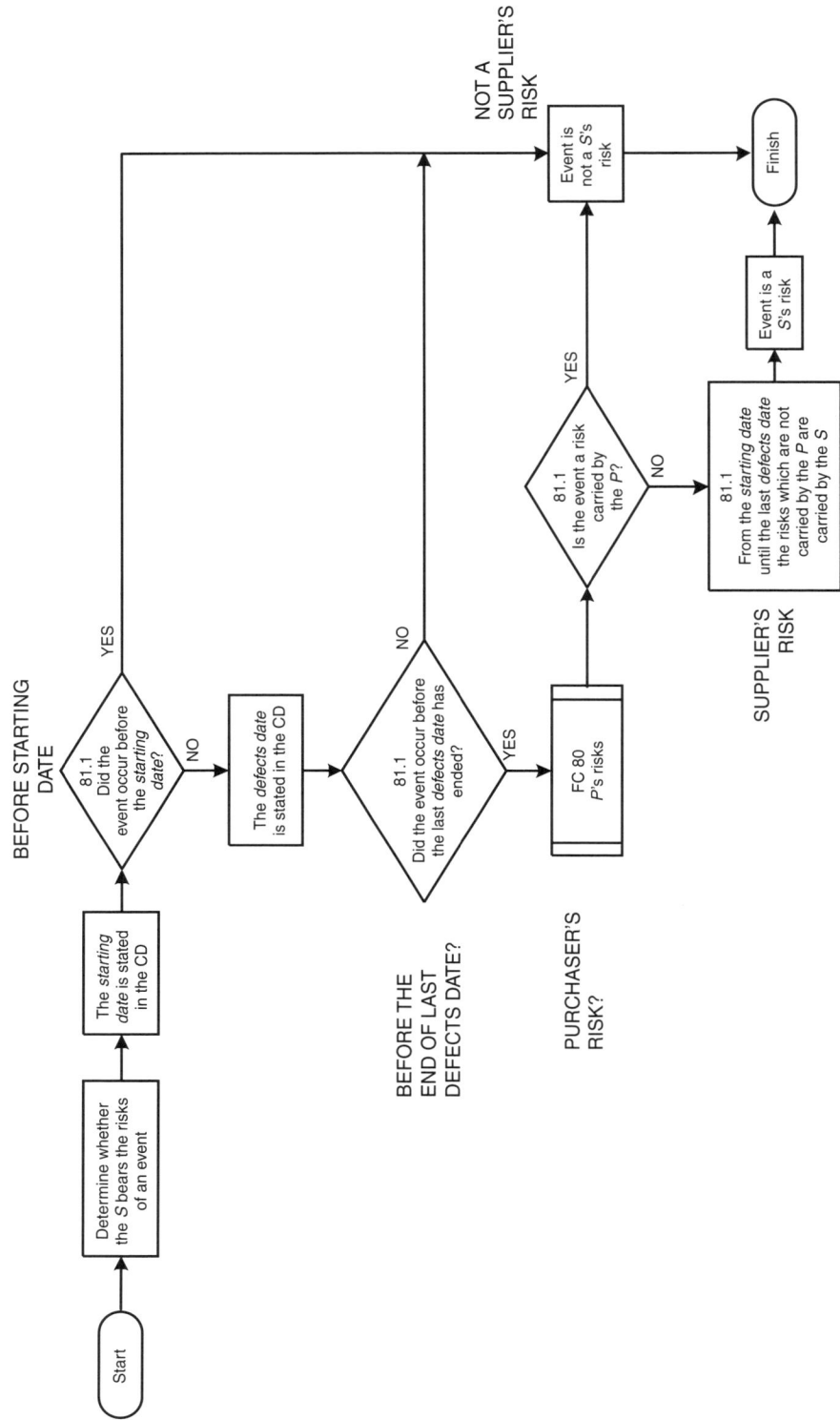

**Flow chart 81
The *Supplier's* risks**

Start

Loss of or damage to the *goods* occurs

**BEFORE THE END OF
LAST DEFECTS DATE?**

82.1
Has the
last *defects date*
passed?

YES →

NO REPLACEMENT OR REPAIR

No replacement or repair is undertaken by the S.

NO →

82.1
Has the
SM instructed
otherwise?

NO →

**REPLACE LOSS OF
AND REPAIR DAMAGE**

82.1
The S promptly replaces loss of and repairs damage to the *goods*.

YES →

SUPPLIER OBEYS INSTRUCTION

FC I3
Instruction

25.3
The S obeys an instruction which is in accordance with this contract and is given to him by the *SM*.

Finish

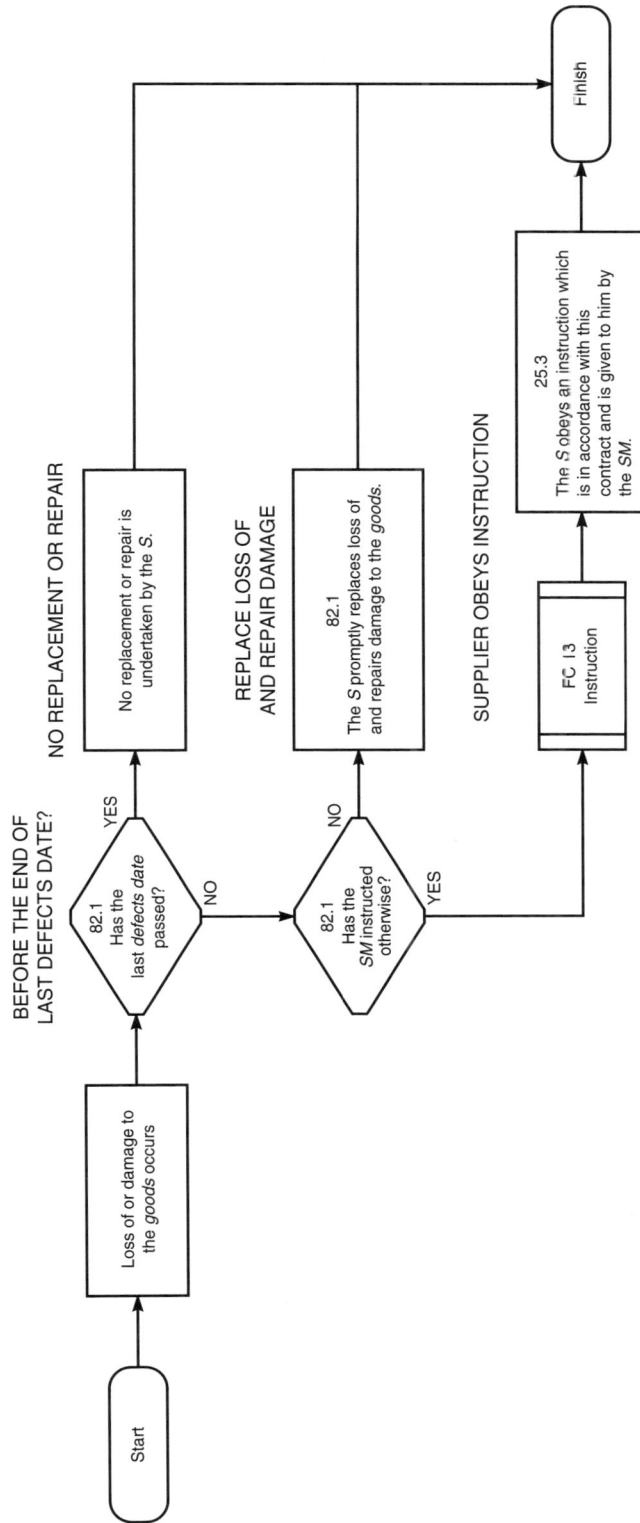

**Flow chart 82
Loss of and damage to the *goods***

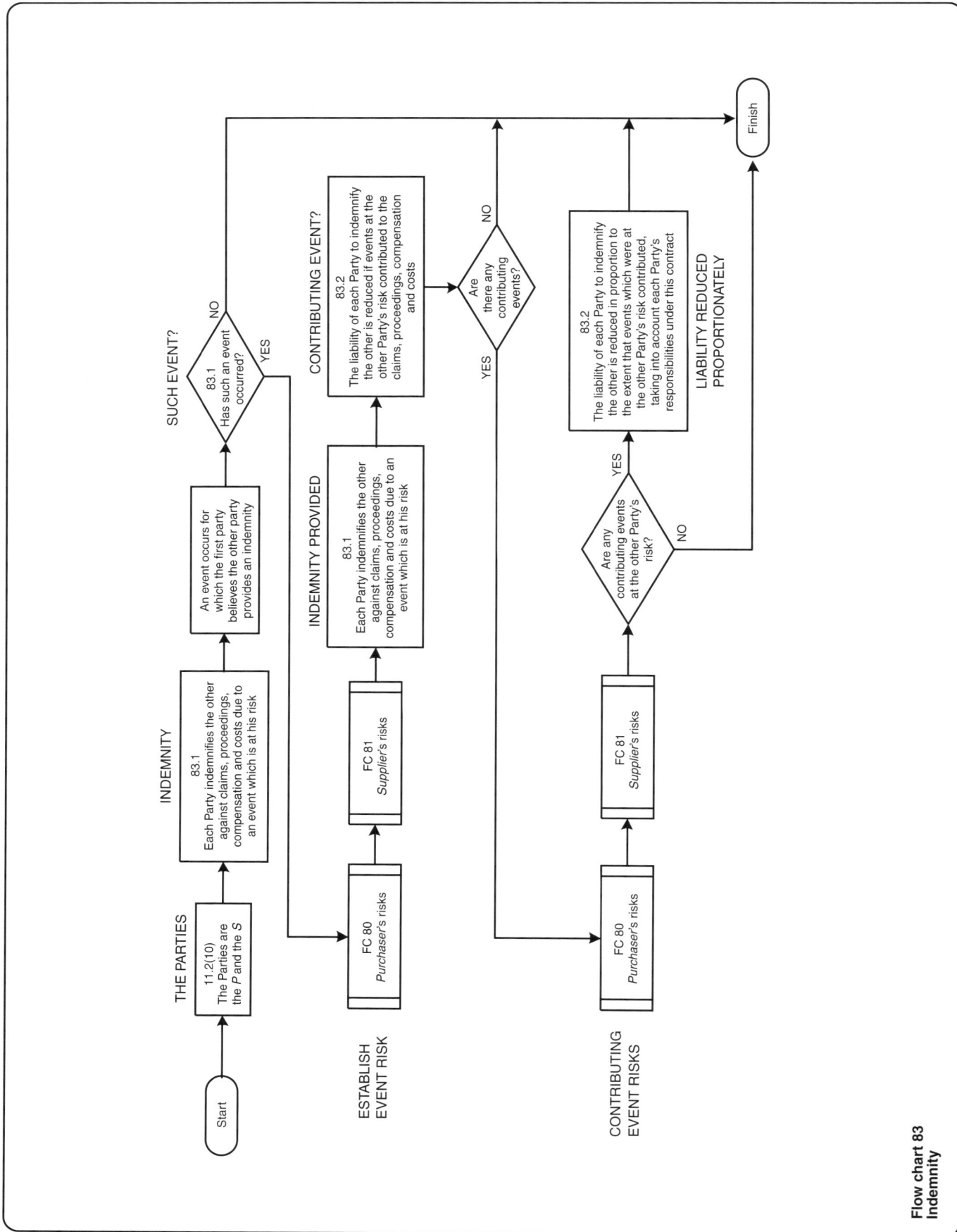

Flow chart 83
Indemnity

INSURANCE TABLE

Insurance against	Minimum amount of cover or minimum level of indemnity
Loss of or damage to the *goods*, P&M	The replacement cost, including the amount stated in the CD for the replacement of any P&M provided by the *P*
Liability for loss of or damage to property (except the *goods*, P&M and equipment) and liability for bodily injury to or death of a person (not an employee of the *S*) caused by activity in connection with this contract	The amount stated in the CD for any one event with cross liability so that the insurance applies to the Parties separately
Liability for death of or bodily injury to employees of the *S* arising out of and in the course of their employment in connection with this contract	The greater of the amount required by the applicable law and the amount stated in the CD for any one event

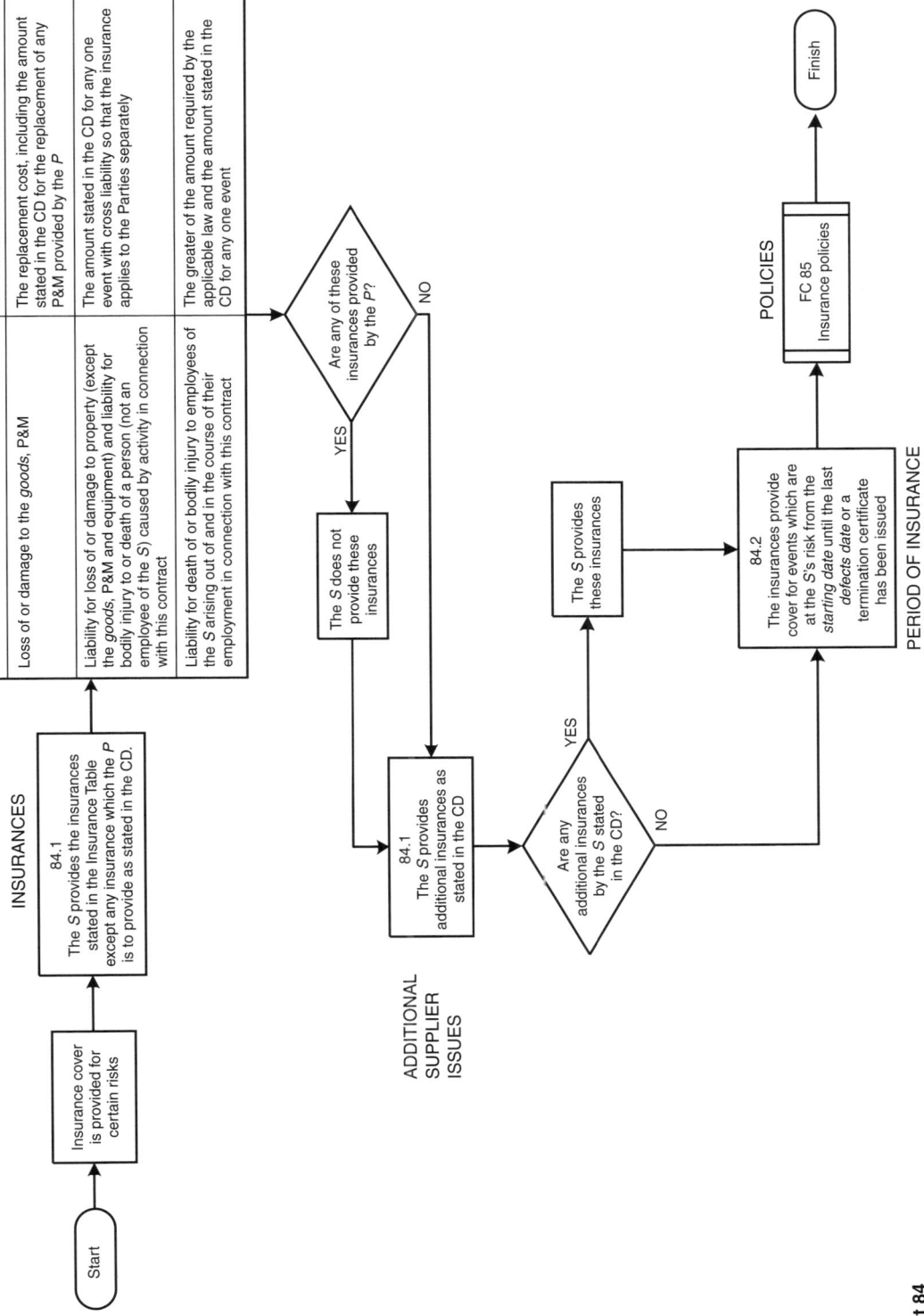

INSURANCES

Start

Insurance cover is provided for certain risks

84.1
The *S* provides the insurances stated in the Insurance Table except any insurance which the *P* is to provide as stated in the CD.

Are any of these insurances provided by the *P?*

YES → The *S* does not provide these insurances

NO →

ADDITIONAL SUPPLIER ISSUES

84.1
The *S* provides additional insurances as stated in the CD

Are any additional insurances by the *S* stated in the CD?

YES → The *S* provides these insurances

NO →

84.2
The insurances provide cover for events which are at the *S's* risk from the *starting date* until the last *defects date* or a termination certificate has been issued

PERIOD OF INSURANCE

POLICIES

FC 85
Insurance policies

Finish

Flow chart 84
Insurance cover

Flow chart 85 Insurance policies

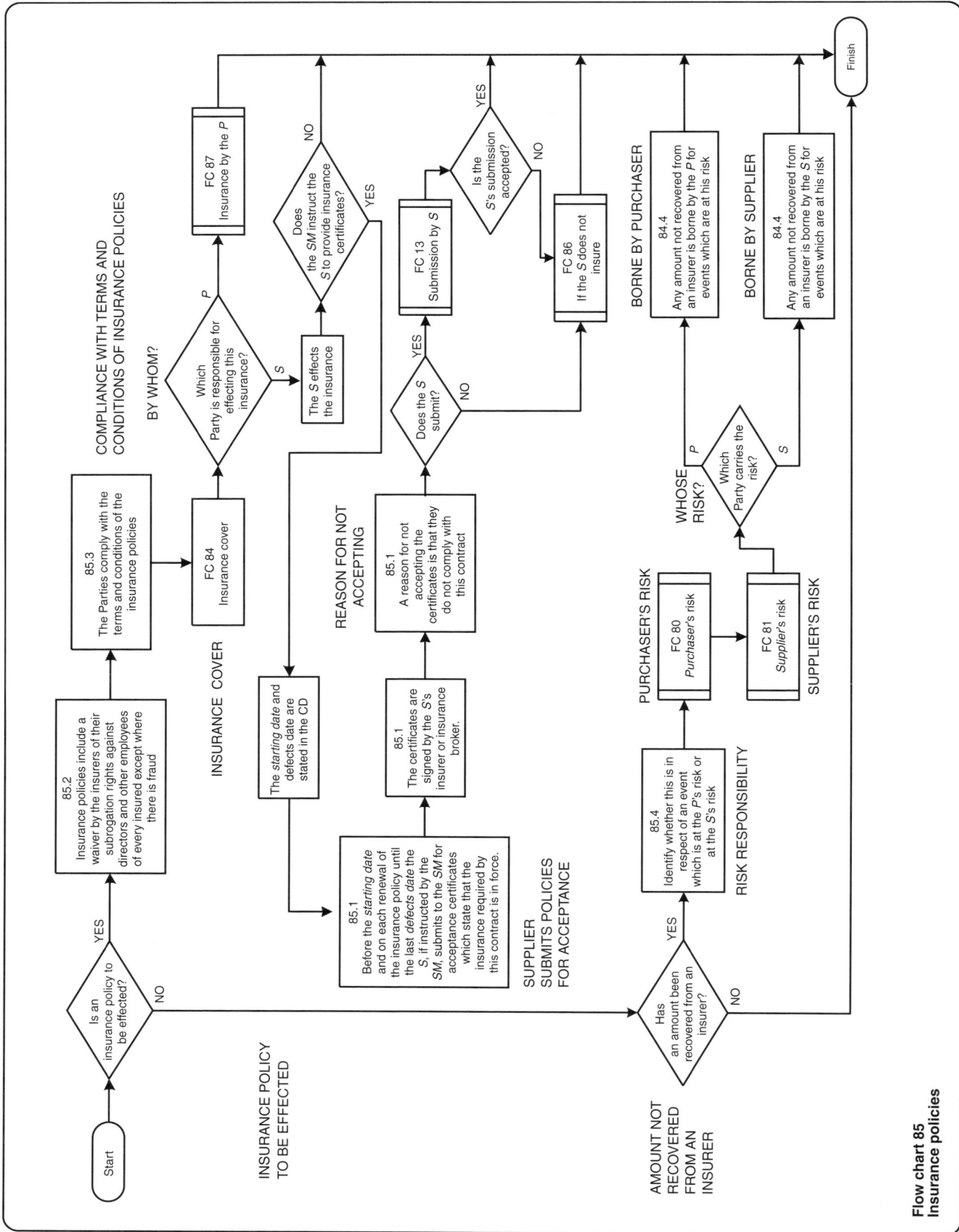

INSURANCE CERTIFICATE
NOT SUBMITTED

Start

86.1
The S has not submitted
a required certificate

86.1
Does the P decide
to insure the risk which
the S should have
insured?

NO

YES

Risk is not
insured

PURCHASER TAKES OUT INSURANCE

86.1
The P may insure a risk which this contract
requires the S to insure if the S does not
submit a required certificate

85.1
The cost of this
insurance to the P is paid
by the S

COST OF INSURANCE PAID BY SUPPLIER

FC 50
Assessing the
amount due

Finish

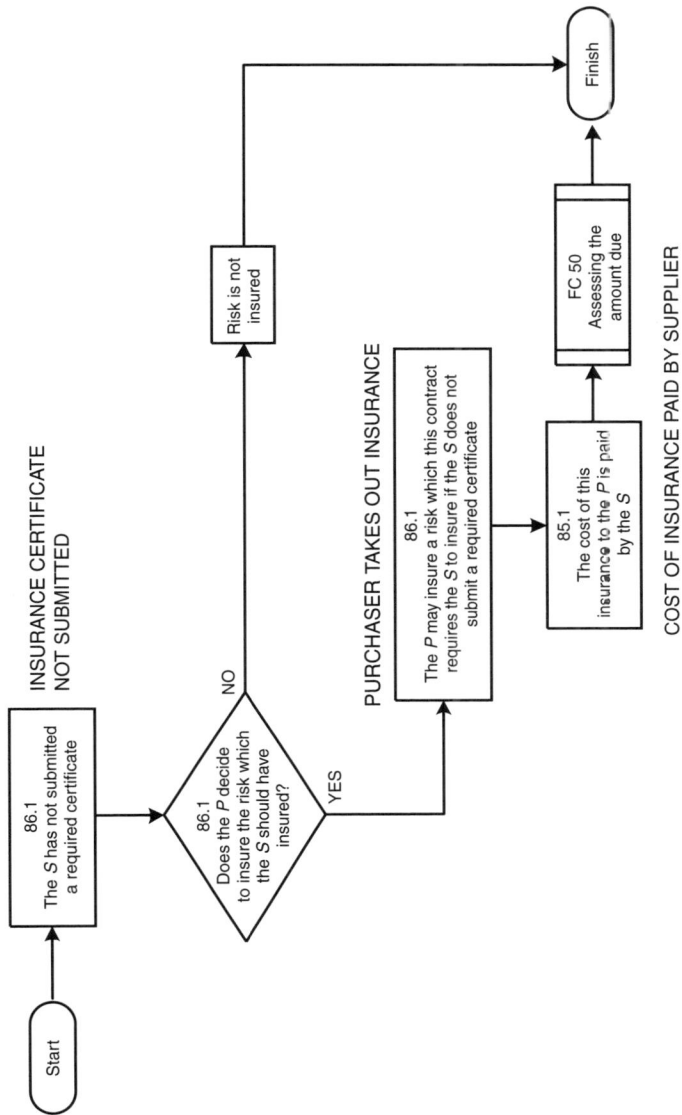

Flow chart 86
If the Supplier does not insure

PURCHASER INSURANCES

Start

84.1
The *P* is to provide insurances as stated in the CD

The *starting date* is stated in the CD

POLICIES AND CERTIFICATES SUBMITTED

87.1
The *SM* submits policies and certificates for insurances provided by the *P* to the *S* for acceptance before the *starting date* and afterwards as the *S* instructs

ACCEPTANCE BY SUPPLIER

87.1
The *S* accepts the policies and certificates if they comply with this contract

FC 13
Submission by the *P* for acceptance by the *S*

PURCHASER'S RESPONSIBILITY TO INSURE

87.2
The *S*'s acceptance of an insurance policy or certificate provided by the *P* does not change the responsibility of the *P* to provide the insurances stated in the CD

87.3
Have the required policies or certificates been submitted to the *S*?

— YES

— NO

87.3
Does the *S* decide to insure the risk which the *P* should have insured?

— NO → Risk is not insured

— YES

SUPPLIER TAKES OUT INSURANCE

87.3
The *S* may insure a risk which this contract requires the *P* to insure if the *P* does not submit a required policy or certificate

COST OF INSURANCE PAID BY PURCHASER

87.3
The cost of this insurance to the *S* is paid by the *P*

FC 50
Assessing the amount due

Finish

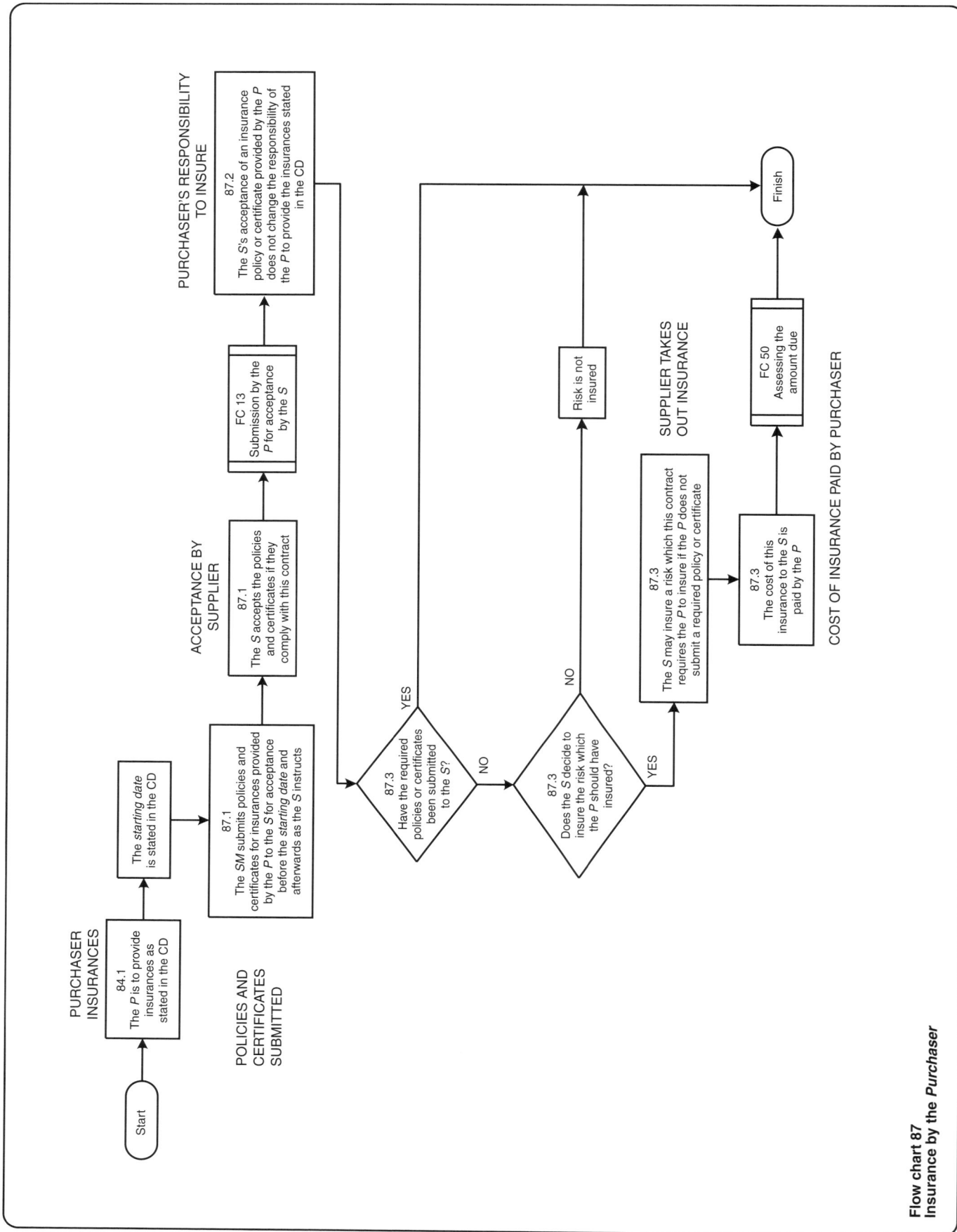

Flow chart 87
Insurance by the *Purchaser*

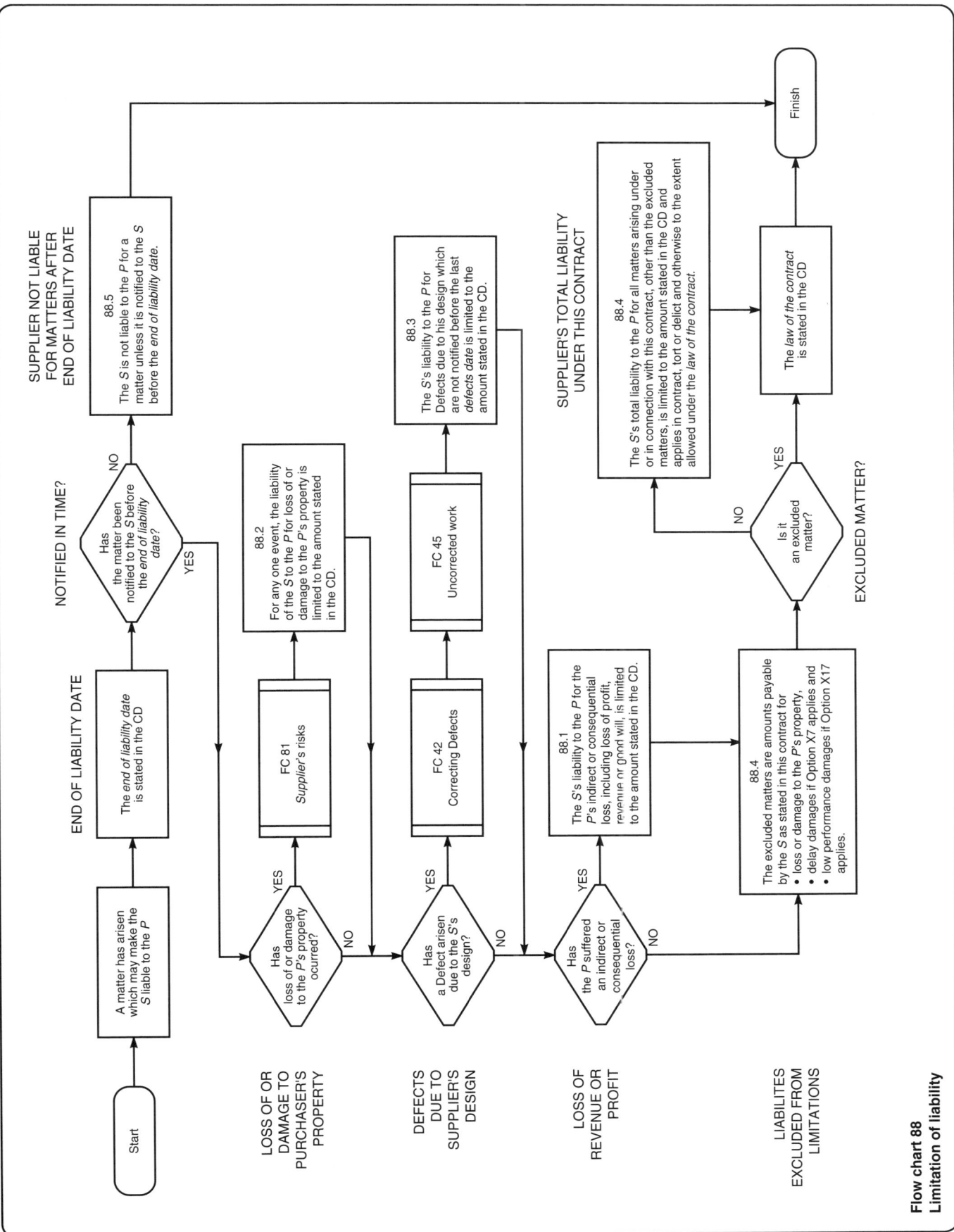

Flow chart 88

NOTIFIED IN TIME?

END OF LIABILITY DATE

SUPPLIER NOT LIABLE FOR MATTERS AFTER END OF LIABILITY DATE

Start

A matter has arisen which may make the *S* liable to the *P*

The *end of liability date* is stated in the CD

88.5
The *S* is not liable to the *P* for a matter unless it is notified to the *S* before the *end of liability date.*

Has the matter been notified to the *S* before the *end of liability date?* — NO →

YES ↓

LOSS OF OR DAMAGE TO PURCHASER'S PROPERTY

Has loss of or damage to the *P*'s property occurred?

YES → FC 81 *Supplier's risks* →
88.2
For any one event, the liability of the *S* to the *P* for loss of or damage to the *P*'s property is limited to the amount stated in the CD.

NO ↓

DEFECTS DUE TO SUPPLIER'S DESIGN

Has a Defect arisen due to the *S*'s design?

YES → FC 42 Correcting Defects → FC 45 Uncorrected work →
88.3
The *S*'s liability to the *P* for Defects due to his design which are not notified before the last *defects date* is limited to the amount stated in the CD.

NO ↓

LOSS OF REVENUE OR PROFIT

Has the *P* suffered an indirect or consequential loss?

YES →
88.1
The *S*'s liability to the *P* for the *P*'s indirect or consequential loss, including loss of profit, revenue or good will, is limited to the amount stated in the CD.

NO ↓

LIABILITES EXCLUDED FROM LIMITATIONS

88.4
The excluded matters are amounts payable by the *S* as stated in this contract for
• loss or damage to the *P*'s property,
• delay damages if Option X7 applies and
• low performance damages if Option X17 applies.

EXCLUDED MATTER?

Is it an excluded matter?

NO →
SUPPLIER'S TOTAL LIABILITY UNDER THIS CONTRACT
88.4
The *S*'s total liability to the *P* for all matters arising under or in connection with this contract, other than the excluded matters, is limited to the amount stated in the CD and applies in contract, tort or delict and otherwise to the extent allowed under the *law of the contract.*

YES →
88.4
The *law of the contract* is stated in the CD

→ Finish

**Flow chart 88
Limitation of liability**

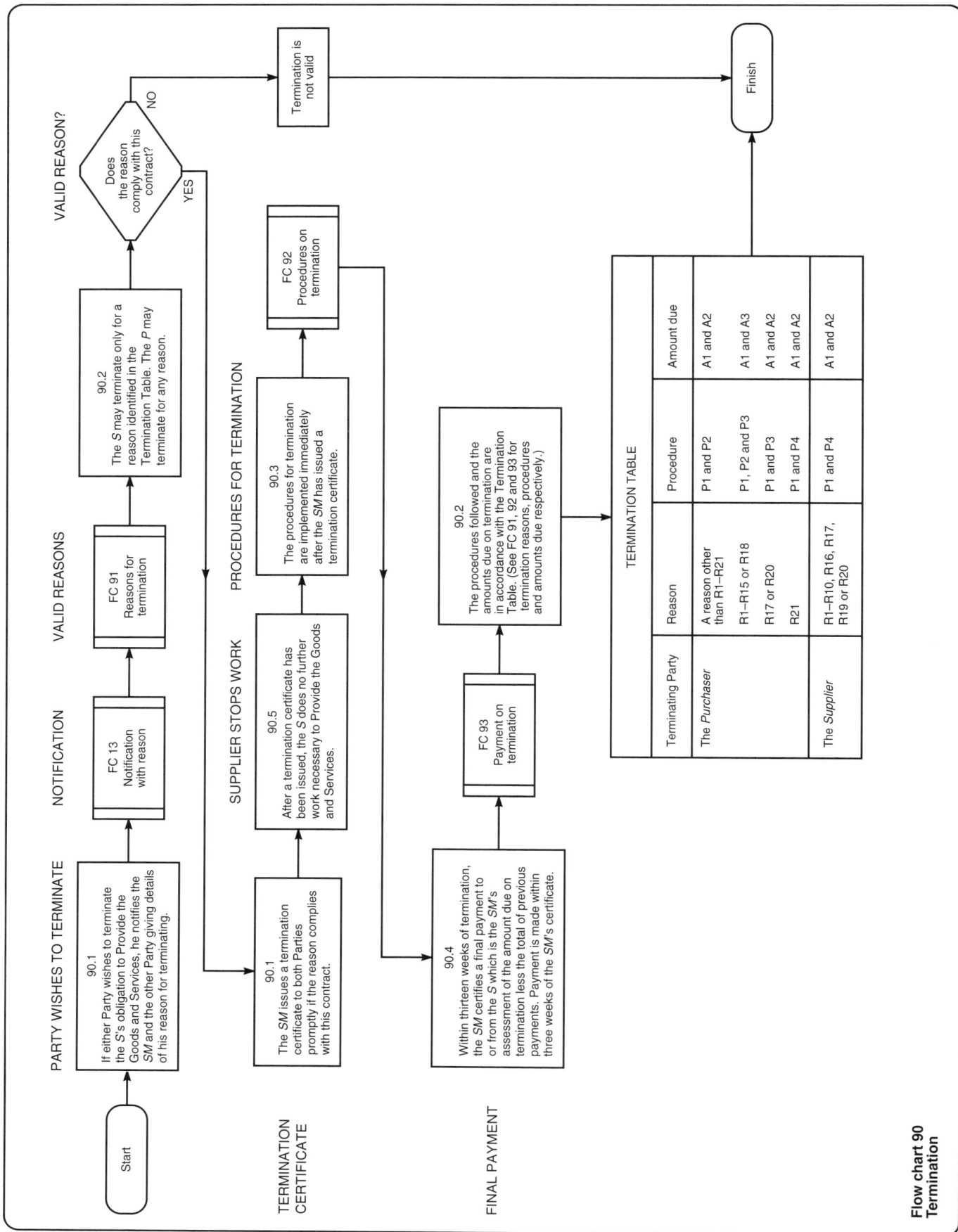

Flow chart 90
Termination

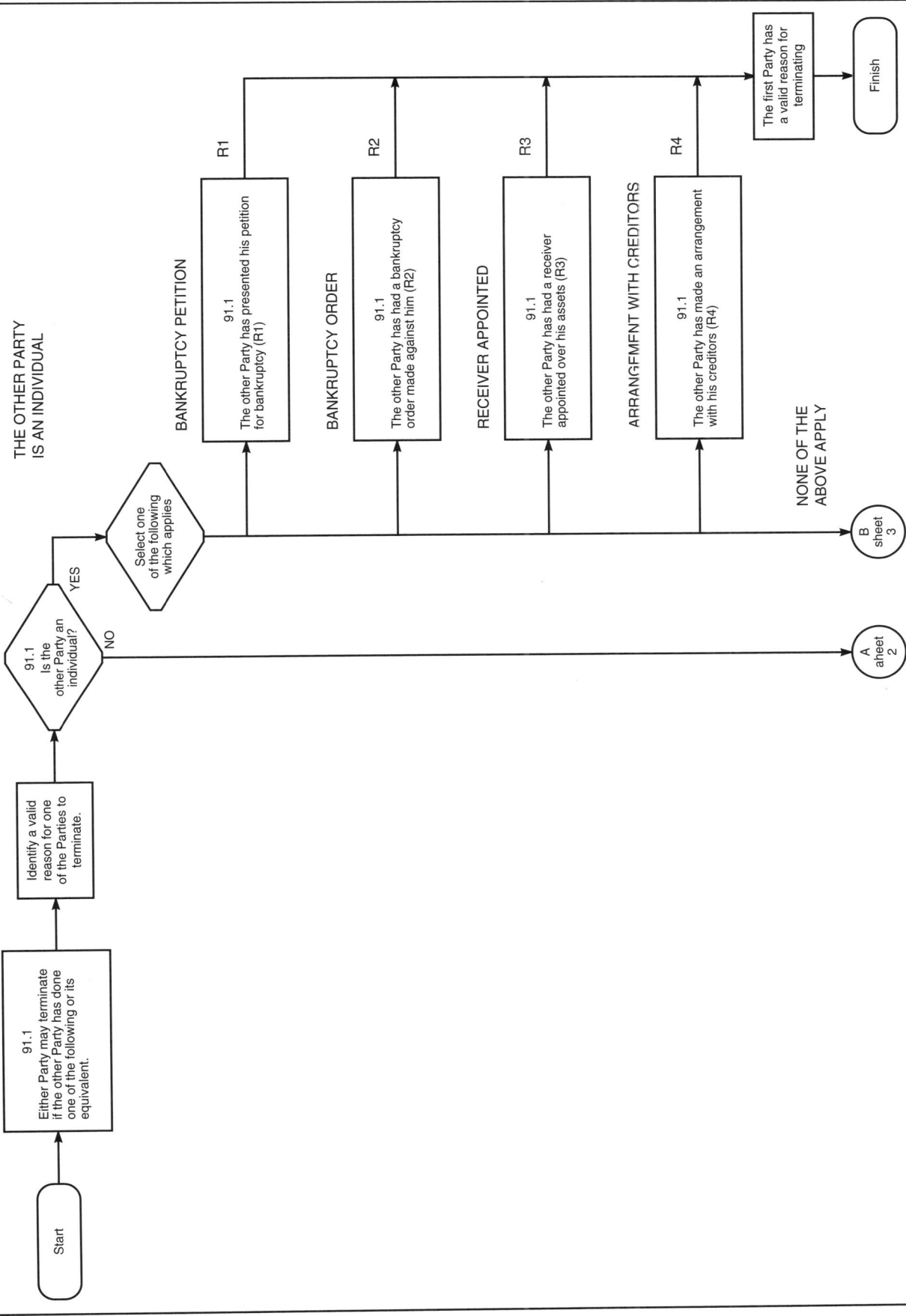

THE OTHER PARTY IS AN INDIVIDUAL

Start

91.1
Either Party may terminate if the other Party has done one of the following or its equivalent.

Identify a valid reason for one of the Parties to terminate.

91.1
Is the other Party an individual?

YES

NO → A sheet 2

Select one of the following which applies

BANKRUPTCY PETITION
91.1
The other Party has presented his petition for bankruptcy (R1)
R1

BANKRUPTCY ORDER
91.1
The other Party has had a bankruptcy order made against him (R2)
R2

RECEIVER APPOINTED
91.1
The other Party has had a receiver appointed over his assets (R3)
R3

ARRANGEMENT WITH CREDITORS
91.1
The other Party has made an arrangement with his creditors (R4)
R4

NONE OF THE ABOVE APPLY → B sheet 3

The first Party has a valid reason for terminating

Finish

Flow chart 91 Sheet 1 of 5
Reasons for termination

```
           ┌─────────────────────┐
           │                     │
    A  →  91.1                   │
  sheet   Is the other  ──YES──→  Select one
    1     Party a company        of the following
          or parnership?         which applies
               │                      │
              NO                      │
               │                      │
```

THE OTHER PARTY
IS A COMPANY OR
A PARTNERSHIP

WINDING-UP ORDER
91.1
The other Party has had a winding-up order made against it (R5)
R5

LIQUIDATOR APPOINTED
91.1
The other Party has had a provisional liquidator appointed to it (R6)
R6

WINDING-UP RESOLUTION
91.1
The other Party has passed a resolution for winding-up (other than in order to amalgamate or reconstruct) (R7)
R7

ADMINISTRATION ORDER
91.1
The other Party has had an administration order made against it (R8)
R8

RECEIVER APPOINTED
91.1
The other Party has had a receiver, receiver and manager or administrative receiver appointed over the whole or a substantial part of its undertaking or assets (R9)
R9

ARRANGEMENT WITH CREDITORS
91.1
The other Party has made an arrangement with its creditors (R10)
R10

The first Party has a valid reason for terminating

Finish

NONE OF THE ABOVE APPLY

B sheet 3

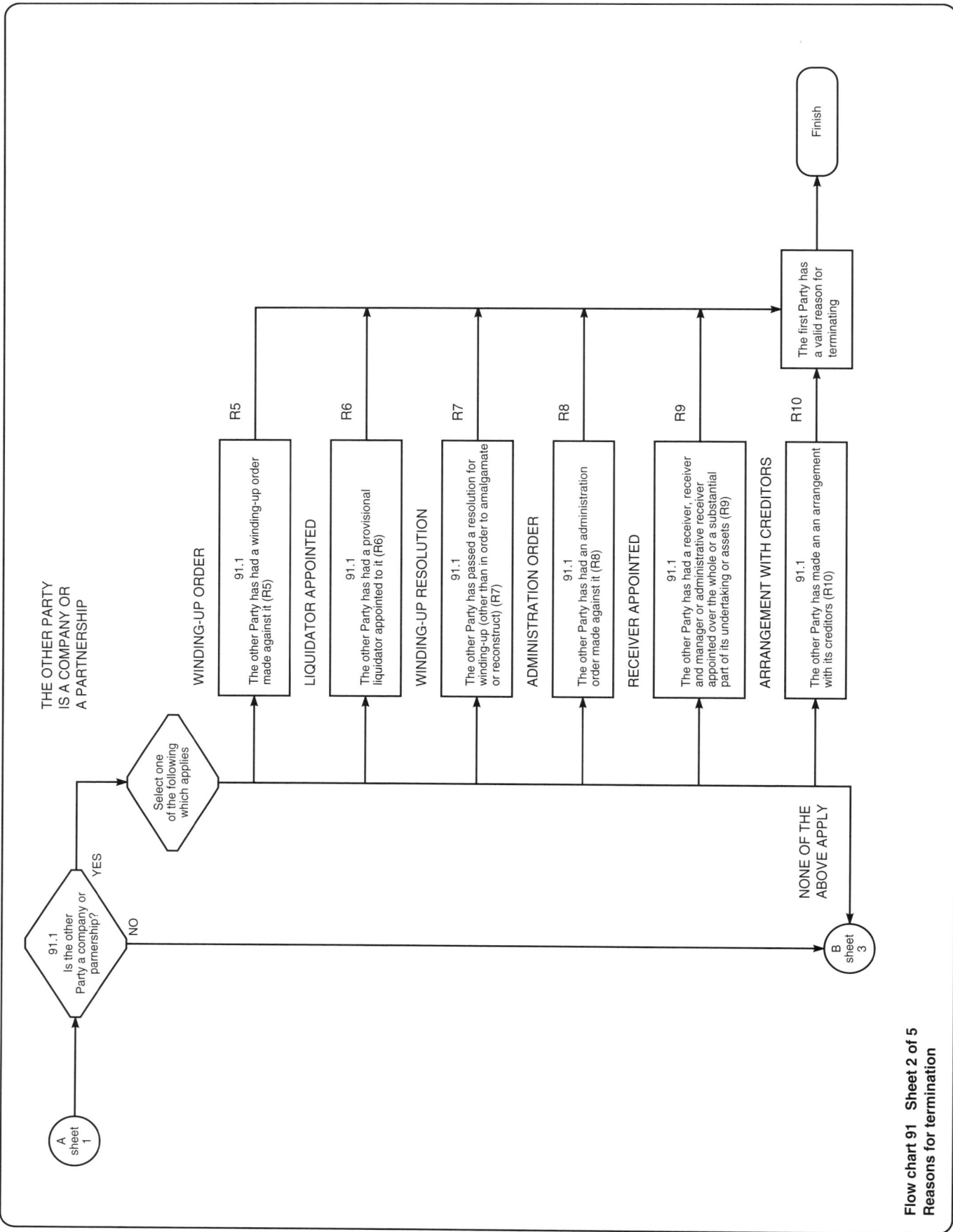

Flow chart 91   Sheet 2 of 5
Reasons for termination

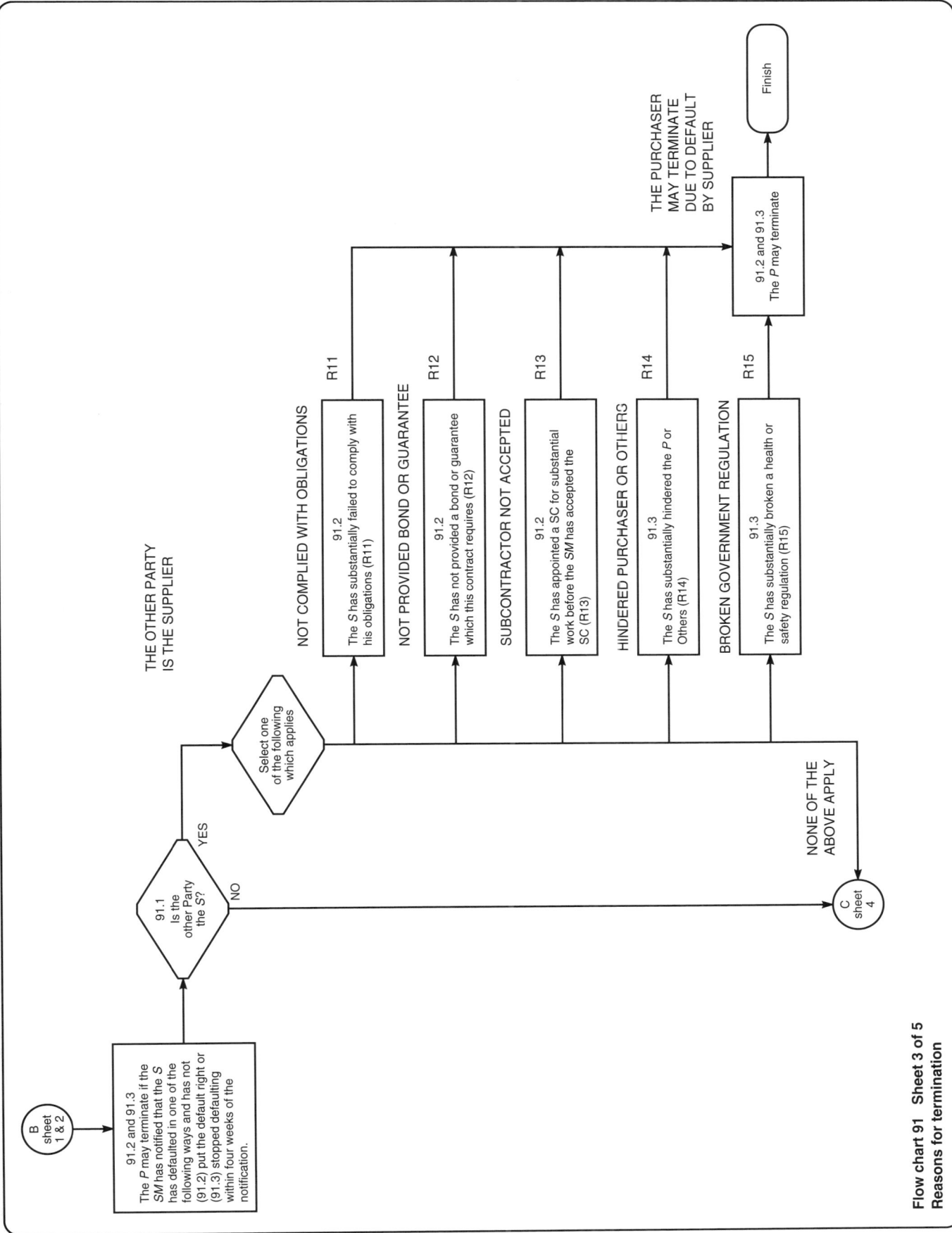

B
sheet
1 & 2

91.2 and 91.3
The *P* may terminate if the *S*
SM has notified that the *S*
has defaulted in one of the
following ways and has not
(91.2) put the default right or
(91.3) stopped defaulting
within four weeks of the
notification.

91.1
Is the
other Party
the *S*?

YES

NO

THE OTHER PARTY
IS THE SUPPLIER

Select one
of the following
which applies

NOT COMPLIED WITH OBLIGATIONS

R11

91.2
The *S* has substantially failed to comply with
his obligations (R11)

NOT PROVIDED BOND OR GUARANTEE

R12

91.2
The *S* has not provided a bond or guarantee
which this contract requires (R12)

SUBCONTRACTOR NOT ACCEPTED

R13

91.2
The *S* has appointed a SC for substantial
work before the *SM* has accepted the
SC (R13)

HINDERED PURCHASER OR OTHERS

R14

91.3
The *S* has substantially hindered the *P* or
Others (R14)

BROKEN GOVERNMENT REGULATION

R15

91.3
The *S* has substantially broken a health or
safety regulation (R15)

NONE OF THE
ABOVE APPLY

C
sheet
4

THE PURCHASER
MAY TERMINATE
DUE TO DEFAULT
BY SUPPLIER

91.2 and 91.3
The *P* may terminate

Finish

Flow chart 91   Sheet 3 of 5
Reasons for termination

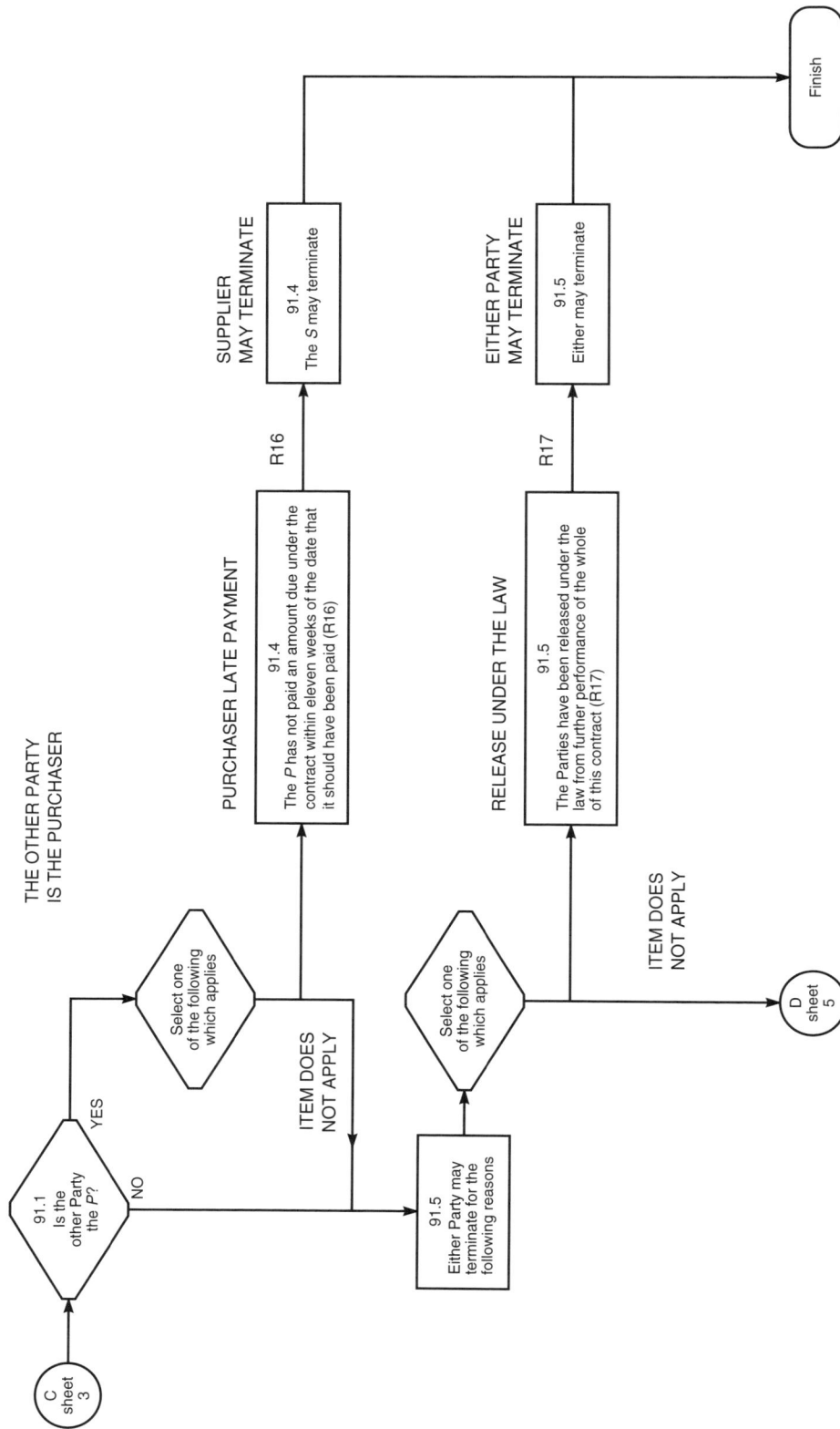

Flow chart 91 Sheet 4 of 5
Reasons for termination

D Sheet 4

91.6
Termination of the contract may occur if the *SM* has instructed the *S* to stop or not to start any substantial work or all work and an instruction allowing the work to re-start or start has not been given within thirteen weeks

AN INSTRUCTION TO STOP OR NOT TO START WORK IS GIVEN

91.6
Does this situation occur?

YES →

NO →

Select one of the following which applies

DUE TO ANY OTHER REASON

91.6
Either Party may terminate if the instruction was due to any reason other than reason R18 and R19 (R20)

R20 → Either Party may terminate

DEFAULT BY PURCHASER

91.6
The *S* may terminate if the instruction was due to a default by the *P* (R19)

R19 → The *S* may terminate

DEFAULT BY SUPPLIER

91.6
The *P* may terminate if the instruction was due to be a default by the *S* (R18)

R18 →

EVENT AFFECTS WORK

91.7
The *P* may terminate if an event occurs which
- stops Delivery or
- stops Delivery by the Delivery Date and is forecast to delay Delivery by more than 13 weeks, and which
- neither Party could prevent and
- an experienced supplier would have judged at the Contract Date to have such a small chance of occurring that it would have been unreasonable for him to have allowed for it (R21)

R21 →

91.7
Termination of this contract may occur if an event occurs which
- stops Delivery or
- stops Delivery by the Delivery Date and is forecast to delay Delivery by more than 13 weeks, and which
- neither Party could prevent and
- an experienced supplier would have judged at the Contract Date to have such a small chance of occurring that it would have been unreasonable for him to have allowed for it

AN EVENT OCCURS WHICH STOPS THE DELIVERY

91.7
Does this situation occur?

YES →

NO →

Does the *P* wish to terminate for some other reason?

YES →

NO →

PURCHASER MAY TERMINATE FOR ANY REASON

90.2
The *P* may terminate for any reason (Not R1–R21)

The *P* may terminate

NO VALID REASON FOR TERMINATION

There is not a valid reason for termination

The *S* may terminate

Finish

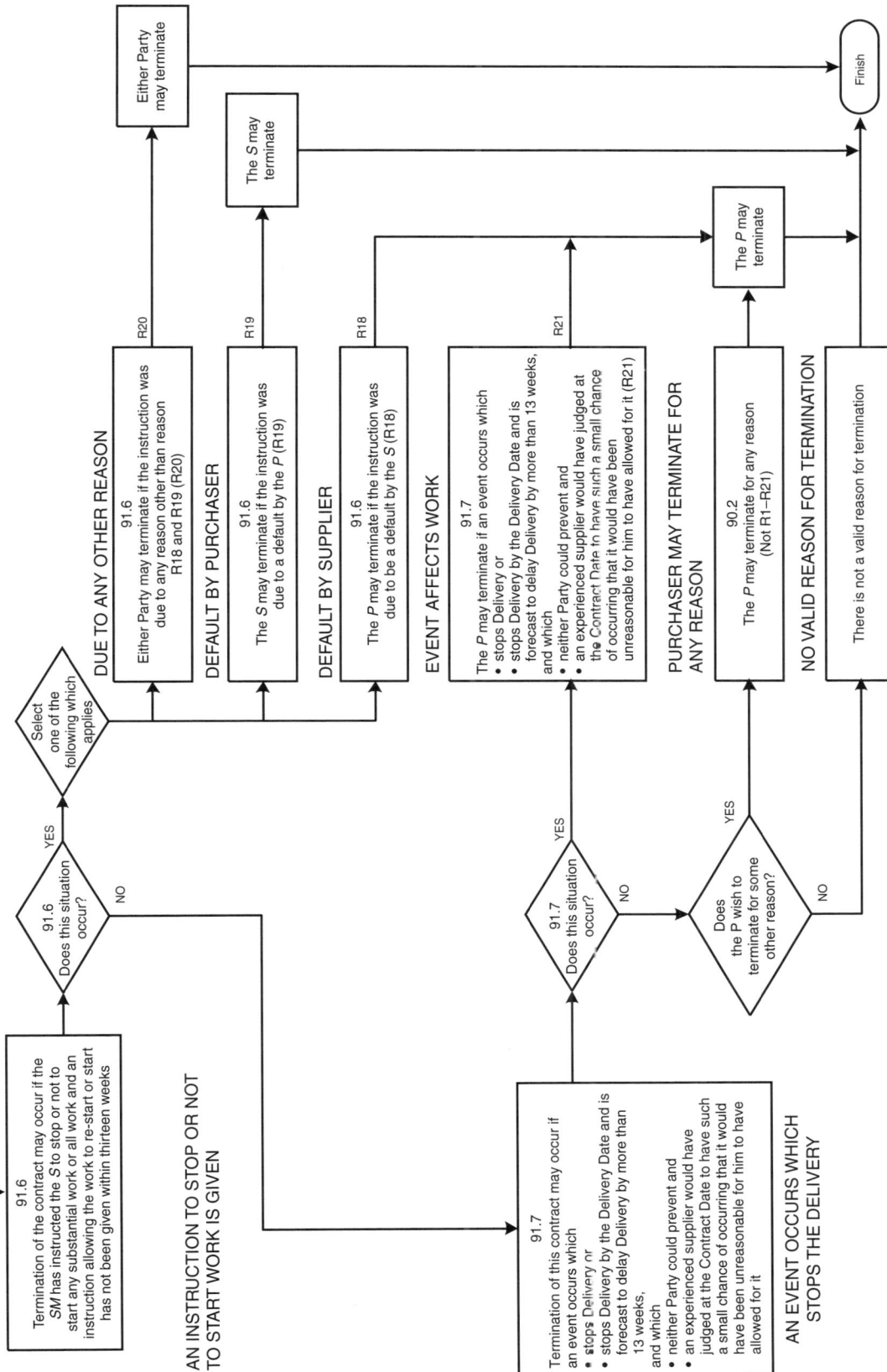

Flow chart 91 Sheet 5 of 5
Reasons for termination

Start

Has a termination certificate been issued?

NO → (to Finish)

YES ↓

PROCEDURE P1

90.3
The procedures for termination are implemented immediately after the *SM* has issued a termination certificate.

92.1
On termination, the *P* may obtain the remaining *goods* and *services* from other suppliers. (P1)

OTHER PROCEDURES

92.2
The procedure on termination also includes one or more of the following (procedures P2 to P4) as set out in the Termination Table.

Does procedure P2 apply?

YES →

92.2
The *P* may instruct the *S* to leave the *P*'s premises, remove any of his equipment, P&M and assign the benefit of any subcontract or other contract related to performance of this contract to the *P*. (P2)

PROCEDURE P2

NO ↓

Does procedure P3 apply?

YES →

92.2
The *P* may use any equipment to which the *S* has title, except equipment fixed in the *S*'s premises, to complete the supply of the *goods* and *services*. The *S* promptly removes the equipment when the *SM* notifies him that the *P* no longer requires it to complete the supply of the *goods* and *services*. (P3)

PROCEDURE P3

NO ↓

Does procedure P4 apply?

YES →

92.2
The *S* leaves the Delivery Place and removes any of his equipment which is on the *P*'s premises. (P4)

PROCEDURE P4

NO →

Finish

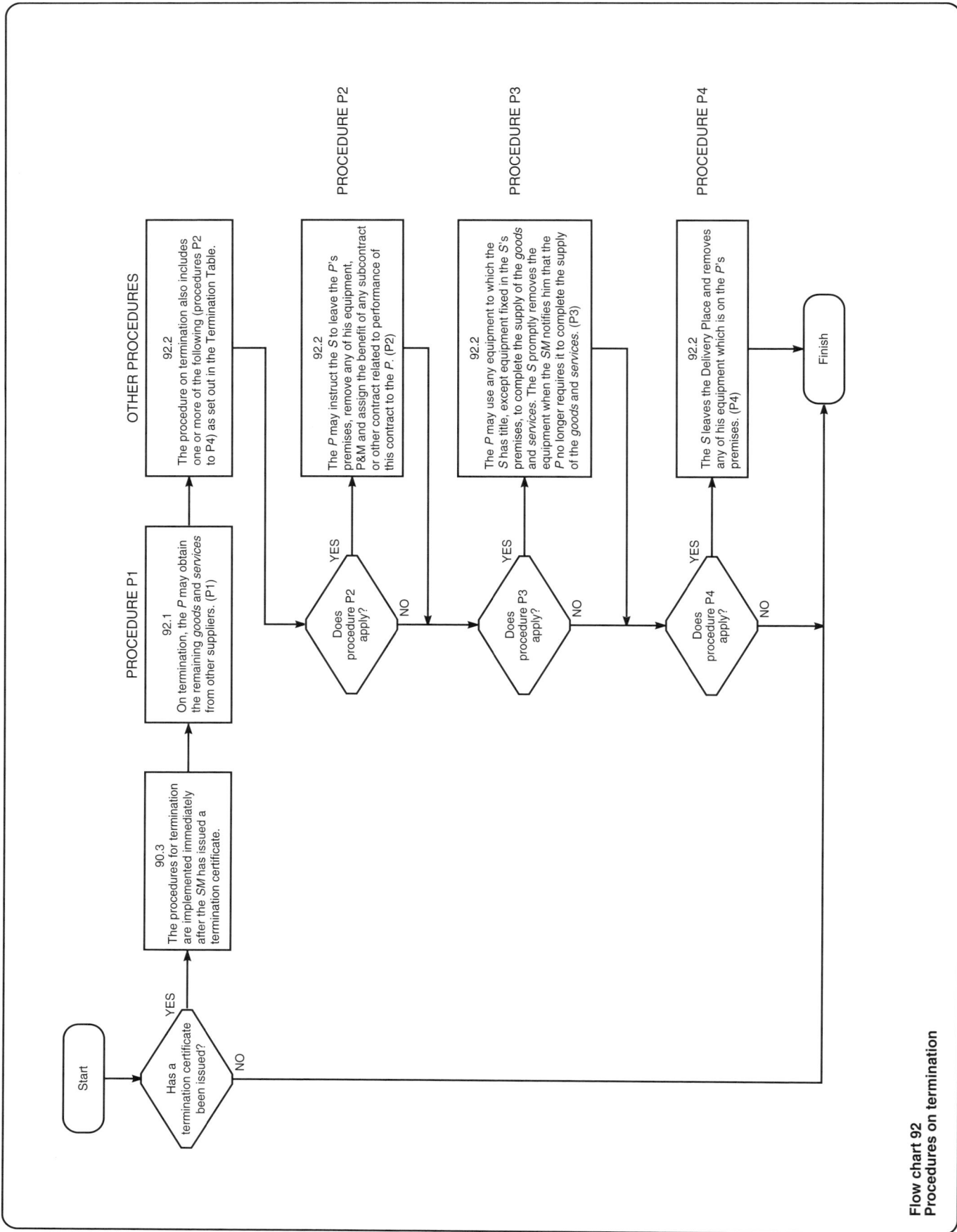

Flow chart 92
Procedures on termination

Start

A payment is due on termination

AMOUNT A1

93.1
The amount due on termination includes (A1)
- an amount due assessed as for normal payments,
- the Defined Cost of goods and services not included in normal payments and reasonably incurred in expectation of completing the whole of the goods and services, less the cost of goods and services which can be resold or used elsewhere,
- any amounts retained by the P and
- a deduction of any un-repaid balance of an advanced payment.

OTHER AMOUNTS

93.2
The amount due on termination also includes one or more of the following (A2 and A3) as set out in the Termination Table.

Include amount A2?

YES

REMOVING EQUIPMENT

93.2
The forecast Defined Cost of removing the equipment. (A2)

NO

Include amount A3?

YES

ADDITIONAL COST TO COMPLETE

93.2
A deduction of the forecast of the additional cost to the P of completing the whole of the goods and services. (A3)

NO

Finish

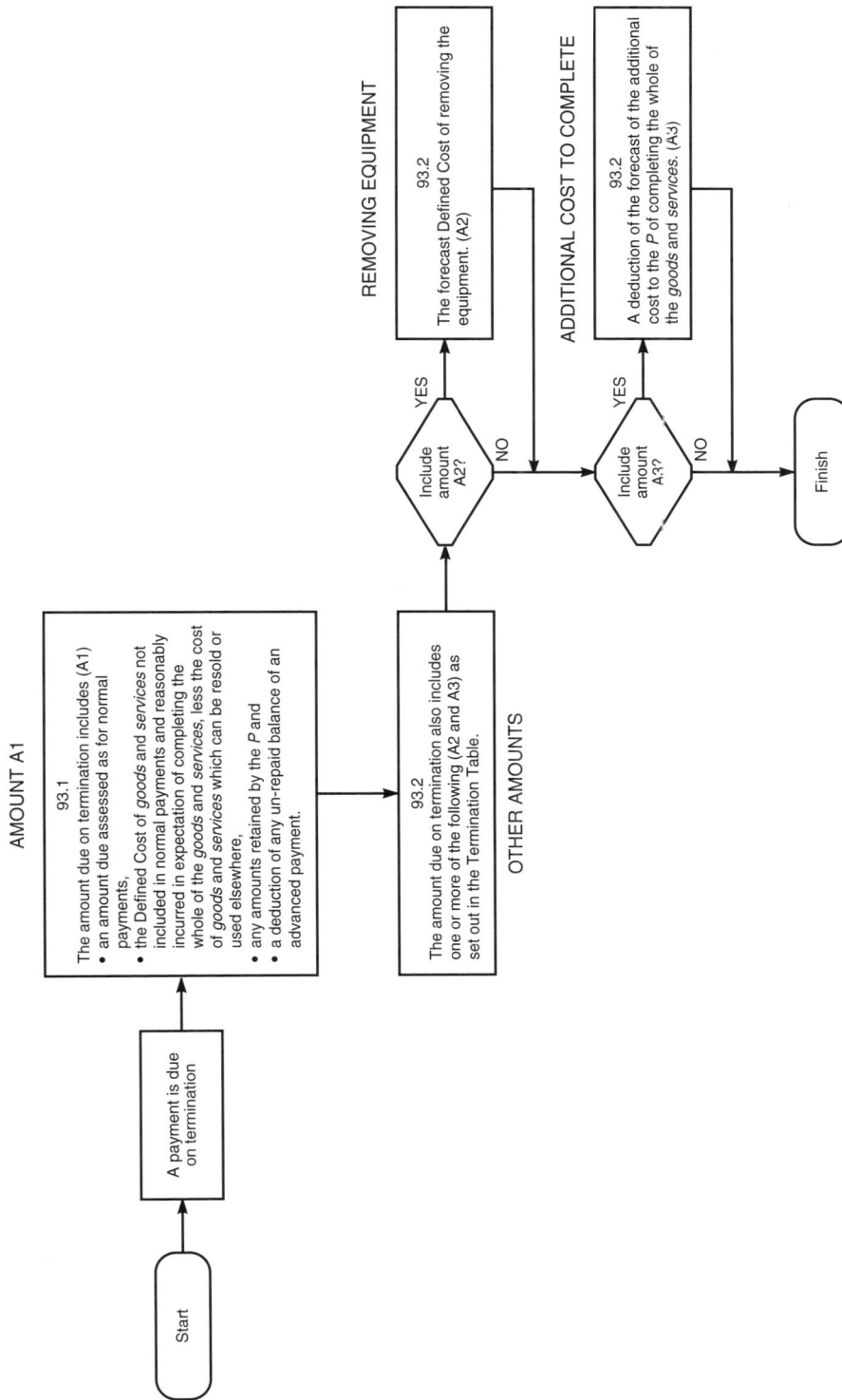

Flow chart 93
Payment on termination

DISPUTE ARISES

A dispute has arisen

DISPUTE RESOLUTION

94.1
Any dispute arising under or in connection with this contract is referred to and decided by the *Adjudicator*

THE PARTIES

11.2(10)
The *Parties* are the *P* and the *S*

APPOINTED UNDER NEC ADJUDICATOR'S CONTRACT

94.2(1)
The *Parties* appoint the *Adjudicator* under the NEC Adjudicator's Contract current at the *starting date*

ADJUDICATOR NOT ARBITRATOR

94.2(2)
The *Adjudicator* acts impartially and decides the dispute as an independent adjudicator and not as an arbitrator

The *starting date* and the *Adjudicator nominating body* are stated in the CD

IDENTIFIED IN THE CD?

94.2(3)
Is the *Adjudicator* identified in the CD? — YES / NO

THE ADJUDICATOR

94.2(3)
Has the *Adjudicator* resigned or become unable to act? — YES / NO

RESIGNED OR UNABLE TO ACT?

ADJUDICATION

A
Sheet 2

CHOSEN JOINTLY?

94.2(3)
Do the *Parties* choose an adjudicator jointly? — YES / NO

NOMINATED

94.2(3)
If the *Parties* have not chosen an adjudicator, either *Party* may ask the *Adjudicator nominating body* to choose one

94.2(3)
The *Adjudicator nominating body* chooses an adjudicator within four days of the request

NEW ADJUDICATOR

94.2(3)
The chosen adjudicator becomes the *Adjudicator*

REPLACEMENT?

94.2(4)
Does the *Adjudicator* replace a previous adjudicator? — YES / NO

INHERITS ANY UNDECIDED DISPUTES

94.2(4)
A replacement *Adjudicator* has the power to decide a dispute referred to his predecessor but not decided at the time when the predecessor resigned or became unable to act. He deals with an undecided dispute as if it had been referred to him on the date he was appointed

NOT LIABLE UNLESS ACTS IN BAD FAITH

94.2(5)
The *Adjudicator*, his employees and agents are not liable to the *Parties* for any action or failure to take action in an adjudication unless the action or failure to take action was in bad faith

Start

Flow chart 94   Sheet 1 of 5
Dispute resolution

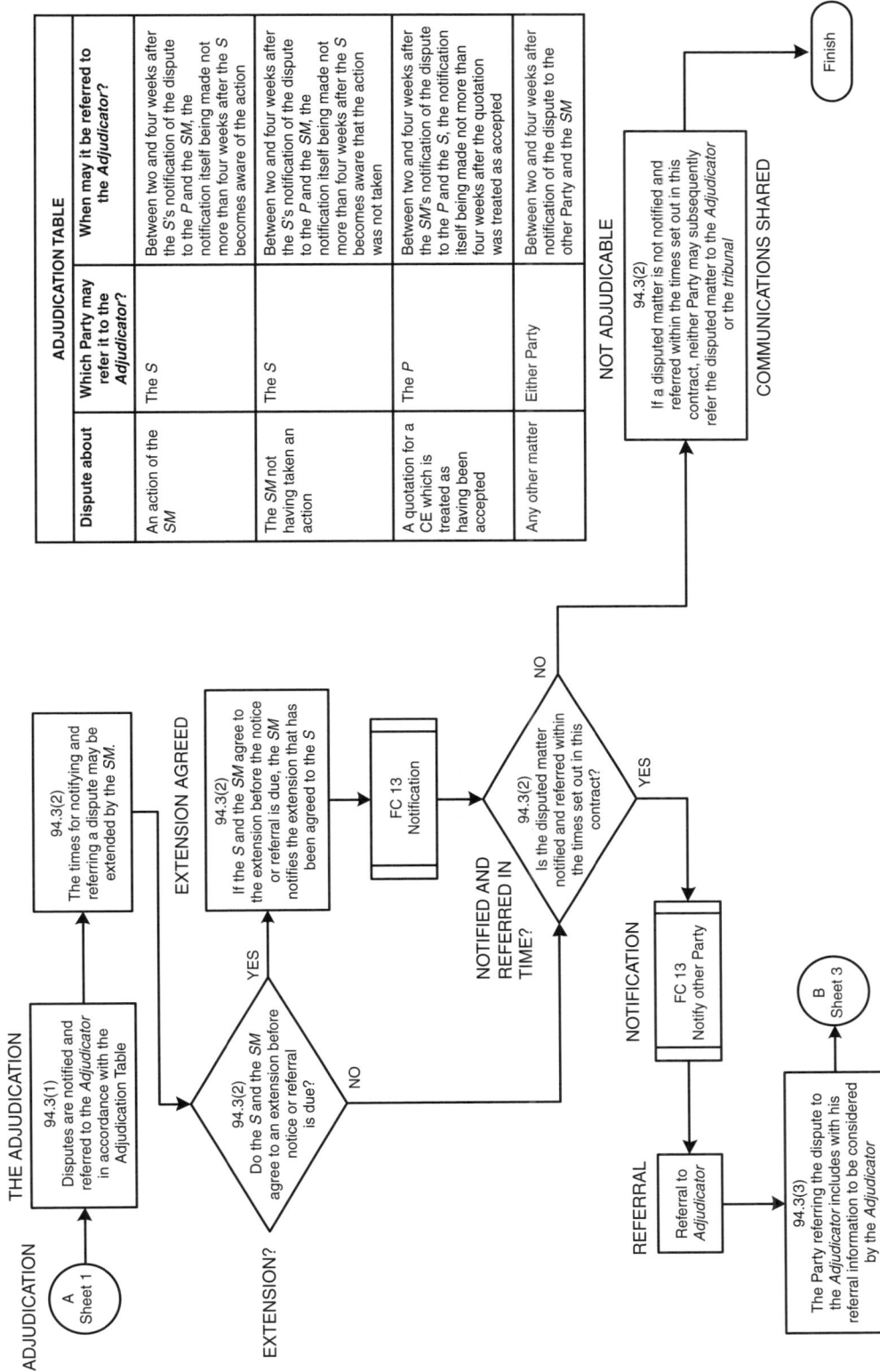

ADJUDICATION TABLE

Dispute about	Which Party may refer it to the *Adjudicator*?	When may it be referred to the *Adjudicator*?
An action of the *SM*	The *S*	Between two and four weeks after the *S*'s notification of the dispute to the *P* and the *SM*, the notification itself being made not more than four weeks after the *S* becomes aware of the action
The *SM* not having taken an action	The *S*	Between two and four weeks after the *S*'s notification of the dispute to the *P* and the *SM*, the notification itself being made not more than four weeks after the *S* becomes aware that the action was not taken
A quotation for a CE which is treated as having been accepted	The *P*	Between two and four weeks after the *SM*'s notification of the dispute to the *P* and the *S*, the notification itself being made not more than four weeks after the quotation was treated as accepted
Any other matter	Either Party	Between two and four weeks after notification of the dispute to the other Party and the *SM*

ADJUDICATION

A
Sheet 1

THE ADJUDICATION

94.3(1)
Disputes are notified and referred to the *Adjudicator* in accordance with the Adjudication Table

94.3(2)
The times for notifying and referring a dispute may be extended by the *SM*.

EXTENSION?

94.3(2)
Do the *S* and the *SM* agree to an extension before notice or referral is due?

YES →

EXTENSION AGREED

94.3(2)
If the *S* and the *SM* agree to the extension before the notice or referral is due, the *SM* notifies the extension that has been agreed to the *S*

→ FC 13
Notification

NO →

NOTIFIED AND REFERRED IN TIME?

94.3(2)
Is the disputed matter notified and referred within the times set out in this contract?

NO →

NOT ADJUDICABLE

94.3(2)
If a disputed matter is not notified and referred within the times set out in this contract, neither Party may subsequently refer the disputed matter to the *Adjudicator* or the *tribunal*

COMMUNICATIONS SHARED

→ Finish

YES →

NOTIFICATION

FC 13
Notify other Party

REFERRAL

Referral to *Adjudicator*

94.3(3)
The Party referring the dispute to the *Adjudicator* includes with his referral information to be considered by the *Adjudicator*

B
Sheet 3

Flow chart 94   Sheet 2 of 5
Dispute resolution

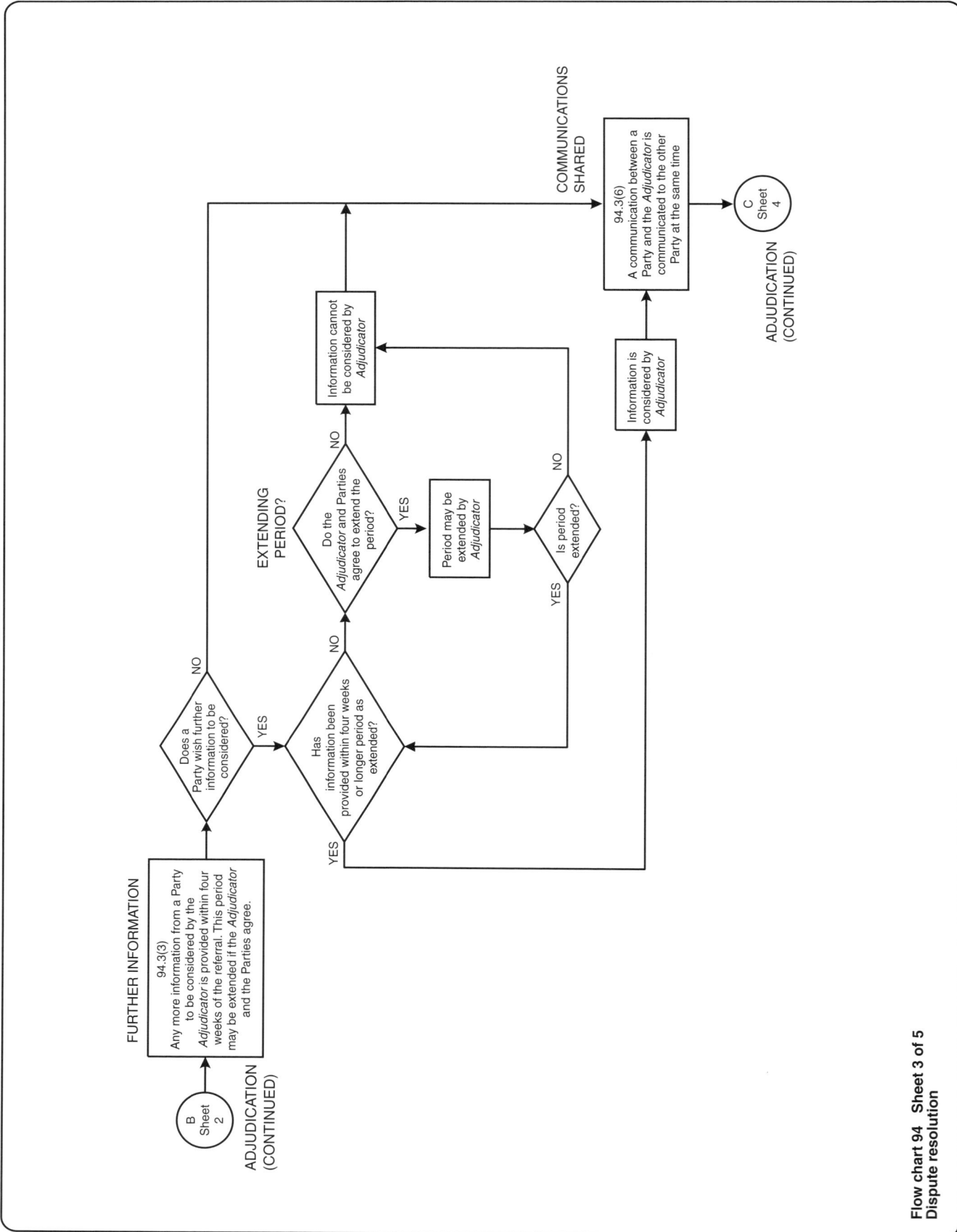

ADJUDICATION (CONTINUED)

B Sheet 2

FURTHER INFORMATION

94.3(3)
Any more information from a Party to be considered by the *Adjudicator* is provided within four weeks of the referral. This period may be extended if the *Adjudicator* and the Parties agree.

Does a Party wish further information to be considered?
- NO
- YES

Has information been provided within four weeks or longer period as extended?
- NO
- YES

EXTENDING PERIOD?

Do the *Adjudicator* and Parties agree to extend the period?
- NO
- YES

Period may be extended by *Adjudicator*

Is period extended?
- NO
- YES

Information cannot be considered by *Adjudicator*

Information is considered by *Adjudicator*

COMMUNICATIONS SHARED

94.3(6)
A communication between a Party and the *Adjudicator* is communicated to the other Party at the same time

C Sheet 4

ADJUDICATION (CONTINUED)

Flow chart 94 Sheet 4 of 5
Dispute resolution

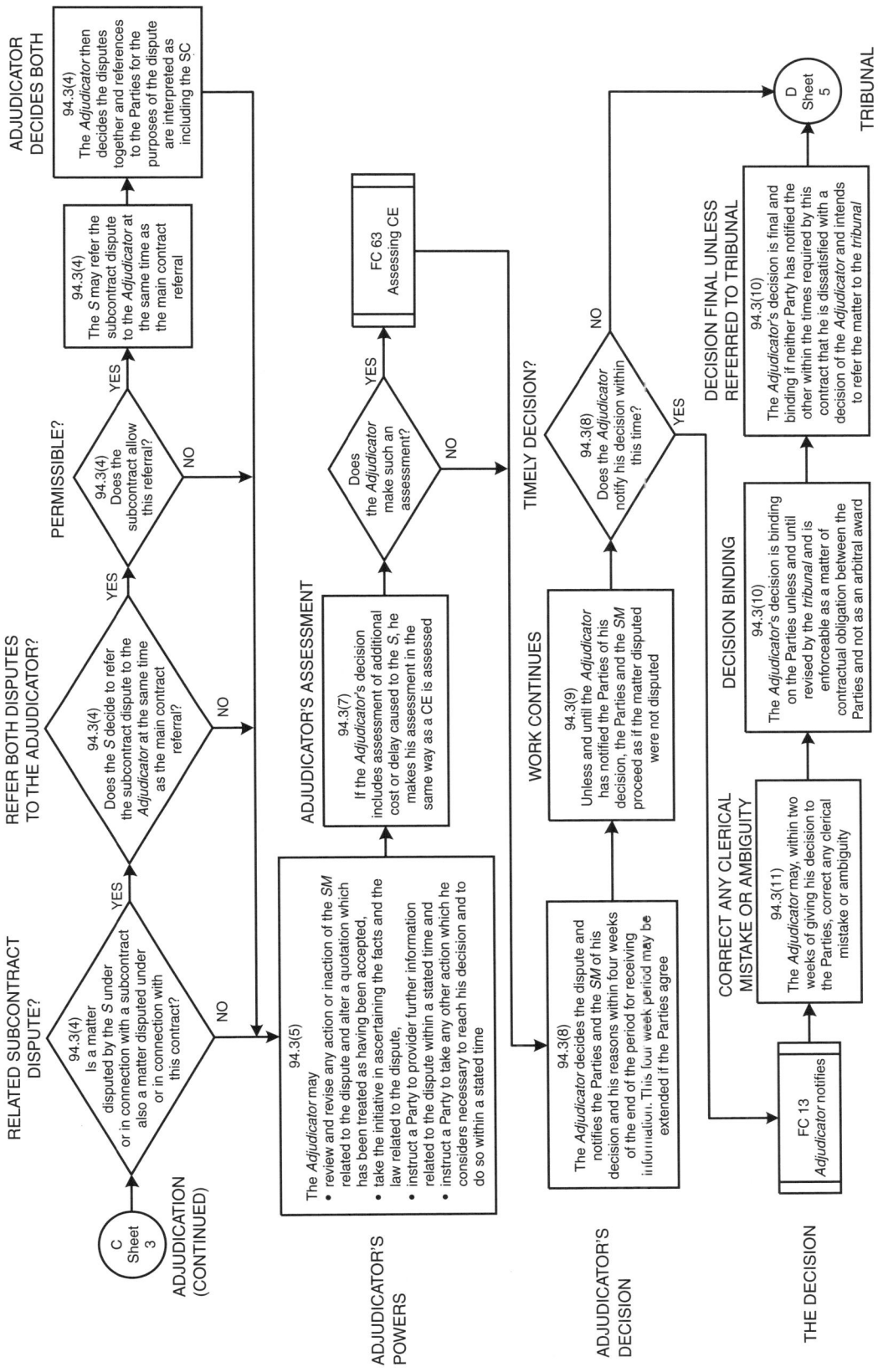

ADJUDICATION (CONTINUED)

C Sheet 3

RELATED SUBCONTRACT DISPUTE?

94.3(4) Is a matter disputed by the S under or in connection with a subcontract also a matter disputed under or in connection with this contract?

REFER BOTH DISPUTES TO THE ADJUDICATOR?

94.3(4) Does the S decide to refer the subcontract dispute to the Adjudicator at the same time as the main contract referral?

PERMISSIBLE?

94.3(4) Does the subcontract allow this referral?

94.3(4) The S may refer the subcontract dispute to the Adjudicator at the same time as the main contract referral

ADJUDICATOR DECIDES BOTH

94.3(4) The Adjudicator then decides the disputes together and references to the Parties for the purposes of the dispute are interpreted as including the SC

ADJUDICATOR'S POWERS

94.3(5) The Adjudicator may
• review and revise any action or inaction of the SM related to the dispute and alter a quotation which has been treated as having been accepted,
• take the initiative in ascertaining the facts and the law related to the dispute,
• instruct a Party to provider further information related to the dispute,
• instruct a Party to take any other action which he considers necessary to reach his decision and to do so within a stated time

ADJUDICATOR'S ASSESSMENT

94.3(7) If the Adjudicator's decision includes assessment of additional cost or delay caused to the S, he makes his assessment in the same way as a CE is assessed

Does the Adjudicator make such an assessment?

FC 63 Assessing CE

ADJUDICATOR'S DECISION

94.3(8) The Adjudicator decides the dispute and notifies the Parties and the SM of his decision and his reasons within four weeks of the end of the period for receiving information. This four week period may be extended if the Parties agree

WORK CONTINUES

94.3(9) Unless and until the Adjudicator has notified the Parties of his decision, the Parties and the SM proceed as if the matter disputed were not disputed

TIMELY DECISION?

94.3(8) Does the Adjudicator notify his decision within this time?

CORRECT ANY CLERICAL MISTAKE OR AMBIGUITY

94.3(11) The Adjudicator may, within two weeks of giving his decision to the Parties, correct any clerical mistake or ambiguity

FC 13 Adjudicator notifies

THE DECISION

DECISION BINDING

94.3(10) The Adjudicator's decision is binding on the Parties unless and until revised by the tribunal and is enforceable as a matter of contractual obligation between the Parties and not as an arbitral award

DECISION FINAL UNLESS REFERRED TO TRIBUNAL

94.3(10) The Adjudicator's decision is final and binding if neither Party has notified the other within the times required by this contract that he is dissatisfied with a decision of the Adjudicator and intends to refer the matter to the tribunal

D Sheet 5

TRIBUNAL

DISPUTES REFERRED FIRST TO THE ADJUDICATOR

94.4(1)
A Party does not refer any dispute under or in connection with this contract to the *tribunal* unless it has first been referred to the *Adjudicator* in accordance with this contract

D
Sheet 4

Has this dispute been referred to the *Adjudicator?*

DECISION IN TIME?

94.4(3)
Has the *Adjudicator* notified his decision in time?

A PARTY DISSATISFIED

94.4(2)
If, after the *Adjudicator* notifies his decisions, a Party is dissatisfied, he may notify the other Party that he intends to refer it to the *tribunal*

Is a Party dissatisfied with the *Adjudicator's* decision?

PERIOD FOR NOTIFICATION

94.4(2)
A Party may not refer a dispute to the *tribunal* unless this notification is given within four weeks of notification of the *Adjudicator's* decision

DECISION NOT NOTIFIED

94.4(3)
If the *Adjudicator* does not notify his decision within the time provided by this contract, a Party may notify the other Party that he intends to refer the dispute to the *tribunal*

PERIOD FOR NOTIFICATION

94.4(3)
A Party may not refer a dispute to the *tribunal* unless this notification is given within four weeks of the date by which the *Adjudicator* should have notified his decision

NOTIFY IN TIME?

Does a Party notify within the time?

This dispute is not referred to the *tribunal*

NO REFERRAL TO TRIBUNAL

Finish

NOTIFICATION OF REFERRAL

FC 13
Notification of referral to the *tribunal*

IF THE TRIBUNAL IS ARBITRATION

94.4(5)
If the *tribunal* is arbitration, the place where the arbitration is to be held and the method of choosing the arbitrator are those stated in the CD

TRIBUNAL'S POWERS

94.4(4)
The *tribunal* has the powers to reconsider any decision of the *Adjudicator* and review and revise any action or inaction of the *SM* related to the dispute

ADMISSIBLE EVIDENCE

94.4(4)
A Party is not limited in the *tribunal* proceedings to the information, evidence or arguments put to the *Adjudicator*

ADJUDICATOR NOT CALLED AS WITNESS

94.4(6)
A Party does not call the *Adjudicator* as a witness in *tribunal* proceedings

TRIBUNAL DECIDES

94.4(4)
The *tribunal* settles the dispute referred to it

Flow chart 94   Sheet 5 of 5
Dispute resolution

Start

Assessment of the amount due adjusted for inflation

The indices, proportions and *base date* are defined in the CD

Calculate the PAF for an assessment date?

YES →

X1.1(a)
The Base Date Index (B) is the latest available index before the *base date*

BASE DATE INDEX

X1.1(b)
The Latest Index (L) is the latest available index before the assessment of an amount due

LATEST INDEX

X1.1(c)
The PAF is the total of the products of each of the proportions stated in the CD multiplied by (L−B)/B for the index linked to it

PRICE ADJUSTMENT FACTOR

NO

INDEX CHANGED

Has an index been changed after it has been used for a PAF?

YES →

X1.2
If an index is changed after it has been used in calculating a PAF, the calculation is repeated and a correction included in the next assessment of the amount due

CORRECTION IN NEXT ASSESSMENT

NO

Is the assessment date later than the Delivery Date?

YES →

X1.2
The PAF calculated at the Delivery Date of the *goods* and *services* is used for calculating price adjustments after this date

PAF NOT ADJUSTED AFTER DELIVERY DATE

NO

COMPENSATION EVENT

Assess CEs?

YES →

X1.3
The change to the Prices for a CE is assessed using the change to the Prices current at the time of assessing the CE adjusted to *base date* by dividing by one plus the PAF for the last assessment of the amount due

DEFINED COST OF COMPENSATION EVENTS ASSESSED AT BASE DATE LEVELS

NO →

Calculate price adjustment →

X1.4
Each amount due includes an amount for price adjustment which is the sum of
• the change in
  • the Price for each lump sum item in the Price Schedule which the *S* has completed and
  • where a quantity is stated for an item in the Price Schedule, the amount calculated by multiplying the quantity which the *S* has completed by the rate, since the last assessment of the amount due multiplied by the PAF for the date of the current assessment,
• the amount for price adjustment included in the previous amount due and
• correcting amounts, not included elsewhere, which arise from changes to indices used for assessing previous amounts for price adjustment

PRICE ADJUSTMENT INCLUDED IN THE AMOUNT DUE

→ **Finish**

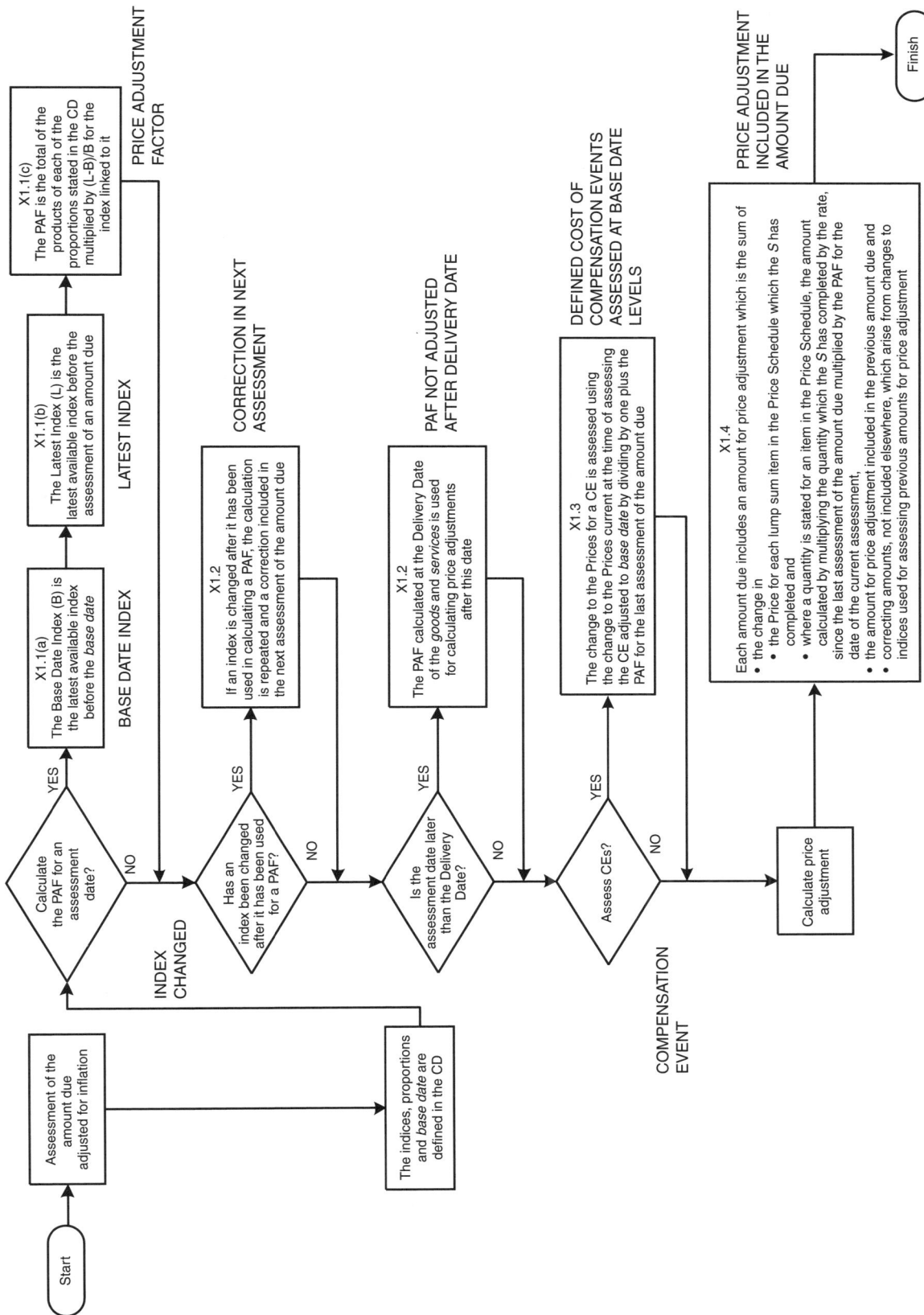

Flow chart X1
Price adjustment for inflation

CHANGE IN THE LAW IS COMPENSATION EVENT

X2.1

A change in the law of the country stated in the CD is a CE if it occurs after the Contract Date

CONTRACT DATE

11.2(2)

The Contract Date is the date when this contract came into existence

Start

CHANGE IN LAW?

Does a change in the law occur after the Contract Date?

NO

YES

SUPPLY MANAGER MAY NOTIFY COMPENSATION EVENT

X2.1

The *SM* may notify the *S* of a CE for a change in the law and instruct him to submit quotations

NOTIFIED BY SUPPLY MANAGER?

Does the *SM* notify a CE?

NO

YES

NOTIFIED BY SUPPLIER?

Does the *C* believe the event is a CE?

NO

YES

FC 61
Notifying CE's 61.3

COMPENSATION EVENT

FC 61
Notify CE X2.1

PRICES MAY BE REDUCED

X2.1

If the effect of a CE which is a change in the law is to reduce the total Defined Cost, the Prices are reduced

Finish

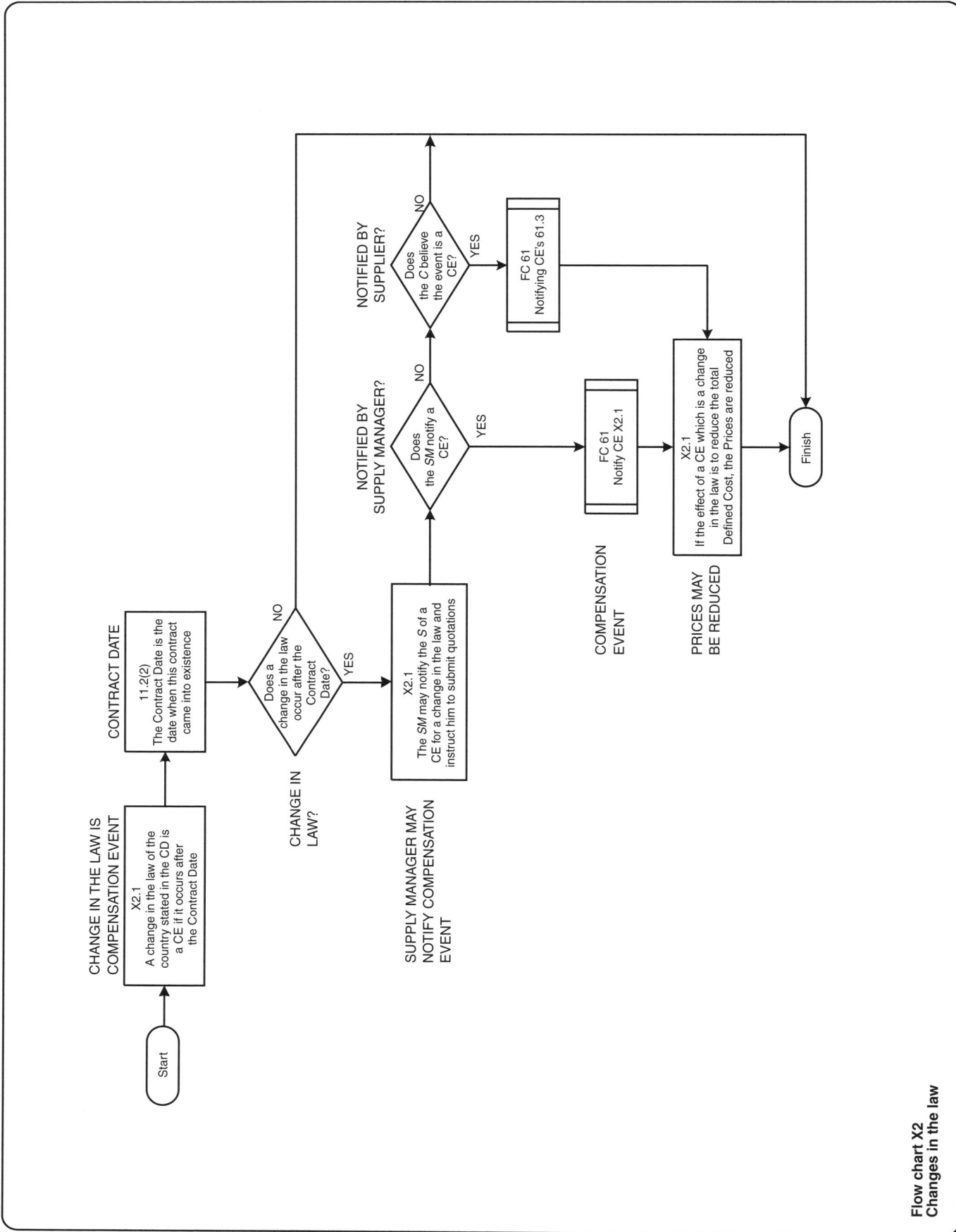

**Flow chart X2
Changes in the law**

PAYMENT DUE IN OTHER CURRENCIES?

Start

SOME PAYMENTS ARE IN OTHER CURRENCIES

X3.1

The S is paid in currencies other than the *currency of this contract* for the items of *goods and services* listed in the CD.

CURRENCY OF THIS CONTRACT

The *currency of this contract* is stated in the CD.

Does the amount due include payments in other currencies for such items or activities?

NO

YES

Finish

CURRENCY CONVERSION

X3.1

The *exchange rates* are used to convert from the *currency of this contract* to other currencies.

EXCHANGE RATES

The *exchange rates* are stated in the CD.

PAYMENTS IN OTHER CURRENCIES DO NOT EXCEED MAXIMUM AMOUNTS

X3.2

Payments to the S in currencies other than the *currency of this contract* do not exceed the maximum amounts stated in the CD.

EXCESS PAID IN CURRENCY OF CONTRACT

X3.2

Any excess is paid in the *currency of this contract*.

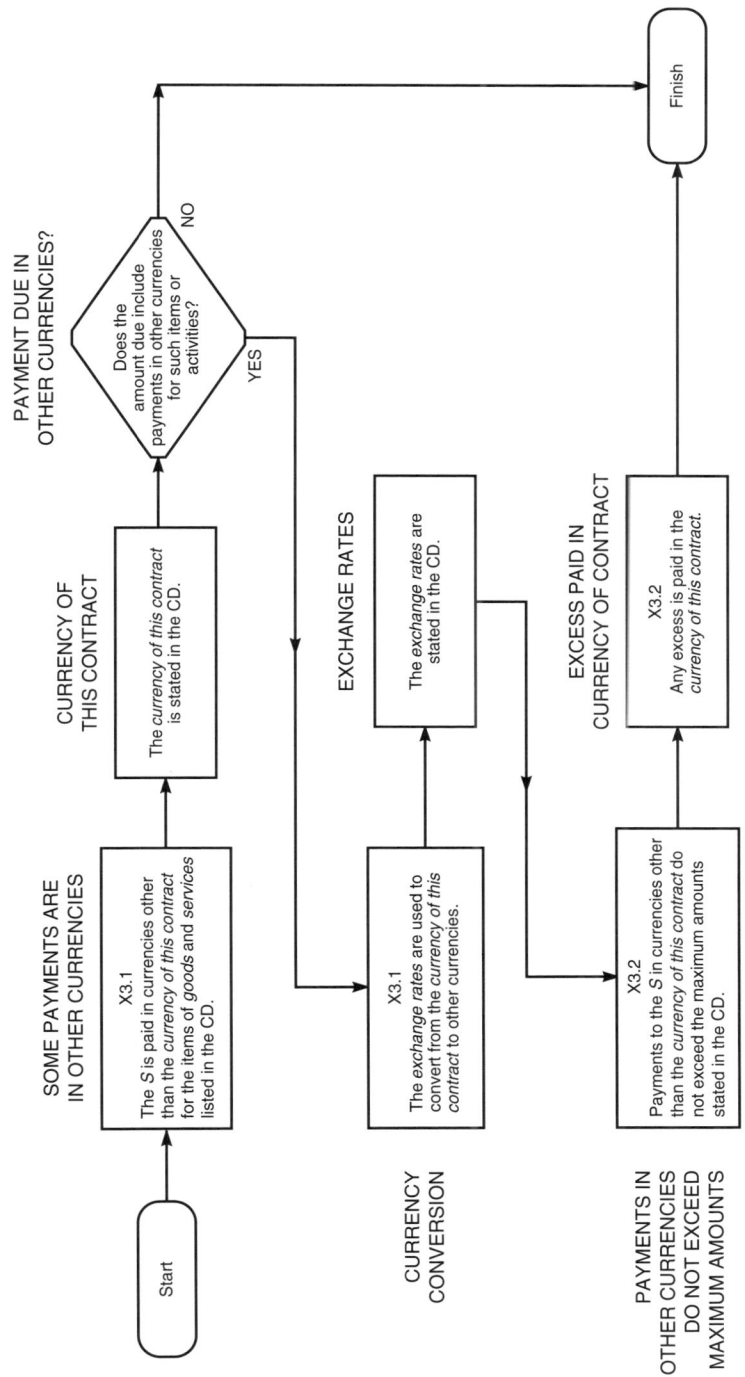

Flow chart X3
Multiple currencies

Start

PARENT COMPANY?

X4.1
Does a parent company own the *S*?

YES →

NO →

PARENT COMPANY GUARANTEE

X4.1
The *S* gives to the *P* a guarantee by the parent company of the *S*'s performance in the form set out in the GI.

CONTRACT DATE

11.2(2)
The Contract Date is the date when this contract came into existence.

GUARANTEE GIVEN BY CONTRACT DATE?

X4.1
Is the guarantee given by the Contract Date?

YES →

NO →

GUARANTEE GIVEN WITHIN FOUR WEEKS

X4.1
The guarantee is given to the *P* within four weeks of the Contract Date.

Is the guarantee given within four weeks?

NO →

YES →

FC90
Termination Reason R12

Finish

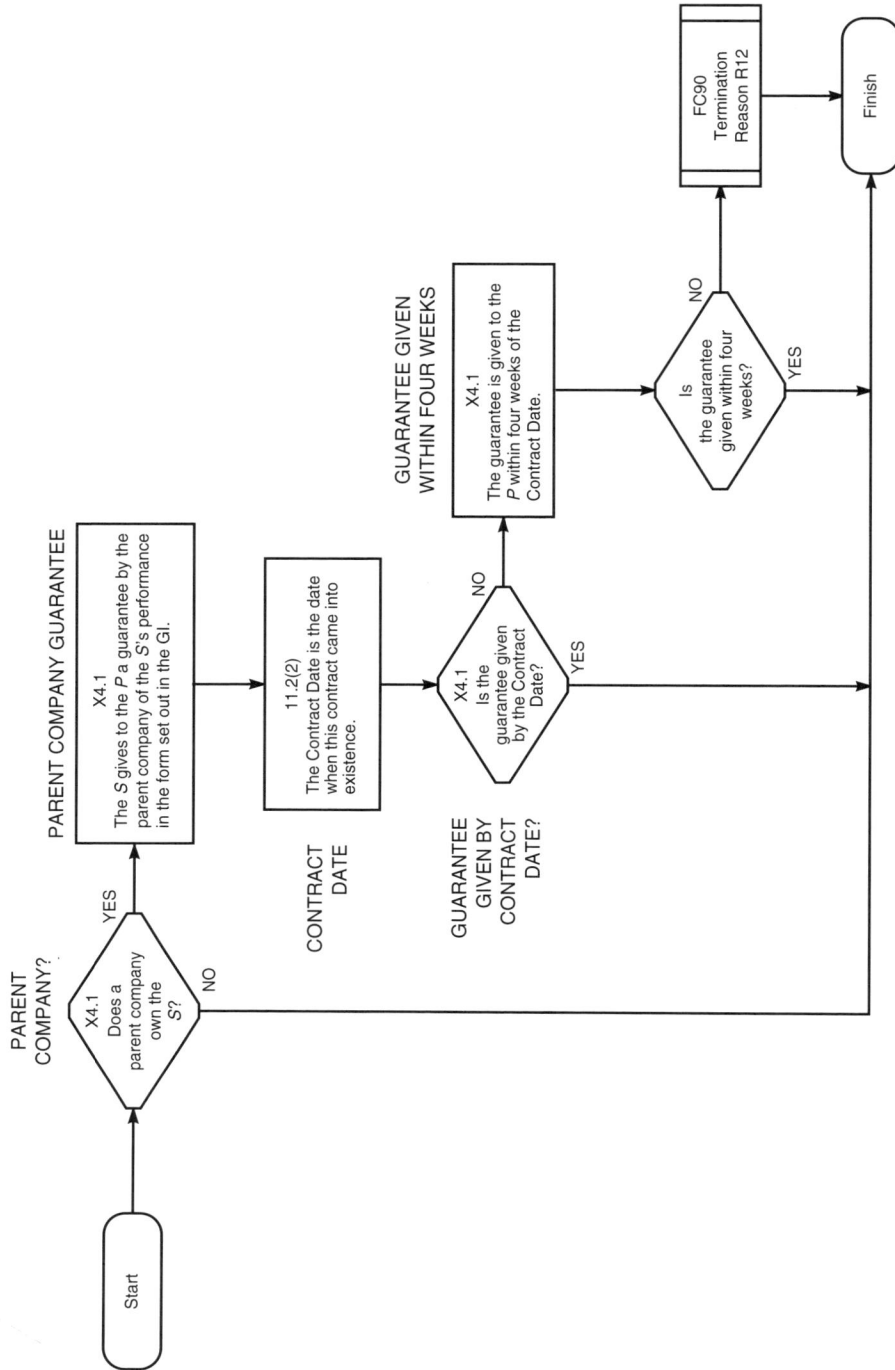

Flow chart X4
Parent company guarantee

www.neccontract.com

Start

DELIVERY

11.2(5)
Delivery is when the *S* has
- done all the work which the GI states he is to do by the Delivery Date and
- corrected Defects which would have prevented the *P* from using the *goods* and *services* and Others from doing their work.

DELIVERY DATE

11.2(6)
The Delivery Date is the *delivery date* (stated in the CD) unless later changed in accordance with this contract.

A DEFECT

11.2(3)
A Defect is
- a part of the *goods* and *services* which is not in accordance with the GI or
- a part of the *goods* designed by the *S* which is not in accordance with the applicable law or the *S*'s design which the *SM* has accepted.

DELAY DAMAGES

The *delay damages* per day for Delivery is stated in the CD.

MULTIPLE DELIVERIES?

Is there more than one Delivery?

MULTIPLE DELIVERIES

12.5
In these *conditions of contract*, each reference and clause relevant to Delivery and the Delivery Date applies to each Delivery and its Delivery Date

DELAY DAMAGES

The *delivery dates* and the delay damages per day are stated in the CD.

LATE DELIVERY?

X7.1
Has the Delivery Date occurred?

DAMAGES PAID?

X7.2
Have delay damages been paid?

LATER DELIVERY DATE?

X7.2
Is the Delivery Date changed to a later date?

REPAYMENT WITH INTEREST

X7.2
The *P* repays the overpayment of damages with interest. Interest is assessed from the date of payment to the date of repayment and the date of repayment is an assessment date.

TIMELY DELIVERY?

X7.1
Has Delivery occurred before the Delivery Date?

PURCHASER USES GOODS AND SERVICES?

X7.1
Has the *P* started to make use of the *goods* and *services* before the Delivery Date?

DELAY DAMAGES

X7.1
The *S* pays delay damages at the rate stated in the CD from the Delivery Date for each day until the earlier of
- Delivery and
- the date on which the *P* starts to make use of the *goods* and *services*.

PURCHASER USES PART OF GOODS AND SERVICES?

X7.3
Has the *P* used part of the *goods* and *services*?

X7.3
If the *P* uses part of the *goods* and *services* before Delivery the delay damages are reduced from the date on which the part is used. The *SM* assesses the benefit to the *P* of using part of the *goods* and *services* as a proportion of the benefit to the *P* of taking over the whole of the *goods* and *services* not previously used. The delay damages are reduced in this proportion.

Finish

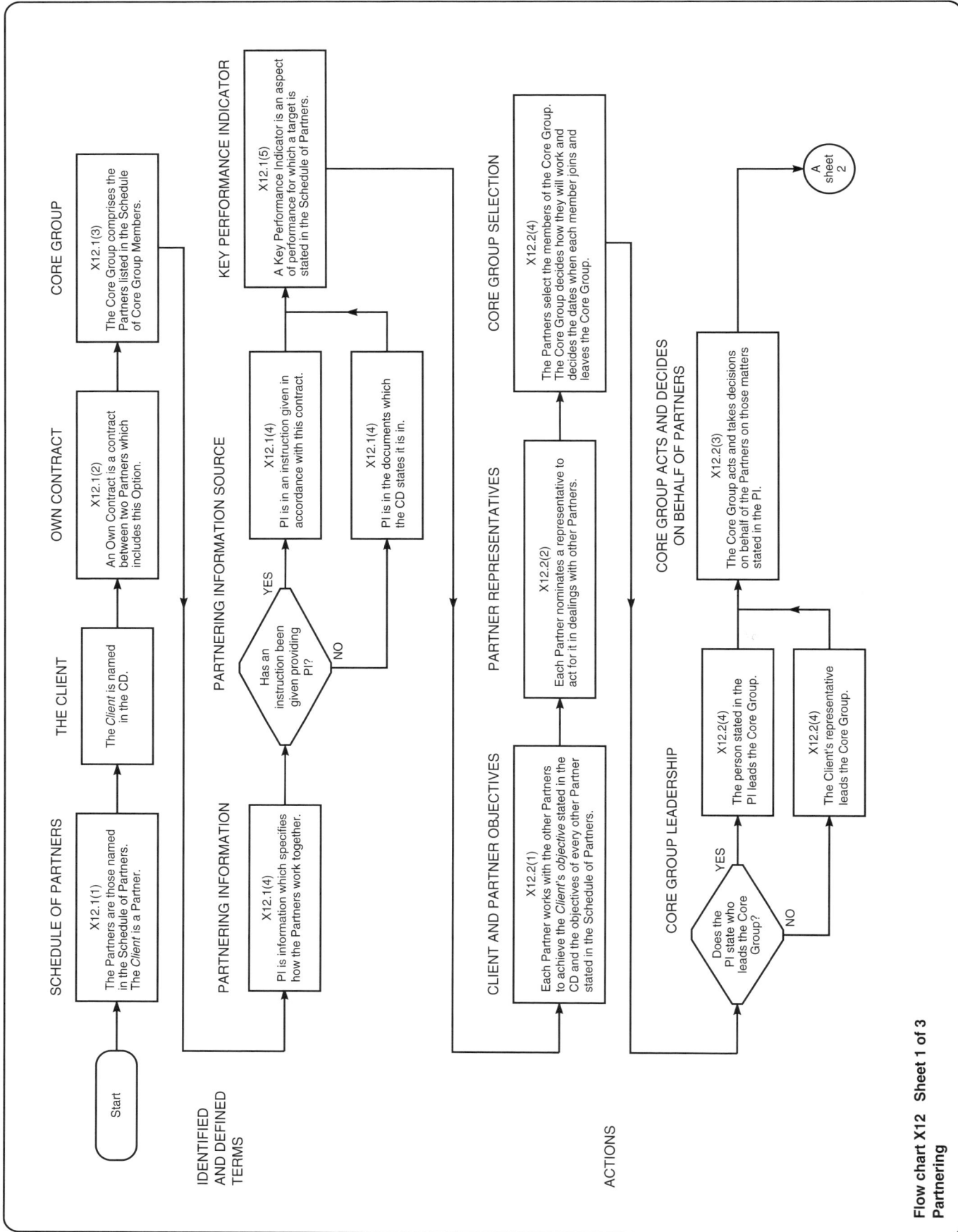

SCHEDULE OF PARTNERS

X12.1(1)
The Partners are those named in the Schedule of Partners. The *Client* is a Partner.

THE CLIENT
The *Client* is named in the CD.

OWN CONTRACT

X12.1(2)
An Own Contract is a contract between two Partners which includes this Option.

CORE GROUP

X12.1(3)
The Core Group comprises the Partners listed in the Schedule of Core Group Members.

PARTNERING INFORMATION

X12.1(4)
PI is information which specifies how the Partners work together.

PARTNERING INFORMATION SOURCE

Has an instruction been given providing PI?

YES → **X12.1(4)** PI is in an instruction given in accordance with this contract.

NO → **X12.1(4)** PI is in the documents which the CD states it is in.

KEY PERFORMANCE INDICATOR

X12.1(5)
A Key Performance Indicator is an aspect of performance for which a target is stated in the Schedule of Partners.

CLIENT AND PARTNER OBJECTIVES

X12.2(1)
Each Partner works with the other Partners to achieve the *Client*'s *objective* stated in the CD and the objectives of every other Partner stated in the Schedule of Partners.

PARTNER REPRESENTATIVES

X12.2(2)
Each Partner nominates a representative to act for it in dealings with other Partners.

CORE GROUP SELECTION

X12.2(4)
The Partners select the members of the Core Group. The Core Group decides how they will work and decides the dates when each member joins and leaves the Core Group.

CORE GROUP LEADERSHIP

Does the PI state who leads the Core Group?

YES → **X12.2(4)** The person stated in the PI leads the Core Group.

NO → **X12.2(4)** The *Client*'s representative leads the Core Group.

CORE GROUP ACTS AND DECIDES ON BEHALF OF PARTNERS

X12.2(3)
The Core Group acts and takes decisions on behalf of the Partners on those matters stated in the PI.

A sheet 2

Start

IDENTIFIED AND DEFINED TERMS

ACTIONS

Flow chart X12   Sheet 1 of 3
Partnering

SCHEDULES OF PARTNERS AND CORE GROUP MEMBERS KEPT

A sheet 1

X12.2(5)
The Core Group keeps the Schedule of Core Group Members and the Schedule of Partners up to date.

Has either of the Schedules been revised?

YES →

REVISED SCHEDULES ISSUED

X12.2(5)
The Core Group issues copies of them to the Partners each time either is revised.

NO →

NOT A LEGAL PARTNERSHIP

X12.2(6)
This Option does not create a legal partnership between Partners who are not one of the Parties in this contract.

PARTNERS WORK TOGETHER IN SPIRIT OF TRUST AND COOPERATION

X12.3(1)
The Partners work together as stated in the PI and in a spirit of mutual trust and co-operation.

PARTNERS PROVIDE INFORMATION

X12.3(2)
A Partner may ask another Partner to provide information which he needs to carry out the work in his Own Contract and the other Partner provides it.

Does the other Partner provide the needed information?

NO →

EARLY WARNING

FC 16
Early warning

YES ↓

PARTNERS GIVE EARLY WARNING

X12.3(3)
Each Partner gives an early warning to the other Partners when he becomes aware of any matter that could affect the achievement of another Partner's objectives stated in the Schedule of Partners.

Does the Partner give the necessary early warning?

YES →

FC 16
Early warning

NO →

CONTRACTS (RIGHTS OF THIRD PARTIES) ACT

Does Option Y(UK)3 apply?

YES →

FC Y(UK)3
Contracts (Rights of Third Parties) Act

NO →

COMMON INFORMATION SYSTEMS

X12.3(4)
The Partners use common information systems as set out in the PI.

IMPLEMENT CORE DECISION

X12.3(5)
A Partner implements a decision of the Core Group by issuing instructions in accordance with its Own Contracts.

CHANGE PARTNERING INFORMATION

X12.3(6)
The Core Group may give an instruction to the Partners to change the PI.

Does the Core Group give an instruction to change the PI?

YES →

COMPENSATION EVENT

X12.3(6)
Each such change to the PI is a CE and may lead to reduced Prices.

FC 63
Assessing CE

→ **B sheet 3**

NO →

WORKING TOGETHER

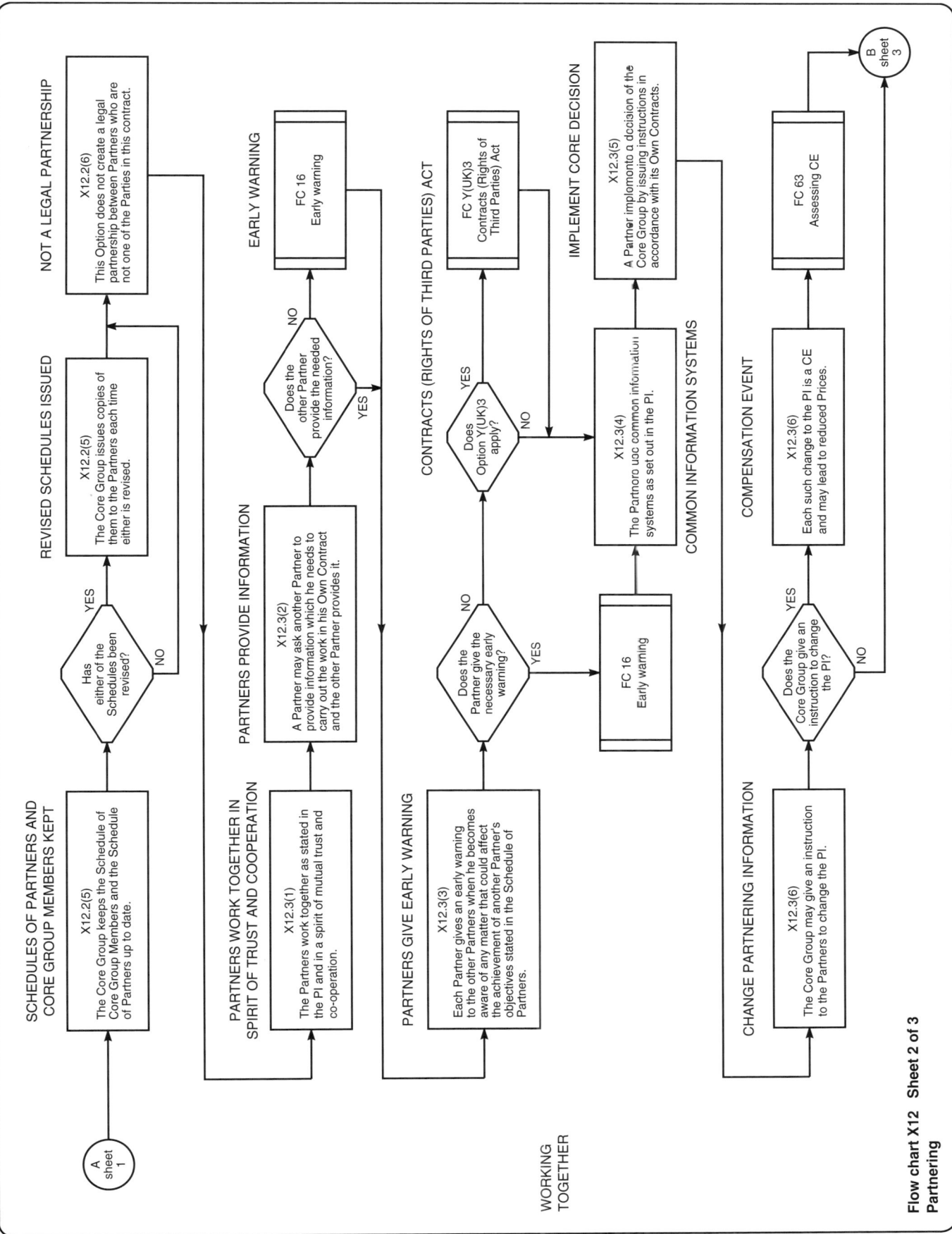

Flow chart X12   Sheet 2 of 3
Partnering

CHANGE CORE TIMETABLE

B
sheet
2

X12.3(7)

The Core Group prepares and maintains a timetable showing the proposed timing of the contributions of the Partners. The Core Group issues a copy of the timetable to the Partners each time it is revised.

COMPENSATION EVENT

Does the Core Group issue a revised timetable?

YES

NO

X12.3(7)

The *S* changes his programme if it is necessary to do so in order to comply with the revised timetable. Each such change is a CE which may lead to reduced Prices.

FC 63
Assessing CE

PARTNERS GIVE ADVICE

X12.3(8)

A Partner gives advice, information and opinion to the Core Group and to other Partners when asked to do so by the Core Group. This advice, information and opinion relates to work that another Partner is to carry out under its Own Contract and is given fully, openly and objectively. The Partners show contingency and risk allowances in information about costs, prices and timing for future work.

SUBCONTRACTING

X12.3(9)

A Partner notifies the Core Group before subcontracting any work.

PARTNER NOTIFIES

FC 13
Notification

ACHIEVEMENT OF TARGET

X12.4(1)

A Partner is paid the amount stated in the Schedule of Partners if the target stated for a Key Performance Indicator is improved upon or achieved.

PAYMENT DUE

Has the target been improved upon or achieved?

YES

NO

X12.4(1)

Payment of the amount is due when the target has been improved upon or achieved and is made as part of the amount due in the Partner's Own Contract.

FC 50
Assessing the amount due

ASSESSMENT

INCENTIVES

ADJUSTING KEY PERFORMANCE INDICATORS

X12.4(2)

The *Client* may add a Key Performance Indicator and associated payment to the Schedule of Partners but may not delete or reduce a payment stated in the Schedule of Partners.

Finish

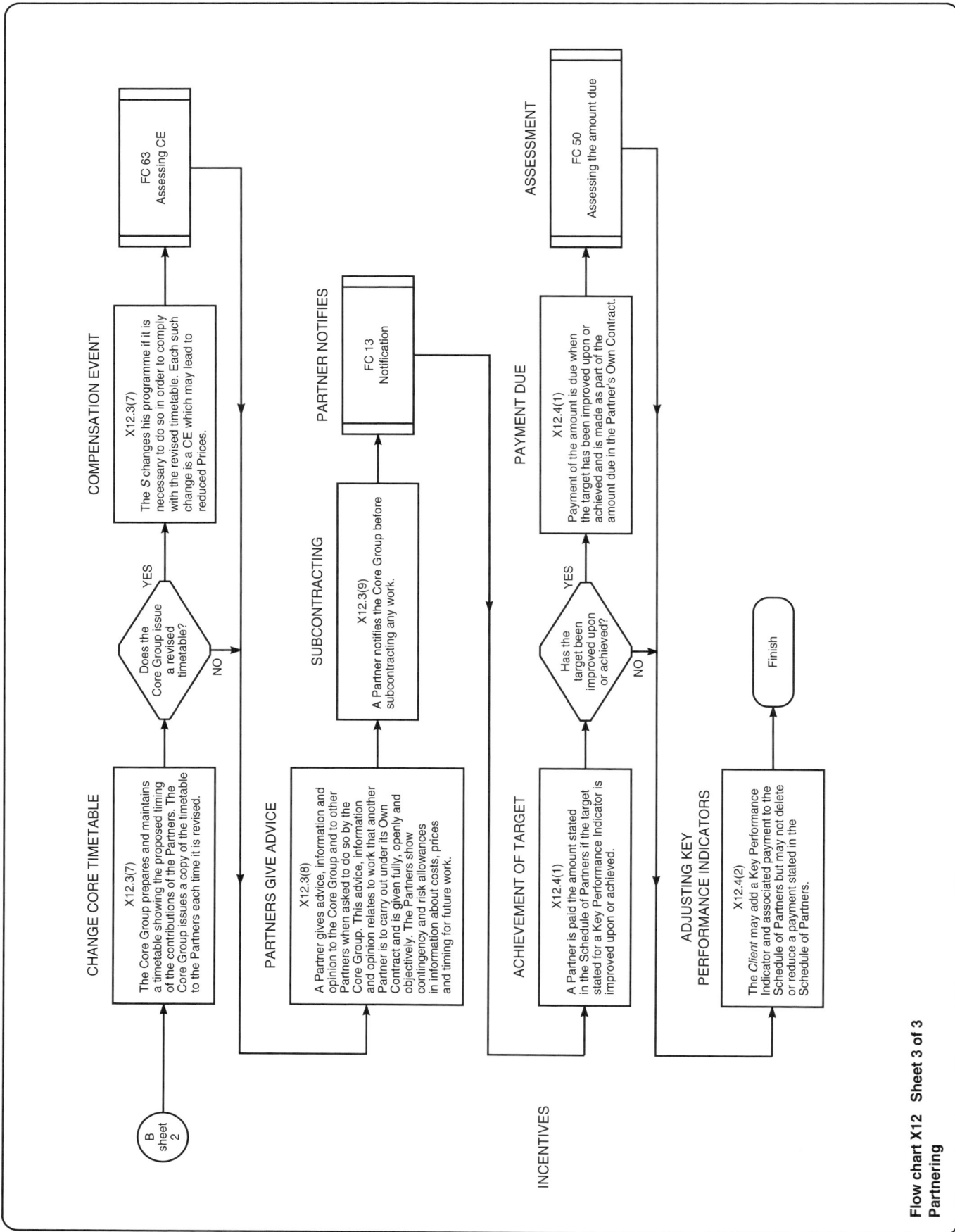

Flow chart X12   Sheet 3 of 3
Partnering

PERFORMANCE BOND

X13.1
The *S* gives the *P* a performance bond, provided by a bank or insurer which the *SM* has accepted, for the amount stated in the CD and in the form set out in the GI

CONTRACT DATE

11.2(2)
The Contract Date is the date when this contract came into existence

Start

A performance bond is required

BOND GIVEN BY THE CONTRACT DATE?

Is the bond given by the Contract Date?

NO →
X13.1
The performance bond is given to the *P* within four weeks of the Contract Date

→ Is the bond given within four weeks?

YES / NO

NO →
FC 90
Termination Reason R12

→ **Finish**

YES →

REASON FOR NOT ACCEPTING

X13.1
A reason for not accepting the bank or insurer is that its commercial position is not strong enough to carry the bond

SUBMISSION FOR ACCEPTANCE

FC 13
Submission for acceptance

ACCEPTED?

Does the *SM* accept the performance bond?

NO → The *S* submits an alternative proposal → **Finish**

YES → **Finish**

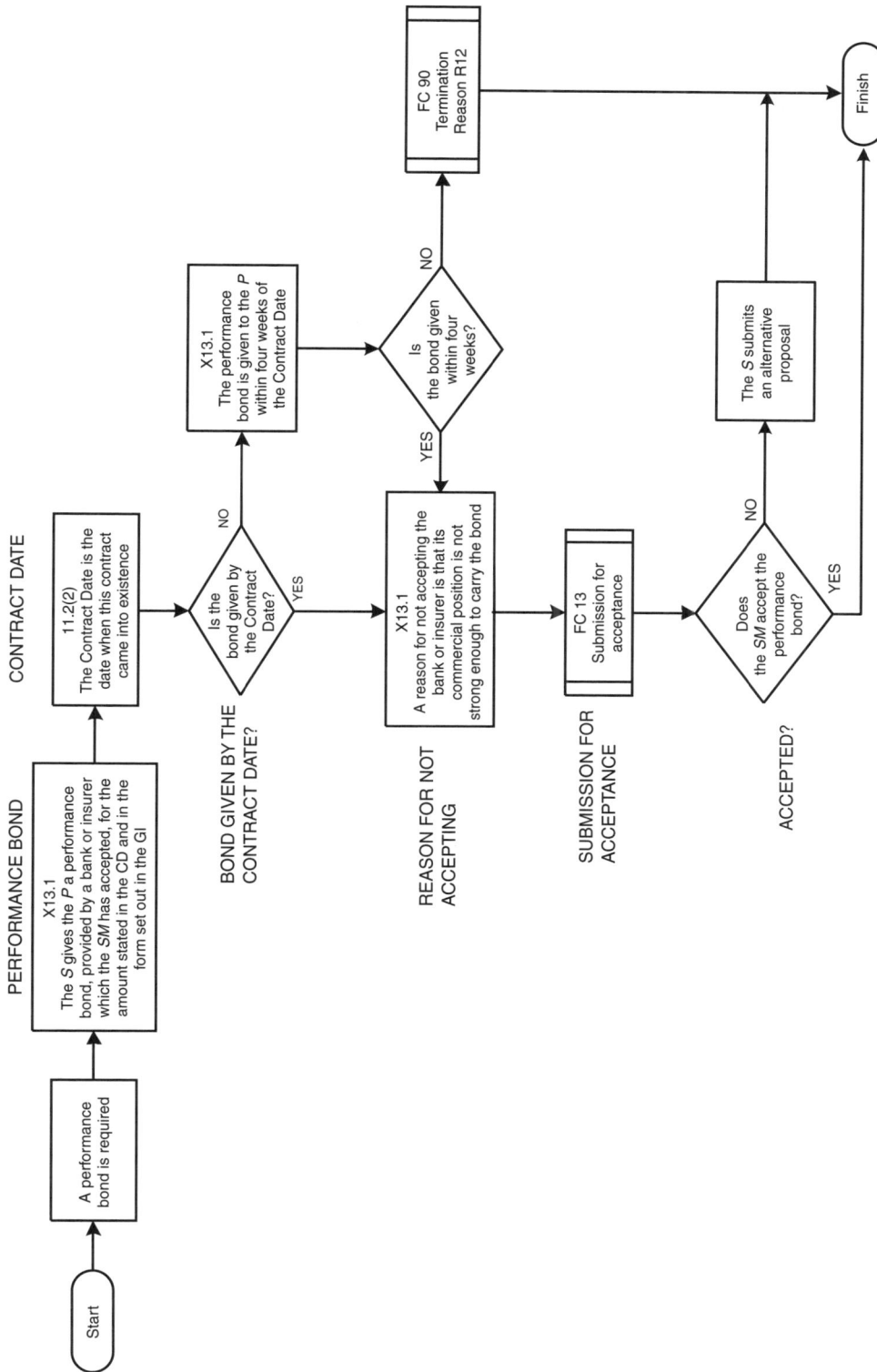

Flow chart X13
Performance bond

Start

PURCHASER MAKING ADVANCED PAYMENT

What is the advanced payment issue?

Payment? →

ADVANCED PAYMENT
X14.1
The P makes an advanced payment to the S of the amount stated in the CD.

ADVANCED PAYMENT BOND?
X14.2
Is an advanced payment bond required?

YES →

ADVANCED PAYMENT BOND
X14.2
The advanced payment bond is issued by a bank or insurer which the SM has accepted. The bond is for the amount of the advanced payment which the S has not repaid and is in the form set out in the GI.

REASON FOR NOT ACCEPTING
X14.2
A reason for not accepting the proposed bank or insurer is that its commercial position is not strong enough to carry the bond.

SUBMIT PROPOSAL
FC 13
Submission for acceptance

ACCEPTED?
Does the SM accept the bond?

YES / NO

RE-SUBMIT
The S re-submits an alternative proposal.

NO →

CONTRACT DATE
11.2(2)
The Contract Date is the date when this contract came into existence.

ADVANCE PAYMENT DATE
X14.2
The advance payment is made either within four weeks of the Contract Date or, if an advanced payment bond is required, within four weeks of the later of
• the Contract Date and
• the date when the P receives the advanced payment bond.

TIMELY PAYMENT?
X14.2
Does the P make the advance payment on time?

YES / NO

COMPENSATION EVENT
X14.2
Delay in making the advanced payment is a CE.

SUPPLIER MAKING REPAYMENTS

Repayment? →

REPAYMENT INSTALMENTS
X14.3
The advanced payment is repaid to the P by the S in instalments of the amount stated in the CD and at the intervals stated in the CD.

REPAYMENT SCHEDULE
X14.3
An instalment is included in each amount due assessed after the period stated in the CD has passed until the advance payment has been repaid.

Finish

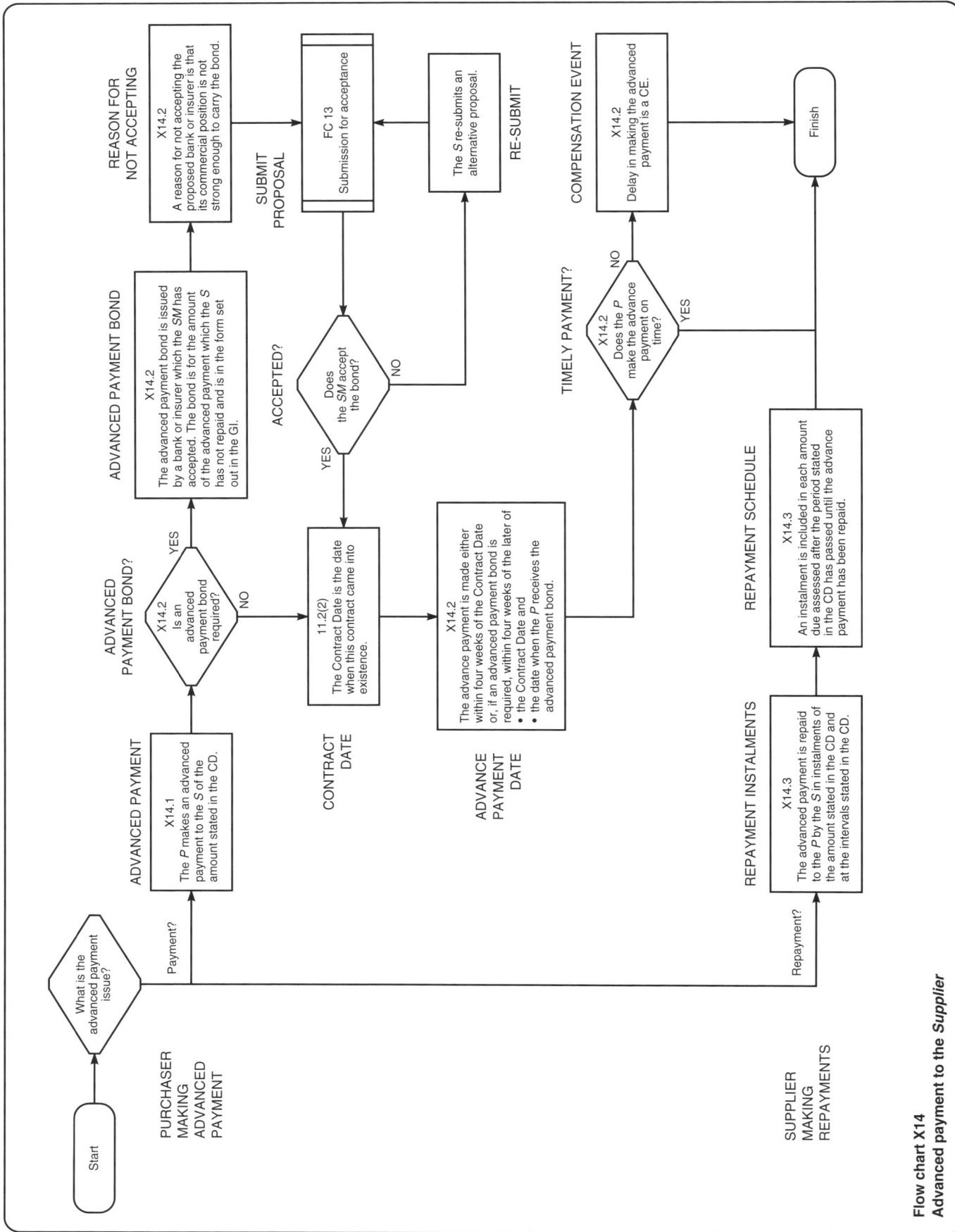

Flow chart X14
Advanced payment to the Supplier

A DEFECT

11.2(3)

A Defect is
- a part of the *goods* and *services* which is not in accordance with the GI or
- a part of the *goods* designed by the *S* which is not in accordance with the applicable law or the *S*'s design which the *SM* has accepted.

Start

DEFECTS DATE

11.2(6)
The *defects date* is stated in the CD.

DEFECT AFTER DEFECT DATE?

X17.1
Is there a Defect which remains uncorrected at its *defect date*?

YES →

NO →

LOW PERFORMANCE

X17.1
A Defect may show low performance with respect to a performance level stated in the CD.

LISTED DEFECT SHOWS LOW PERFORMANCE?

X17.1
Does the Defect show low performance?

YES →

NO →

LOW PERFORMANCE DAMAGES

X17.1
The *S* pays the amount of low performance damages stated in the CD.

X17.1
The GI is treated as having been changed to accept the Defect.

Finish

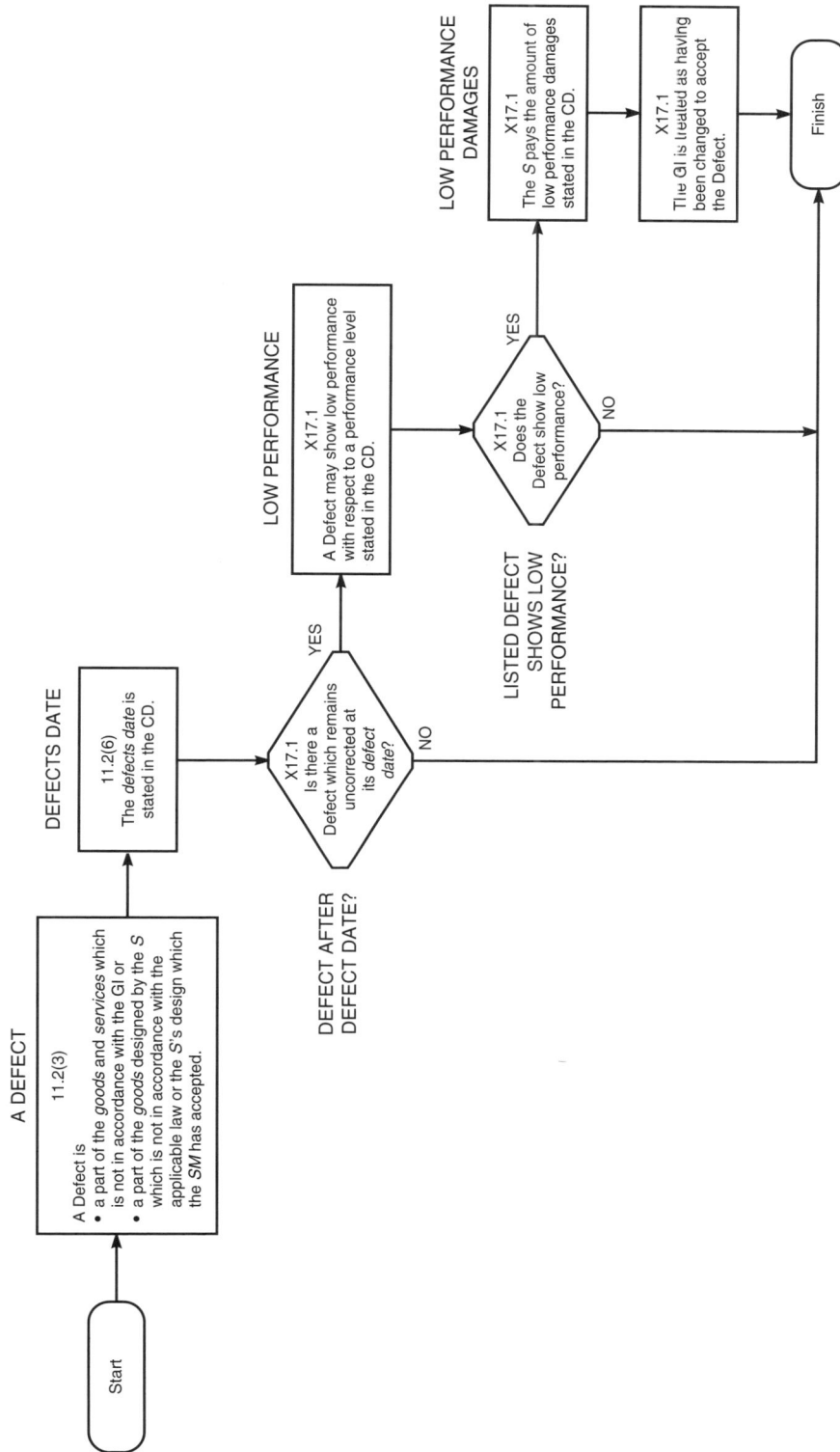

Flow chart X17
Low performance damages

STARTING DATE AND DEFECTS DATE

The *starting date* and *defects date* are stated in the CD.

INCENTIVE SCHEDULE

The Incentive Schedule is the *incentive schedule* (stated in the CD) unless later changed in accordance with this contract.

ADDING AN INCENTIVE

X20.5

The *P* may add a Key Performance Indicator and associated payment to the Incentive Schedule but may not delete or reduce a payment stated in the Incentive Schedule.

KEY PERFORMANCE INDICATOR

X20.1

A Key Performance Indicator is an aspect of performance by the *S* for which a target is stated in the Incentive Schedule.

Start

REPORT CONTENTS

X20.2

Reports are provided at intervals stated in the CD and include the forecast final measurement against each indicator.

PERFORMANCE REPORTS

X20.2

From the *starting date* until the past defects date, the *S* reports to the *SM* his performance against each of the Key Performance Indicators.

FORECAST PERFORMANCE ACHIEVED?

X20.3

Does the *S*'s forecast final measurement against a Key Performance Indicator achieve the target stated in the Incentive Schedule?

YES

NO

PERFORMANCE IMPROVEMENT

X20.3

The *S* submits to the *SM* his proposals for improving performance.

TARGET ACHIEVED?

X20.4

Has the target for a Key Performance Indicator stated in the Incentive Schedule been improved upon or achieved?

YES

NO

INCENTIVE PAID

X20.4

The *S* is paid the amount stated in the Incentive Schedule if the target stated for a Key Performance Indicator is improved upon or achieved. Payment of the amount is due when the target has been improved upon or achieved.

Finish

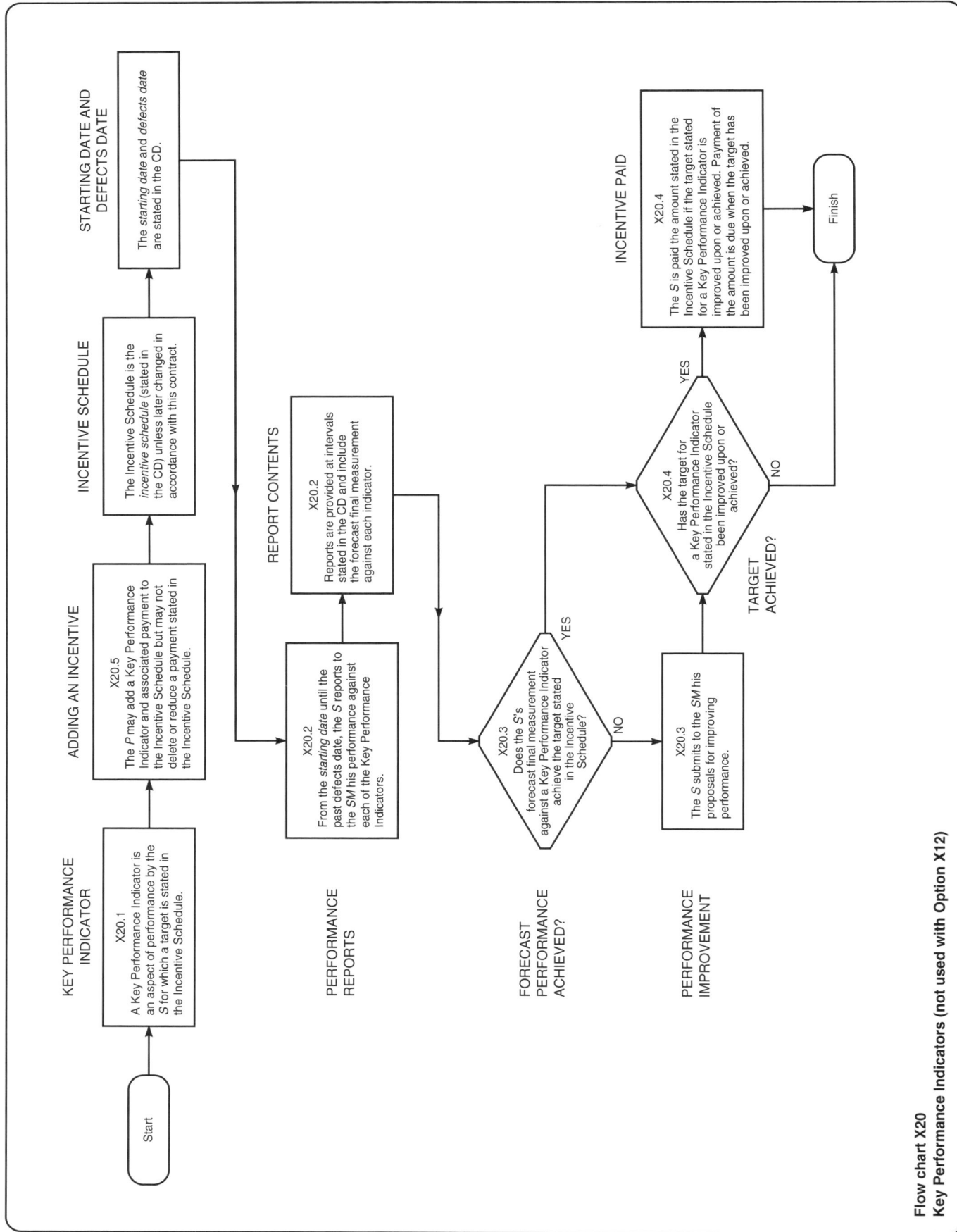

Flow chart X20
Key Performance Indicators (not used with Option X12)

Start

Y1.1(2)
Trust Deed is an agreement in the form set out in the contract which contains provisions for administering the Project Bank Account.

Is the S identified as a Named Supplier in the Contract Data for the P's contract with his employer

YES →

Y1.5
The P, his employer and the S sign the Trust Deed before the first assessment date in the contract between the P and his employer.

NO ↓

Y1.5
The P, his employer and the S sign the Joining Deed before the first assessment date.

Y1.1(1)
Project Bank Account is the account established by the P and used to make payments to the S.

Is payment due from the P to the S?

NO →
YES ↓

Is payment due from the S to the P?

YES →
NO ↓

Y1.3
A payment which is due from the S to the P is not made through the Project Bank Acccount

ECC FC 51
Payment

Y1.2
The S receives payment from the Project Bank Acccount of the amount certified by the SM as soon as practicable after the Project Bank Account receives payment.

Y1.4
Payments made from the Project Bank Acccount are treated as payments from the P to the S in accordance with this contract.

Has the SM issued a termination certificate?

YES ↓
NO →

Y1.6
If the SM issues a termination certificate, no further payment is made into the Project Bank Acccount.

Finish

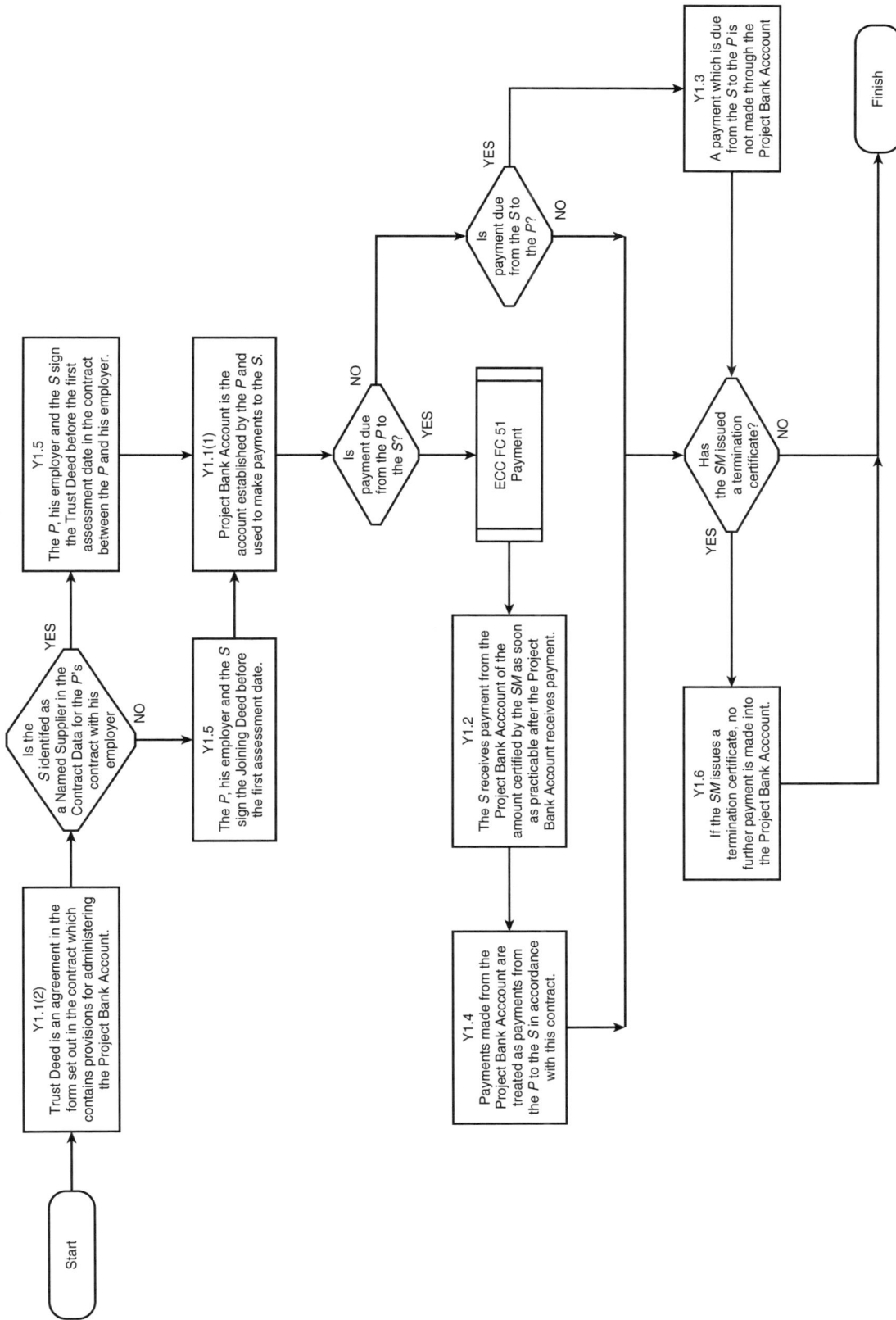

Flow chart Y(UK)1
Project Bank Account

THE PARTIES

Start

11.2(10)
The Parties are the *Purchaser* and the *Supplier*.

RIGHTS OF THIRD PARTIES TO ENFORCE CONTRACT TERM

Y3.1
A person or organisation who is not one of the Parties may enforce a term of this contract under the Contracts (Rights of Third Parties) Act 1999 only if the term and the person or organisation are stated in the CD.

IS THE PERSON OR ORGANISATION ONE OF PARTIES?

Y3.1
Is the person or organisation a Party to this Contract?

— YES

— NO

IS THE TERM AND THE THIRD PARTY STATED IN THE CONTRACT DATA?

Y3.1
Is the term and the person or organisation stated in the CD?

— YES

— NO

THE THIRD PARTY CAN ENFORCE CONTRACT TERM

Y3.1
Term of contract can be enforced under Act.

THE THIRD PARTY CANNOT ENFORCE CONTRACT TERM

Y3.1
Term of contract cannot be enforced under Act.

Finish

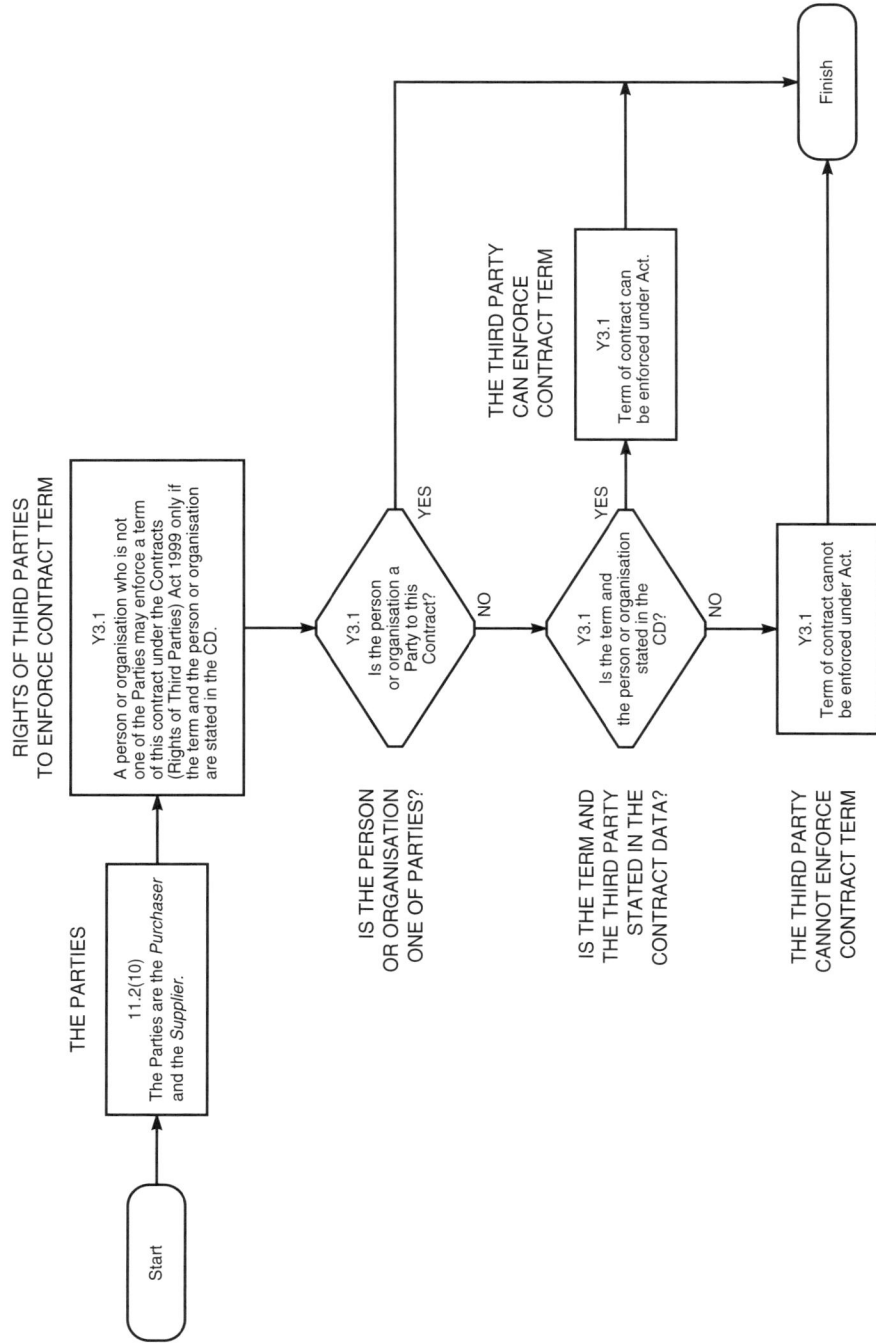

Flow chart Y(UK)3
The Contracts (Rights of Third Parties) Act 1999